"In this long-awaited contribution, the Halls offer an irenic corrective to modern individualism and rationalism that continue to influence much Christianity in the twenty-first century, through this accessible and sophisticated integration of Scripture, Christian theology, contemporary psychological theory and research, and even some Christian philosophy. Building on the deep coherence evident in biblical teaching on the love of the Trinity and contemporary research on attachment and social neuroscience, the authors construct a rich and profound Christian model of human love that takes into account the impact of childhood experience yet gives hope of healing transformation. Some will question the equation of mindfulness and contemplative prayer, but there is simply no better introduction today to the formative role that interpersonal relationships play in human development, maturation, flourishing, and eternal life."

Eric L. Johnson, professor of Christian psychology, Gideon Institute of Christian Psychology and Counseling at Houston Baptist University

"*Relational Spirituality* is a significant contribution that brings together attachment psychology, neuroscience, theology, spirituality, and other disciplines in an emerging and dynamic conversation, all for the sake of a deeply relational vision of Christian spiritual formation. Frankly, this is a book I've been waiting and hoping for, one that will be well used by my students in years to come."

Chuck DeGroat, professor of pastoral care and Christian spirituality at Western Theological Seminary, senior fellow at Newbigin House of Studies

Relational Spirituality

A Psychological-Theological Paradigm for Transformation

TODD W. HALL

with M. ELIZABETH LEWIS HALL

iVp
Academic
An imprint of InterVarsity Press
Downers Grove, Illinois

InterVarsity Press
P.O. Box 1400, Downers Grove, IL 60515-1426
ivpress.com
email@ivpress.com

InterVarsity Press® is the book-publishing division of InterVarsity Christian Fellowship/USA®, a movement
of students and faculty active on campus at hundreds of universities, colleges, and schools of nursing in the
United States of America, and a member movement of the International Fellowship of Evangelical Students.
For information about local and regional activities, visit intervarsity.org.

Unless otherwise indicated, all Scripture quotations are taken from the Holy Bible, New Living Translation,
copyright ©1996, 2004, 2007, 2013. Used by permission of Tyndale House Publishers, Inc., Carol Stream,
Illinois 60188. All rights reserved.

In order to protect the privacy of individuals, all client names and other identifying information
have been changed, and some cases are composites of several people.

The publisher cannot verify the accuracy or functionality of website URLs used in this book beyond
the date of publication.

Cover design and image composite: Autumn Short
Interior design: Daniel van Loon
Images: abstract landscape © SOCIAL.CUT / unsplash.com
        butterfly image © Fleur / unsplash.com
        abstract circle image © MirageC / Moment Collection / Getty Images

ISBN 978-0-8308-5118-8 (print)
ISBN 978-0-8308-9957-9 (digital)

Printed in the United States of America ∞

Library of Congress Cataloging-in-Publication Data
Names: Hall, Todd W., author. | Hall, M. Elizabeth Lewis, 1968- author.
Title: Relational spirituality : a psychological-theological paradigm for transformation / Todd W. Hall with
        M. Elizabeth Lewis Hall.
Description: Downers Grove, IL : IVP Academic, [2021] | Includes bibliographical references and indexes.
Identifiers: LCCN 2021002227 (print) | LCCN 2021002228 (ebook) | ISBN 9780830851188 (hardcover) |
        ISBN 9780830899579 (ebook)
Subjects: LCSH: Interpersonal relations—Religious aspects—Christianity. | Spiritual formation—Psychology. |
        Christianity—Psychology.
Classification: LCC BV4597.52 .H35 2021 (print) | LCC BV4597.52 (ebook) | DDC 248—dc23
LC record available at https://lccn.loc.gov/2021002227
LC ebook record available at https://lccn.loc.gov/2021002228

| P | 25 | 24 | 23 | 22 | 21 | 20 | 19 | 18 | 17 | 16 | 15 | 14 | 13 | 12 | 11 | 10 | 9 | 8 | 7 | 6 | 5 | 4 | 3 |
| Y | 43 | 42 | 41 | 40 | 39 | 38 | 37 | 36 | 35 | 34 | 33 | 32 | 31 | 30 | 29 | 28 | 27 | 26 | 25 | 24 |

To Lary Sharp and Charlie Garbarini

My pastors and spiritual mentors who showed me the family of God

Contents

Acknowledgments

MANY PEOPLE HAVE HELPED this book come to fruition.

I am grateful to all my Rosemead colleagues, past and present, for creating a wonderful, stimulating environment in which to work and pursue scholarship. In particular, I want to thank Keith Edwards and John Coe for their mentoring, support, and formative influence on my scholarship throughout my career. In addition, I'm grateful to Steve Porter and Jason McMartin, with whom I've had the pleasure of coteaching a graduate integration course for nearly a decade. They have sharpened my thinking regarding the theological foundations of relational spirituality.

I'm very grateful to many Rosemead students who have read and provided helpful feedback on various chapters in the anthropology class. I owe a debt of gratitude to a number of former Rosemead students who have worked on related projects with me, which helped shape the book: Annie Fujikawa, John Teal, Lauren Maltby, Brian Augustyn, Evonne Edwards, Kendra Bailey, and Brendon Jones.

I want to express my deep gratitude to my clients, past and present, who have given me the privilege of coming alongside them in their journey of growth and healing. Their courage has inspired me, and I have learned a great deal from our work together about myself and the growth process.

I'm thankful to my fellow members at the Institute for Research on Psychology and Spirituality (IRPS) at Rosemead/Biola for being stimulating dialogue partners over the last two decades. Many outstanding scholars have also served as dialogue partners and influenced my thinking, but in particular I want to highlight and thank Steve Sandage, Eric Johnson, and David Benner, whose work and encouragement have been a formative influence in my scholarship for which I am grateful.

I am grateful to the Rosemead administration, especially my former dean Clark Campbell, for two sabbaticals that supported the writing of this book. I also want to express my gratitude to the John Templeton Foundation, and the Center for Christian Thought (CCT) at Biola University for a semester-long fellowship that allowed me to focus on writing. In particular, I'd like to thank the CCT leadership during my fellowship: Steve Porter, Greg TenElshof, Tom Crisp, and Evan Rosa for creating a very special environment for deep, collaborative scholarship. I'm also very grateful to my cofellows at CCT who provided invaluable feedback on several chapters and the book as a whole: Kaye Cook, Eric Johnson, Christopher Kaczor, Jonathan Lunde, Alan Padgett, and Judy TenElshof. I'm grateful to Gene and Judy TenElshof for graciously allowing me to stay at their beautiful retreat center, Hilltop, so I could get away and focus on writing.

I owe a dept of gratitude to the entire IVP team, who have been wonderful partners in this project. In particular, I want to thank my editors, Gary Deddo who first believed in this book, David Congdon who encouraged me to keep the project going, and Jon Boyd who worked most closely with me to shape the book and bring it to completion. Jon's editing and conceptual expertise significantly improved the book, for which I am deeply grateful. I also wish to thank Rebecca Carhart, whose eye for detail in the editing process gave the book a much-needed final polish.

Finally, I am extremely grateful to my wife, Liz, for her unwavering support throughout this project. She provided emotional and practical support in countless ways, without which I could not have written the book. Ultimately, Liz became a contributor to the book, which undoubtedly improved it significantly. She updated some of the content and contributed significantly to several chapters. It has been an honor and delight to work with my wife on this book, which has been such big part of my life over the past ten years.

Author Note

For simplicity, the authorial voice throughout the book is the "I" of Todd Hall.

Introduction

The Emergence of a Relational Spirituality Paradigm

AS OUR SOCIETY IS BECOMING more socially fragmented and polarized, more Christians are feeling disconnected and struggling to grow spiritually. The recent COVID-19 pandemic has, of course, contributed to a sense of isolation, but the signs of a connection crisis were present prior to COVID-19.[1] Loneliness, for example, has increased in the past forty years to the point that it is now considered by some authorities to be a "growing health epidemic."[2] Over the same period, there has been a corresponding weakening of the family unit and communities.[3] The family unit, parent-child relationships in particular, is the most important social context in which children develop attachment bonds,

---

[1] Niobe Way, Alisha Ali, Carol Gilligan, and Pedro Noguera, *The Crisis of Connection: Roots, Consequences, and Solutions* (New York: NYU Press, 2018).

[2] In a recent article in *Harvard Business Review*, former US Surgeon General Vivek Murthy stated, "Loneliness is a growing health epidemic." He goes on to note that, despite being more technologically connected than ever, rates of loneliness have more than doubled since the 1980s. According to researcher Julianne Holt-Lunstad, loneliness is associated with a reduced lifespan similar to that caused by smoking fifteen cigarettes per day, and greater than the reduced lifespan predicted by obesity. Loneliness overlaps with a growing sense of disconnection and insecure attachment, which impacts people's connection to God. See Vivek Murthy, "Work and the Loneliness Epidemic: Reducing Isolation at Work Is Good for Business," *Harvard Business Review*, September 2017, https://hbr.org/cover-story/2017/09/work-and-the-loneliness-epidemic. See also Julianne Holt-Lunstad, Theodore F. Robles, and David A. Sbarra, "Advancing Social Connection as a Public Health Priority in the United States," *American Psychologist* 72, no. 6 (2017): 517-30.

[3] Regarding the decline of the family unit, see Judith S. Wallerstein, Julia M. Lewis, and Sandra Blakeslee, *The Unexpected Legacy of Divorce* (New York: Hyperion, 2000). Regarding the decline of community, see Robert D. Putnam, *Bowling Alone: The Collapse and Revival of American Community* (New York: Simon & Schuster, 2000).

which—as we will see—greatly impact our relationship with God. Related to these trends, millennials, more so than other generations, desire spiritual growth for the purpose of helping them work through struggles they have experienced.[4] More followers of Christ, it seems, need emotional healing as an integral part of their spiritual growth process.

Within many sectors of the evangelical movement, there is a growing recognition that our conceptual models of spiritual transformation[5] are not addressing these paramount issues. A recent study on the current state of discipleship, for example, noted that in many churches "there is an assumption that the appropriation of biblical knowledge will by itself lead to spiritual maturity."[6] This assumption gets to the heart of the problem this book addresses: a rationalistic paradigm of knowing God, ourselves, and others.

This rationalistic approach to Scripture and God, with long-standing historical roots we'll trace in chapter one, caused some segments of the evangelical movement to de-emphasize the messy process of growth and change. If the Bible is a set of facts to be properly arranged, and God is known *strictly* through explicit knowledge of propositions, then knowing God, ourselves, and others—indeed the entire task of theology—becomes a linear rationalistic process rather than a non-linear relational process.

This movement led to an unintended split between doctrine and Christian life, which has contributed to the growing sense of spiritual disconnection. In this vein, Donald Fairbairn states: "Part of the reason there is a divorce between doctrine and Christian life is that contemporary evangelicals normally understand 'doctrines' as concepts, teachings, true ideas (to which we often give the word *propositions*), and we unwittingly see these doctrines as the objects of our faith."[7] In reality,

---

[4]Barna Group, *The State of Discipleship* (Ventura, CA: Barna, 2015), 84. Thirty-six percent of millennials (compared to 33 percent of Gen-Xers, 30 percent of boomers, and 27 percent of elders) reported that spiritual growth would help them because they have "been through a lot."

[5]I primarily use the terms *spiritual development* and *spiritual transformation* throughout the book, and view these terms as parallel to the concept of sanctification within the theological literature.

[6]Barna Group, *The State of Discipleship* (Ventura, CA: Barna, 2015), 60.

[7]Donald Fairbairn, *Life in the Trinity: An Introduction to Theology with the Help of the Church Fathers* (Downers Grove, IL: IVP Academic, 2008), 4.

however, we do not believe in abstract doctrinal propositions such as justification per se. Rather we believe in—or perhaps it is better to say we *commit ourselves to or put our trust in*—the triune God who justifies us through our faith in Christ's sacrifice for our sins. If we approach knowing God strictly through explicit propositions, we risk making propositions the object of our faith, rather than God. Our doctrinal beliefs become separated from our relationship with God, which is constituted by participation in the divine love of the Trinity.

While there are ongoing problems caused by a rationalistic paradigm of knowing God, this is not the end of the story. In recent decades a new relational paradigm of human and spiritual development has been emerging from multiple fields. There is now a critical mass of evidence that human beings are fundamentally relational—that we develop, heal, and grow to become more loving and Christlike through relationships. This critical mass of evidence points to a relational spirituality paradigm.

A Relational Spirituality Paradigm

This new relational paradigm that is emerging provides a coherent picture of spiritual development—both the end goal and the process of how we get there. Beginning in the 1940s, there was a relational turn in psychology and related fields,[8] which converged with the growing interest in contemporary theology in the Trinity and community over the same period.[9] When we synthesize recent insights from fields such as trinitarian theology, spiritual theology, attachment theory, affective neuroscience, emotion theory, and interpersonal neurobiology, to name a few, we see common findings that converge on one unified reality and one big idea: *human beings are fundamentally relational, reflecting the relational nature of our triune God.*

---

[8]This relational turn can be traced back to the 1940s with the rise of relational theories within the field of psychoanalysis, such as object-relations theory and attachment theory. See Jay R. Greenberg and Stephen A. Mitchell, *Object Relations in Psychoanalytic Theory* (Cambridge, MA: Harvard University Press, 1983) and John Bowlby, *Attachment and Loss*, 3 vols. (New York: Basic Books, 1969–1976).

[9]Roderick Leupp, *The Renewal of Trinitarian Theology: Themes, Patterns & Explorations* (Downers Grove, IL: IVP Academic, 2008).

The revival in trinitarian theology during the second half of the twentieth century has brought into clearer focus the notion that God is fundamentally a relational being who exists in a community of mutual love within the three persons of the Trinity. This renewed interest in the Trinity places relationality and love, or God's loving relational presence, at the center of all theology. In this vein, recent scholarship has argued that God's relational presence is the "cohesive center" of biblical theology—that is, the through line of the entire biblical narrative.[10] This relational perspective also informs what it means to be created in the image of God. Just as God is intrinsically relational, so humans are created as relational beings. From a theological vantage point, a relational spirituality paradigm is showing us more clearly that we are born to love and created to connect.

Spiritual theology extends trinitarian theology by asking how our understanding of God as triune impacts our understanding of development in the Christian life across the entire spectrum of maturity. Within Protestant circles, there has been a renewed interest in spiritual theology and spiritual formation in the past few decades.[11] The growing sense of a disconnect or gap between doctrine and the Christian life has led to a renewed focus on the process of spiritual development—at the intellectual and experiential levels, and in church leadership and academic domains. We see here a parallel movement to that of the revival of trinitarian theology—a response to the split between theological reflection and spiritual life.

Spiritual theology focuses on our subjective experience of relationship with the triune God, and on the processes involved in growth toward spiritual maturity. As such, it explores both explicit theological concepts and experience, but the theoretical focus is on the inner workings of the spiritual development process. Within the field of spiritual theology, the conceptualization of this process is informed by a trinitarian spirituality,

---

[10]J. Scott Duvall and J. Daniel Hays, *God's Relational Presence: The Cohesive Center of Biblical Theology* (Grand Rapids, MI: Baker Academic, 2019).

[11]Simon Chan, *Spiritual Theology: A Systematic Study of the Christian Life* (Downers Grove, IL: IVP Academic, 1998).

which points toward relationality and loving presence. For example, Simon Chan suggests that a trinitarian spirituality includes three emphases.[12] First, salvation is conceptualized as a personal relationship with God. If God is a personal-relational being, then salvation must be understood as a relational notion. The goal of salvation so construed is intimacy with God. True salvation, as Chan notes, "must partake of the trinitarian life itself, which can be nothing other than an explicit knowledge of Christ and a conscious personal relationship that progresses toward intimacy and union."[13]

Second, spiritual life is relational, yet particular. I refer to this notion in chapter two as *being-in-relation*. Believers are connected to God and to the body of Christ as constituent members. However, this mutual dependence and relationality within the church coexists with individual particularity, and each dimension informs the other. Spiritual growth, then, involves becoming more interconnected with God and others while at the very same time inhabiting our unique personhood, which indeed requires being formed by others. Psychological theory and research in recent decades have significantly advanced our understanding of the inner workings of these processes, and we will return to this throughout the book. The loving presence within the Trinity further suggests that spiritual life and the body of Christ are constituted by deep family-type relationships. Thus, spiritual development requires loving presence and secure attachment, as well as Christian community. Finally, a trinitarian spirituality seeks participation in a unified mission of God that weaves together extending trinitarian life through the gospel message and developing full life in Christ within the body of Christ.

Psychological fields such as object-relations theory, relational psychoanalysis, and attachment theory have advanced our understanding of this trinitarian vision of spiritual development. All of these fields suggest that early relational experiences, particularly those in attachment relationships, are deeply imprinted into our social-emotional brain circuits, creating internal working models which then subconsciously guide the

---

[12]Chan, *Spiritual Theology*.
[13]Chan, *Spiritual Theology*, 53.

way we relate to God and others. Neuroscience and emotion theory further suggest that emotion and implicit memory are the mechanisms by which the implicit self evaluates the meaning of experiences for our well-being, always filtered by our relational history. We are gaining a deeper picture of how relationships profoundly shape our spiritual development and capacity to love.

With this relational spirituality paradigm that is emerging, we can begin to understand the proper roles of explicit theology and implicit spirituality, and to bring them into a unified process of spiritual transformation in which we become more loving and more like Christ. Loving presence, indeed, is the central goal of the spiritual development process. Spiritual maturity is about growing in love for God and others by participating in the mutual love of the Trinity in the context of the body of Christ. In short, we are loved into loving.

Purpose and Organization of the Book

The purpose of this book is to integrate these insights from multiple fields in order to present a new relational spirituality paradigm of spiritual transformation. My hope is that this broad synthesis will stimulate further dialogue with scholars from the many fields that touch on this topic, thereby advancing our understanding. At a practical level, the purpose of this book is to provide a working model to guide spiritual leaders and practitioners, including graduate students, pastors, pastoral counselors, spiritual directors, counselors, psychologists, missionaries, educators, and parachurch leaders.

The book is divided into three parts. Part one sets the stage for the need for a relational spirituality paradigm. Chapter one describes how theological reflection and lived spirituality, while once unified, became split apart, leaving us with disconnected doctrine or disconnected experience, each of which hinders a deep relationship with God and others.

Part two moves into the (relational) nature and goal of spiritual transformation. Chapter two presents a trinitarian-relational view of the image of God—a theology of being-in-relation. I draw on trinitarian theology to propose that human beings have a relational nature, which in turn manifests in a relational goal (what I refer to as *loving presence*) and a relational process of spiritual development. Chapter three describes evidence from infant research, attachment theory, and social neuroscience, among other fields, demonstrating that human beings are prewired or created to connect. In chapter four, we'll extend the idea that we are prewired to connect by discussing the role of different types of knowledge in the growth process. The chapter describes two distinct ways of knowing—explicit knowledge and implicit relational knowledge— and presents evidence from neuroscience, emotion theory, and clinical psychology that, while both are important, implicit relational knowledge is foundational for spiritual transformation.

Chapter five turns to relational knowledge in a very formative type of relationship—attachment relationships. Taking a broad view of attachment, we'll review research suggesting that the patterned experiences in attachment relationships form mental models (what I call *attachment filters*) of how relationships work for us, which then dynamically shape how we relate to others. I review common attachment patterns and present evidence that they tend to play out in our relationship with God. In chapters six and seven, we'll extend the implications of our relational nature to the relational *goal* of spiritual development, suggesting that it is *loving presence.* In chapter six it is proposed that the love among the three persons of the Trinity is the foundation for Christian love. Building on this foundation, the chapter discusses two essential components of love: goodwill and connection. In chapter seven we'll discuss some of the practical challenges in loving others—the art of love—and conclude with the contours of a model of distinctively Christian love.

In part three, the focus shifts to the relational process of spiritual transformation. In chapter eight, we'll consider how our deep relational knowledge, or attachment filters, change so that we grow in our love for God and others. I draw on the concept of nonlinear dynamic systems to show that spiritual development unfolds in a nonlinear way. The chapter then outlines how we change through relational processes with God and others, exploring the context, the process, and the practices of change.

The book concludes with chapter nine by putting spiritual transformation in the context of spiritual community. In the communal context of the church—the new family of God—we most fully express the image of God. The church is the context in which we both grow in love and shine forth God's love to the world. We'll highlight four key characteristics of spiritual community that help us create the kind of communities in which our souls are transformed by connecting our stories to God's grand story. We'll then explore how the two ways of knowing help us understand the function of spiritual community in our growth process. The goal of all of this is to help followers of Christ participate ever more deeply in the love of the Trinity, as we build the new family of God and reflect God's love back to the world. Now, let us embark on this journey and turn to part one, the need for a relational spirituality paradigm.

PART 1

The Need for a Relational Spirituality Paradigm

Theology and Spirituality

Their Fundamental Unity and Historical Split

WHY IS IT NECESSARY to reclaim relationality? We live in a world in which we take for granted distinctions between reason and experience, fact and value, theology and spirituality. We have a hard time imagining these polarities meeting in some meaningful way and have difficulty envisioning what a more unified outlook would entail. Yet it is also important to recognize that our current polarized vision of how we obtain truth, grow, and flourish has not always existed. The relational spirituality paradigm proposed in this book is actually a return to relationality—specifically, the grounding of all of our knowing in our relationship with God. What did this look like in the early church? We see important foundations for a relational spirituality paradigm in the holistic notion of theology, or *theologia*, in the early church.

Many of the great theologians prior to the thirteenth century viewed the intellectual exploration of the Christian faith and of the world God created as inseparable from a personal relationship with God and the practical outworking of one's faith and ministry. Sustained intellectual contemplation of the life of faith and thinking about the world in light of one's faith and Scripture went hand in hand with the development of one's heart, character, and love for God. There was a seamless connection between knowing about God and knowing God. Likewise, there was a close link between studying God's creation, including human nature and development, and living the Christian life. In fact, until the thirteenth century, theology (*theologia*) was foundationally *a deeply experiential way of knowing*. There were not distinct terms, such as *spirituality*, referring to experiential or even mystical knowledge of God on the one hand, and *theology*, representing academic, conceptual knowledge of God on the other hand.

Practical or experiential knowledge was viewed as the foundational way of knowing for theology and the Christian life. Early theologians certainly engaged in intellectual reflection, but this was viewed as intrinsically connected to prayer, loving God, and loving one's neighbor. Theology included conceptual analysis, but it was always more than this—analysis was never the central goal of *theologia*. Intellectual reflection was not pursued for its own sake; rather, it was pursued for the primary purpose of experiential knowledge of God, which is to say, growth in one's capacity to love God and others. The early church fathers' attempts to understand the relation of the soul to God and progress in the Christian life were the central organizing principles of their theology.

Likewise, mystical theology for the patristic fathers was not, generally speaking, a separate area of explicit, conceptual knowledge, or a special experience for the elite. Rather, it related to the breadth of the Christian life and incorporated both explicit and experiential knowledge of God. The word *mysticism* did not identify a distinct mode of spiritual knowledge or experience for the patristic fathers. However, the adjective *mystikos*, on which the word *mysticism* is based, was used frequently (for example, in the writings of Dionysius the Areopagite, author of *Mystical Theology*).[1] The noun *mysterion* means, most simply, a "secret," and so the adjective *mystikos* essentially means "simple or hidden." The word represented the notion of the secret life available in Christ, because the depth of the gospel has unending implications for our lives.

It was also used in intimate connection with the sacraments and the Eucharist, and thus was a communal experience. It did not refer to an ecstatic experience with a focus on an individual's experience of rapture, and it was not disconnected from doctrine. Rather, the *mystikos* life in

---

[1] Andrew Louth, *The Origins of the Christian Mystical Tradition* (New York: Oxford University Press, 2007).

Christ was precisely the working out of doctrine in the lived experience of Christians—a working out that went hand in hand with the gradual working out of the major doctrinal formulations during the first five centuries of Christianity. We may suggest, then, that the ecclesial, sacramental, and doctrinal were all seamlessly woven together in the mystical dimension for the Fathers. Andrew Louth put it this way: "'Mysticism,' in this sense, is not esoteric but exemplary, not some kind of flight from the bodily but deeply embedded (not to say: embodied), not about special 'experiences' of God but about a radical opening of ourselves to God."[2]

In part two, we will connect this experiential knowledge with the contemporary scientific concept of "implicit relational knowledge." Modern science elaborates on this way of knowing as essentially *relational*, which sheds light on the church fathers' approach, as well as elaborates on it. We need to recapture this focus in our contemporary context and bring the insights of the early notion of *theologia* into conversation with new understandings of relational knowledge.

The unity that existed in the early centuries of Christianity of what we now call theology, spirituality (including mysticism) eventually fractured. We now turn our attention to the main objective of this chapter, examining the development of a split between theology and spirituality and between two ways of knowing. In the remainder of the chapter, we trace the split from the harmonious coexistence of faith and reason in the early church fathers, through the development of scholastic theology in the Middle Ages, to the solidification of the split in the Enlightenment. We close by describing the implications of this split for contemporary evangelicalism, and particularly for our understanding and pursuit of spiritual development.

The Early Church Fathers: Faith and Reason in Harmony

When Christianity emerged in the centuries-old Roman Empire, early Christian scholars were faced with the question of what to do with the

---

[2]Louth, *Origins of the Christian Mystical Tradition*, 201.

secular learning inherited from pagan Greek sources, most notably Plato, Aristotle, Cicero, and the Stoics. Two conflicting attitudes developed. One tradition sought to protect Christianity by disengaging from the intellectual traditions of the pagan society out of which the Roman Empire was birthed. The classic expression of this tradition was articulated by Tertullian (ca. 150–ca. 225) when he wrote:

> What indeed has Athens to do with Jerusalem? What concord is there between the academy and the Church? What between heretics and Christians? . . . Away with all attempts to produce a mottled Christianity of Stoic, Platonic, and dialectic composition! We want no curious disputation after possessing Christ Jesus, no inquisition after enjoying the gospel! With our faith we desire no further belief.[3]

A second tradition proposed that pagan thought foreshadowed Christianity, and therefore, could provide insight to Christian scholars. This line of thought, which can be traced back to Philo,[4] held that Christians should take what is of value from pagan thought and use it for their own purposes, just as God instructed Moses to plunder the wealth of the Egyptians (Exodus 3:22; 11:2; 12:35).[5] This approach is thus sometimes referred to as "spoiling the Egyptians." A second rationale for seeking wisdom from secular philosophers was to use their own ideas as an apologetic against them. Christians, then, came to adopt the fundamental view of philosophy and science as "handmaids to theology."

This tradition is exemplified by Clement in early antiquity and Augustine in late antiquity. In responding to his objectors who argued that God had replaced philosophy (based on reason) with faith, Clement argued that the Greek poets and philosophers prepared the way for the gospel. Through natural reason, God guided philosophers toward truth, even if indirectly. According to Clement, "Jewish law and Greek philosophy have been two rivers, at whose confluence Christianity sprung

---

[3]Tertullian, *On Prescription Against Heretics*, chap. 7, trans. Peter Holmes, in *The Ante-Nicene Fathers*, ed. Alexander Roberts and James Donaldson, 10 vols. (New York: Charles Scribner's Sons, 1896–1903), 3:246.

[4]See Henry Chadwick, "Philo," in *The Cambridge History of Later Greek and Early Medieval Philosophy*, ed. A. H. Armstrong (Cambridge: Cambridge University Press, 1967), chap. 8.

[5]Edward Grant, *God and Reason in the Middle Ages* (New York: Cambridge University Press, 2001).

forth, like a new source, powerful enough to carry, along with its own waters, those of its two feeders."[6] Thus, the handmaiden tradition developed the ambition to grasp all truth that is accessible to humans. The search for truth through pagan learning and reason, however, was kept in check. Clement urged Christians to use secular learning without mistaking it for true Christian wisdom for which philosophy prepares us. While the gospel is sufficient for salvation, and encompasses a direct relationship with God, philosophy and reason can help lead people to Christ and help them understand the meaning of their Christian faith after accepting it. The significance of Clement lies in this deep articulation of the harmonious relationship between philosophy/reason and the Christian faith.

Augustine's conviction was that secular knowledge should not be sought as an end in itself.[7] The goal in plundering pagan philosophy is the search for Christian wisdom. Only studies that serve this purpose should be pursued. Reason, for Augustine and many of his followers, was not to follow logical arguments beyond the confines of revealed doctrine. When it came to theology and the spiritual life, which were highly intertwined for Augustine and the church fathers, the purpose of reason was to shed light on the truth of doctrine and deepen one's relationship and experiential knowledge of God. This stance of the handmaiden tradition assumed that one accepted faith prior to striving to understand it more deeply. For Augustine, to truly understand reason and logic, one must have a deep faith and relationship with God. This is reflected in the well-known phrase "faith seeking understanding" (*fides quaerens intellectum*). Faith, then, is primary in some sense and involves knowing God through direct relationship, and not merely through logic or reason.

What we see in this approach during this era is that faith and reason (including secular philosophy) were viewed as operating in harmony with one another. Reason and logic were applied to doctrine in order to

---

[6]Clement, *Miscellanies* 6.8, in Etienne Gilson, *History of Christian Philosophy in the Middle Ages* (New York: Random House, 1955), 32.

[7]Augustine, *On Christian Doctrine*, in *The Works of Saint Augustine, A Translation for the 21st Century, Vol. II: Teaching Christianity*, ed. John E. Rotelle, OSA (Hyde Park, NY: New City Press, 1996), 159-60.

bolster one's faith. Moreover, faith involved a direct relationship with God and a relational/experiential way of knowing, which was distinct from reason and assumed to be valid. The validity of this experiential way of knowing tied to faith gradually eroded as reason and explicit knowledge came to take center stage. This split began in the transition to the Middle Ages.

The Transition to the Middle Ages: The Foundations of the Split Between Faith and Reason

In the transition to the Middle Ages, Boethius, who has been referred to as the "Last of the Romans, first of the scholastics,"[8] reinforced and extended Augustine's approach to reason in relation to faith. As the Roman Empire fell, and the Goths of Theodoric's kingdom rose to power, the new Nordic-Germanic nations sought to master and assimilate the massive body of accumulated knowledge they came across, including patristic theology and the wisdom of classical antiquity. This required that the entire knowledge base be translated and systematized. The man who took on this task of selection and translation was Boethius (480–525).[9] In doing this, he compiled the most significant contribution to the history of reason in the early Middle Ages: the literature known as the old logic (*logica vetus*).

In considering the enormous undertaking and accomplishments of Boethius, it is not difficult to understand why he is considered one of the founders of the Middle Ages.[10] More important for our considerations, however, is that he is considered the first scholastic. Although scholasticism did not emerge as the primary method of thought in medieval universities until centuries later, Boethius started something altogether new that was to have major implications for the tension between two ways of knowing: faith (*fides*) and reason (*ratio*).

---

[8]Henry Chadwick, *Boethius: The Consolations of Music, Logic, Theology, and Philosophy* (Oxford: Clarendon Press, 1981), xi.

[9]This work was referred to as the scholarly endeavors to which the name *scholasticism* would later be attached in the eleventh century.

[10]See E. K. Rand, *Founders of the Middle Ages,* 2nd ed. (Cambridge, MA: Harvard University Press, 2013), 135-80.

What, then, was new? Boethius extended Augustine's approach of applying Aristotelian logic to theological issues. In his introduction to the tractate on the Trinity, Boethius probed the oneness of God. In so doing, he declared his intention to explain the doctrine of the Trinity "only so far as the insight of man's reason is allowed to climb the height of heavenly knowledge."[11] Thus, his goal was to make the trinitarian nature of God understandable to the rational mind using solely rational means. While a rational understanding of belief was assumed in prior times, the novelty of Boethius's approach was his overt emphasis on reason. The last sentence of Boethius's letter on the Trinity, addressed to Pope John I, shows this emphasis: "As far as you are able, join faith to reason."[12] It was more than just this explicit emphasis on reason that was new, however. It was also Boethius's method, the way in which he carried out this principle of rational examination, that was extraordinarily new.[13] His tractates did not include a single Bible quotation, despite the fact that they deal entirely with theological subjects. He used only logic and mathematics as his models. Henry Chadwick notes that Boethius

> taught the Latin West, above all else, the method of axiomatization, that is, of analyzing an argument and making explicit the fundamental presuppositions and definitions on which its cogency rests. He taught his successors how to state truths in terms of first principles and then to trace how particular conclusions follow therefrom. The West learnt from him demonstrative method.[14]

While this logical and extrabiblical approach is a thread of scholasticism, a central characteristic of scholasticism that emerged from Boethius is the explicit principle of joining faith and reason. As we can see throughout history, this is a most difficult endeavor. However, some of the leading thinkers of the scholastic era, such as Thomas Aquinas, attempted to coordinate knowledge of revealed truth through faith, on the one hand, and knowledge through reason on the other hand. Josef Pieper

---

[11]Boethius, *The Theological Tractates*, trans. H. F. Steward, E. K. Rand, and S. J. Tester (London: William Heinemann Ltd.; Cambridge, MA: Harvard University Press, 1973), 5.

[12]Quoted in Josef Pieper, *Scholasticism* (South Bend, IN: St. Augustine's Press, 2001), 37.

[13]Josef Pieper, *Scholasticism* (South Bend, IN: St. Augustine's Press, 2001).

[14]Henry Chadwick, *Boethius: The Consolations of Music, Logic, Theology, and Philosophy* (Oxford: Clarendon Press, 1981), 210.

notes that they succeeded in balancing the tensions between faith and reason for a brief moment in the period referred to as "high scholasticism" that came to a close at the end of the thirteenth century.[15]

We have, then, a curious and complex situation. On the one hand, we have a principle that seeks to bring together faith and reason. On the other, we have the seeds of a line of thinking that led to a focus on reason and rationalism—to an approach to knowledge of God that at its worst reduced the mysteries of God to that which can be understood by the rational mind. This seed goes back to Boethius. Perhaps Boethius took knowledge by faith for granted and assumed reason and logic would bolster's one's faith. Indeed, during his time up through the late Middle Ages, scholars universally held that there was a single, true account of humankind and the universe and that there was an omnipotent God. In other words, theology was always the context for doing philosophy until the late Middle Ages, when philosophy began to develop as an independent field from theology.

However, despite the task of joining faith and reason, and despite the varying degrees of success in this endeavor by some of the leading thinkers of this era, Boethius appears to have paved the way for a method and approach to knowledge that focused heavily—and at times exclusively—on reason and logic and did not make explicit connections to a more personal knowledge of faith. As Gilson notes, "His theological tractates set the example, which was to obsess certain fine minds in the middle ages, of a scientific theology, systematically deduced from previously-defined terms."[16]

The Late Middle Ages: The Beginnings of the Tension Between Faith and Reason

A shift in the medieval outlook can be seen when Anselm, the abbot of Bec, developed the analytic introspective method in 1079. Anselm's pupils at Le Bec had asked him to demonstrate God's existence without appealing to authority or revelation. Pondering this, one day he entered

---

[15]Pieper, *Scholasticism*.
[16]Gilson, *History of Christian Philosophy*, 106.

the "chamber of his mind," focused his attention solely on the word "God," and found that "the word articulated itself into a demonstration of God's existence, which he believed to be both new and true."[17] This was new for the times—that an individual could gain universal insight and knowledge from introspection was not part of the medieval mindset prior to this time. This coincided with the general trend of major technological advances, leading to an intellectual shift in which "man moved away from a confused trial-and-error approach, became objective and impersonal in his efforts, and grew aware of the complex structures of realities governed by natural laws."[18]

All of these developments combined to stimulate a new passion for learning that led to a proliferation of schools in the latter decades of the eleventh century and into the twelfth century. This led to a period of great intellectual and artistic flourishing, often referred to as the "twelfth-century renaissance." This scientific view of humanism was built on three interrelated ideas: the dignity of humanity, the dignity of nature itself, and the notion that the universe is orderly, intelligible, and accessible to human reason.[19] Underlying all these notions is a certain confidence in human powers to understand God and the universe.

Abelard and the rise of scholasticism. This overall intellectual zeitgeist gave birth to a very different approach to theology. Scholasticism began in the context of this humanistic revival, which influenced all fields, including philosophy and theology. Peter Abelard emphasized humankind's capacity for reason. He latched onto the new dialectic method stemming from Aristotelian logic and applied this to theology. He seems to have pursued learning for the sake of learning and

---

[17]While this proof appears to have come to Anselm suddenly, as if by intuition, the demonstration itself was based on logic. R. W. Southern, *Medieval Humanism and Other Studies* (New York: Harper & Row, 1970), 33.

[18]M. -D. Chenu, *Nature, Man, and Society in the Twelfth Century* (Chicago: University of Chicago Press, 1968), 43.

[19]R. W. Southern makes this distinction between a scientific view of humanism, and a literary view of humanism. He argues that to start with the literary humanism of the Renaissance misses a significant humanist theme of the early twelfth century, which focuses on the nobility of humanity, reason, and the intelligible order of the universe. See Southern, *Medieval Humanism and Other Studies*, 29-60.

his own reputation. Rather than pursuing conceptual or explicit knowledge for the sake of spiritual growth and the kingdom of God, Abelard became enchanted with the power of dialectic to oppose and defeat those who would debate him, as the opening paragraphs of his autobiography reveal:

> I preferred the weapons of dialectic to all the other teachings in philosophy, and armed with these I chose the conflicts of disputation instead of the trophies of war. I began to travel about in several provinces disputing, like a true peripatetic philosopher, wherever I had heard there was keen interest in the art of dialectic.[20]

Abelard represents a new class of teacher in the eleventh century—the individual master. This was a professional master who moved from school to school bringing a following with him and attracting new students due to his reputation and personal qualities.[21] They took the title of "sophist," aware of the parallels with the Greek sophists of Socrates's age. These teachers accepted fees and engaged in dialectic, the method that defined scholasticism more than anything else.

The rise of these masters of logic in the mid-eleventh century marks the beginning of scholasticism, which lasted from approximately 1050 to 1350.[22] The term *scholasticism* has been frequently used by historians as a synonym for medieval thought, which has hindered a more precise definition and understanding of this phenomenon. The term *scholastic* originally referred simply to one who learned or taught in a school in the Middle Ages. Scholastic philosophy was thus the type of philosophy taught in those schools. This broad notion, however, tells us little about the content of scholasticism. There is disagreement about the main pillars of the content of scholastic thought. However, there is more agreement that the term refers to a method of inquiry in medieval thought. Scholasticism was a method of discovering truth by means of a dialectic based on Aristotelian logic. Throughout the phases of

---

[20]Quoted in Sister Edmee, "Bernard and Abelard," in *The Influence of Saint Bernard*, ed. Sister Benedicta Ward (London: SLG Press, 1976), 96.

[21]David Knowles, *The Evolution of Medieval Thought* (New York: Vintage Books, 1962).

[22]Knowles, *Evolution of Medieval Thought.*

medieval thought, dialectic used a basic pattern of question (*quaestio*), argument (*disputatio*), and conclusion or opinion (*sententia*). This can be seen in a wide range of forms of medieval thought, from the dialogues of Saint Anselm, to Peter Lombard's *Sentences*, to the *Summae* of the thirteenth century.

Dialectic was initially used for exposition of texts, but Peter Abelard developed it as an independent method. The dialectic method led to the distinction between commentary/exposition (*lectio*) and articulating the relationships and patterns between ideas (*quaestio*). Before dialectic was developed, the order of questions was arbitrary, but works began to sequence questions in a rational order, which revealed the logical relationships between the questions.

Despite Abelard's emphasis on logic, he was not a rationalist in the modern sense. He didn't use reason to challenge Christian doctrine as formulated by tradition. After his theological views were condemned at Sens in 1141, he expressed this view in a letter: "I will never be a philosopher, if this is to speak against Saint Paul; I would not be an Aristotle, if this were to separate me from Christ."[23] "These," as David Knowles notes, "are not the words of a deliberate heretic or of a professed rationalist."[24] He viewed divine authority as supreme and never continued to teach theological views that had been censured by the church.

However, Abelard believed that logic and reason were paramount for understanding faith that is accepted on the authority of God and the church. He sought to explain, whenever possible, Christian doctrine by dialectic and reason. One of the purposes for doing this was to defend the faith against heretics. Heretics often attacked the faith using philosophical arguments, and it was commonly held in the twelfth century that defenders of the faith should use heretics' own tactics against them. "Those who attack our faith," he stated, "assail us above all with philosophical reasonings. It is those reasonings which we have principally enquired into and I believe that no one can fully understand them

---

[23] As translated in Knowles, *Evolution of Medieval Thought*, 123.
[24] Knowles, *Evolution of Medieval Thought*, 123.

without applying himself to philosophical and especially to dialectical studies."[25]

Abelard's motive for applying reason to theology appears to have been broader than just defending the faith. He was in essence a logician and seems to have been somewhat obsessed with reason, which permeated his theological works. David Knowles captures the sentiment of Abelard well:

> The dogmas of the faith are not for him wells of infinite depth, the reflection in words of luminous supernatural truth. Rather, they are so many propositions or facts thrown, so to say, to the Christian philosopher, upon which he may exercise his ingenuity and to which he can apply no laws but those of logic and grammar. A modern analogy may perhaps be found in the attitude towards the gospels of many sincerely religious scholars, who subject the texts to the rigours of "form criticism," without any regard to the interpretation of past ages, and without any explicit consideration of the words as bearing a deep and divine weight of meaning which can only be grasped by one whose mind and heart are attuned to a spiritual purpose.[26]

It was Abelard who first used the word *theologia* in its contemporary sense—that is, as a discipline with a methodology and body of explicit content. The term previously had been used to refer to a contemplative, experiential knowledge of God. This shift in the meaning of the term, initiated by Abelard, is reflected in the development of theology as a discipline in the universities, which he helped to solidify with the application of dialectic and his introductions to theology. We turn now to the formalization of scholastic theology in the medieval universities.

The development of scholastic theology in medieval universities. Toward the middle of the twelfth century, a monumental series of events occurred that would change the face of the medieval university forever: the translation and availability of ancient Greek and more recent Arabic and Jewish thought.[27] The greatest impact in philosophy and theology was from Aristotle's thought, which was revealed gradually over time

[25]As translated in D. E. Luscombe, "Peter Abelard," in *A History of Twelfth-Century Western Philosophy*, ed. Peter Dronke (Cambridge: Cambridge University Press, 1988), 294, n. 57.
[26]Knowles, *Evolution of Medieval Thought*, 124.
[27]Knowles, *Evolution of Medieval Thought*.

until it dominated the university curriculum and Aristotle replaced Plato as "the Philosopher" in the schools. This had a profound effect on the universities and on theology because of the supremely rational character of Aristotle's thought. Boethius's earlier translations of some of Aristotle's work served as a basis for these later translations. The translation of ancient Greek, Arabic, and Jewish thought, and the rediscovery of Aristotle as part of that process, took well over a century, lasting from the early 1100s until about 1270.[28]

Aristotle's so-called new logic (in contrast to the "old logic" compiled by Boethius) focused on different modes of propositions, syllogisms, argumentation methods, and the detection of fallacies. The impact of the new logic, available at least by 1158, on the universities and faculty of theology is difficult to overstate. John of Salisbury illustrates the impact when, in 1159, he declared that the new logic was the sine qua non for future dialecticians.[29]

The new logic had an immediate impact as it built on the dialectical tradition that was already in full swing. As David Knowles notes, the new logic "canonized, for the whole of the middle ages and beyond, the question and disputation as the basic form of all teaching and discovery."[30] Since this was the requirement for the bachelor of arts degree, which was a prerequisite to study in the higher faculties of theology (as well as medicine and law), it became the common curriculum and had an enormous impact on theology. All masters of theology (professors) had studied the new logic prior to studying theology. Likewise, all students entering the faculty of theology had studied the new logic, as well as natural philosophy (or natural science).[31] Thus, they were immersed in the Aristotelian rationalistic approach to the world and were eager to apply this to their theological studies. The spiritual emphasis of the

---

[28]Knowles, *Evolution of Medieval Thought.*

[29]Knowles, *Evolution of Medieval Thought.*

[30]Knowles, *Evolution of Medieval Thought*, 190.

[31]Natural philosophy, sometimes called natural science, involved the systematic application of logic and reason to the natural world and was the first phase in the process that would later become modern science. It focused on studying physical bodies that are capable of motion and subject to change. See Grant, *God and Reason in the Middle Ages*, 148-206, for a discussion of natural philosophy.

monastic culture was supplanted over time, contributing to a highly scientific approach to theology.

As the new logic was being imported into the universities, some within the faculty of arts began extending it into the realm of theology in ways that opposed orthodox theological teaching. Conservative ecclesiastical authorities and theology faculty members in Paris became concerned about the secular learning being brought into the West, particularly in the latter half of the twelfth century.[32] Part of what the conservative group from the faculty of theology was concerned about was the notion of "double truth."[33] This teaching proposed that philosophical truth could exist in parallel to contradictory theological truth.[34] Theology has its own truth, and natural philosophy has its own truth, and they are completely separate domains that never impinge on each other—or so they seemed to imply. This seemed to be a move by the faculty of arts to protect themselves from the more conservative theologians setting parameters around the knowledge claims that were possible through reason and natural philosophy. The trend of embracing the idea of double truth clearly shows the foundational emphasis that was given to the new logic. While this notion emerged first within the faculty of arts, the underlying mindset it represents was gradually permeating the entire university, including the faculty of theology. We can see here a foreshadowing of the separation between faith and reason a century later, in which faith was no longer considered to be knowledge.

As theology gradually became a "faculty," or department in the medieval universities, it became institutionalized as a discipline. With this institutionalization came a standard course of study, a methodology, and a body of content that had to be mastered by students. The university context for studying theology simply reinforced *theologia* as explicit knowledge. To engage in theology was to engage in a rational, dialectic process of question, dispute, and conclusion, and to master a body of

---

[32]Grant, *God and Reason in the Middle Ages.*

[33]This teaching had its roots in Averroes, the great Arabian commentator on Aristotle, and was imported by the Latin Averroists of Paris in the thirteenth century. See Grant, *God and Reason in the Middle Ages.*

[34]Knowles, *Evolution of Medieval Thought,* 273.

standard, explicit content about God, Scripture, and increasingly, natural philosophy as well. Moreover, this was now done in a very systematic way in the university, the goal of which was to obtain a degree reflecting one's learning of explicit knowledge, not to grow in one's spiritual life as was generally the case in the monastic context.

Over time, experiential or contemplative knowledge was relegated to the domains of mysticism, spirituality, and faith (in revelation), which lost their epistemic status as knowledge. This split, which was solidified by the end of the Middle Ages, was exacerbated in certain ways by the Enlightenment. The seamless unity between what we now call theology and spirituality began to separate with scholastic theology in the twelfth century. History would see this split reinforced with the advent of the Enlightenment, the dominant intellectual movement during the modern period, to which we now turn.

The Enlightenment: The Consolidation of the Split Between Faith and Reason

In very broad terms, the Enlightenment project sought to use reason to free human knowing from any reliance on God and subjectivity. The general approach was to derive principles and laws based on logical analysis of empirical observations.[35] Anything outside the parameters of reason was gradually relegated to the inferior domain of faith. The Enlightenment saw the development of a rationalistic model of knowledge that was imported into theology, which, as we have seen, was already a discipline based on reason that was separated in both context and ethos from a deep experiential knowledge of God. Thus, deeper, more personal ways of knowing involving emotion and intuition played little role in the knowing process in the rationalistic paradigm. This further removed *theologia* from experiential knowledge of God, or our contemporary notion of spirituality. As we will see, it was also particularly disastrous to our understanding of persons and the knowing process in relationships, including our relationship with God.

---

[35]Ernst Cassirer, *The Philosophy of the Enlightenment* (Princeton, NJ: Princeton University Press, 1951).

The Enlightenment took on a particular sensibility in the United States, where its ideals provided the intellectual material needed for an American synthesis that allowed a harmonious existence between empirical science, the self-evident principles of the American Revolution, and evangelical Christianity.[36] It became the basis for stability in a new social order in a new nation, and the basis by which evangelicals defended the place of traditional faith in a traditionless society.[37]

Enlightenment thinkers in this context argued that all humans possess a common set of capacities that allow them to perceive the realities of nature and morality. A combination of empirical observation and common-sense reason would unfailingly reveal the moral truths that undergird Scripture and a new society. The scientific methods of Francis Bacon became so popular in America that they were incorporated into revivals in the Second Great Awakening. Charles Finney, for example, believed that producing a revival follows orderly scientific principles just as much as natural sciences do. This empirical, common-sense way of knowing became the lens through which the Bible and spirituality were viewed.

Leonard Woods Jr., an orthodox Congregationalist, argued in 1822 that the method of physics was the best method for studying the Bible because such methods were regulated "by the maxims of Bacon and Newton." The empirical method of Bacon and Newton, Woods argued, "is as applicable in theology as in physics, although in theology we have an extra-aid, the revelation of the Bible. But in each science reasoning is the same—we inquire for facts and from them arrive at general truths."[38]

By the end of the nineteenth century, Charles Hodge defined the "science" of theology as the collection and arrangement of the truths contained in the Bible:

> The Bible is to the theologian what nature is to the man of science. It is his store-house of facts; and his method of ascertaining what the Bible teaches, is

---

[36]George M. Marsden, *Understanding Fundamentalism and Evangelicalism* (Grand Rapids, MI: Eerdmans, 1991).

[37]Mark A. Noll, *The Scandal of the Evangelical Mind* (Grand Rapids, MI: Eerdmans, 1994).

[38]Quoted in Marsden, *Understanding Fundamentalism and Evangelicalism*, 97.

the same as that which the natural philosopher adopts to ascertain what nature teaches. . . . The duty of the Christian theologian is to ascertain, collect, and combine all the facts which God has revealed concerning himself and our relation to him. These facts are all in the Bible.[39]

A rationalistic approach to Scripture was exemplified by dispensational theology, brought to North America in the mid-nineteenth century by John Nelson Darby, a leader in the Plymouth Brethren tradition. This emphasis grew with the rise of fundamentalism as a result of the liberal-fundamentalist controversy in the early 1900s, but dispensationalist teachings had been promoted for nearly half a century through prophecy conferences, Bible institutes, and the Scofield Reference Bible (1909). Mark Noll argues that dispensationalism was particularly dependent on Enlightenment views of the systematizing purposes of science.[40] Scofield justified his study Bible by arguing that "the old system of references, based solely upon the accident of the English words, was unscientific and often misleading."[41] Lewis Sperry Chafer likewise argued that he arrived at his conclusions about the meaning of Scriptures by "the most exacting of proofs."[42] His *Systematic Theology* exudes the Enlightenment rational methodology: "Systematic Theology is the collecting, scientifically arranging, comparing, exhibiting, and defending of all facts from any and every source concerning God and His work. . . . Contemplation of the doctrine of human conduct belongs properly to a science which purports to discover, classify, and exhibit the great doctrines of the Bible."[43]

At least in part, the dispensationalist approach to Scripture can be viewed as an outgrowth of the Enlightenment methodology, focusing on rational, explicit knowledge, and its confidence in the scientific method to validate Scripture and illuminate the path toward spiritual growth. The level of certitude claimed by some writers in this tradition can be associated with a methodology that embraces explicit knowledge to the exclusion of experiential knowledge of God.

---

[39]Charles Hodge, *Systematic Theology*, 3 vols. (Grand Rapids, MI: Eerdmans, 1952), 1:10-11.
[40]Noll, *Scandal of the Evangelical Mind*.
[41]*Scofield Reference Bible*, rev. ed. (New York: Oxford University Press, 1917), iii.
[42]Lewis Sperry Chafer, *Dispensationalism* (Dallas: Dallas Seminary Press, 1936), 7.
[43]Lewis Sperry Chafer, *Systematic Theology*, 8 vols. (Dallas: Dallas Seminary Press, 1947), 1:115.

The almost blinding focus on explicit knowledge represented in early dispensational theology, and rationalist evangelicalism in general, may explain the primary difficulty of the Enlightenment approach, which Mark Noll argues is the "lack of self-consciousness characteristic of the nineteenth century's confidence in science."[44] It is not difficult to see how the evangelical Enlightenment attitude toward Scripture carried over to the ethos of spiritual life in general. If Scripture is a collection of facts to be arranged and grasped through scientific, Baconian principles, then spiritual transformation becomes a detached, scientific exercise. If the mysteries of God can be validated through empirical science, then one's spirituality can be reduced to the application of explicit knowledge of the Bible—to a set of propositions that can be scientifically validated. Just as the Enlightenment scientific method would unfailingly reveal truth to anyone applying common-sense reason to empirical observation (regardless of presuppositions), objective knowledge of God would pave the way toward spiritual transformation. The evangelical Enlightenment set off a chain of events that contributed to the rise of fundamentalism, which further exacerbated a thin, rationalistic model of spiritual transformation.

The Legacy of the Enlightenment on Contemporary Evangelicalism

Two centuries later, we continue to see the impact of the Enlightenment paradigm on evangelical sensibilities regarding human development and sanctification, which now occupy a very small and truncated piece of the theological pie. As mentioned previously, the story of the Enlightenment played out in a unique way in North America due its sociocultural context. It is a well-known story, and yet the degree to which it colors our contemporary view of spirituality within certain sectors of evangelicalism is difficult to overstate.

In the wake of the Enlightenment, numerous developments occurred in the Protestant tradition in North America that came to be called

---

[44]Noll, *Scandal of the Evangelical Mind*, 129.

evangelicalism that deeply affected our understanding and approach to sanctification. A set of interrelated sociocultural and theological influences converged, resulting in an overriding emphasis on doctrinal knowledge, which eclipsed the value of experiential knowledge and led to a thin conceptual model of spiritual development. There are undoubtedly many factors that contributed to this, but two interrelated themes are particularly germane for our purposes in understanding theology and spirituality, and the place of sanctification and relationality vis-à-vis the broader evangelical movement: the rise of the modern university and the conservative-liberal split.

The rise of the modern university. In 1850, most American college presidents were evangelical clergymen who promoted an evangelical stance in many important courses.[45] Science during this time was also dominated by evangelical Christians. They were busy verifying the Bible through scientific methods. By the end of the century, however, all this had changed. Colleges became universities based on the German scientific model. New universities were started, such as Johns Hopkins University in 1876, to pursue modern science and research. These universities were not funded by Christian communities but by a new generation of wealthy entrepreneurs.[46] As such, concern about the orthodoxy of faculty and administrators diminished, and gradually a new class of businessmen replaced clergymen as the higher education leaders. Disciplines became increasingly specialized and professional, a trend to which evangelicals contributed.

Evangelicalism's attraction to the Enlightenment science contributed to the separation of science and theology, sometimes referred to as "methodological secularization." Science and theology were viewed as two separate but harmonious realms, but science was viewed as the foundational proof for religion. This was already a concession to a naturalistic epistemology. Science was given an epistemological job it was not capable of carrying out, which led to further problems. This was most pronounced in the natural sciences, where the points of contact between

---

[45]Noll, *Scandal of the Evangelical Mind*, 129.
[46]Noll, *Scandal of the Evangelical Mind*.

Christianity and science were not entirely clear. Evangelicals contributed to this methodological secularization unwittingly by pursuing science in isolation from theology and spirituality, which extended the trend that developed in the Middle Ages of pursuing natural philosophy apart from theology.

These evangelicals believed that rational moral science and Scripture would reveal completely harmonious findings, so it was therefore not a problem to pursue the two independently. Francis Wayland, for example, proclaimed, "So complete is this coincidence as to afford irrefragable proof that the Bible contains the moral laws of the universe; and hence, that the Author of the universe—that is of natural religion—is also the Author of the Scriptures."[47] In the natural sciences, the most common way of relating science to Christianity was the "doxological"—that science should lead one to worship God.[48] While there is something right in the doxological sentiment, over time the Enlightenment epistemological underpinnings of this approach led to a gradual drifting apart of science and religion, which was exacerbated by the professionalization of the American academy that was occurring in parallel. The disciplines became increasingly narrow and isolated from theology.

It is difficult to overestimate the devastating effect of this separation of science from theology. While there were certainly limitations in the work of premodern theologians, in a general sense they did seem to better integrate knowledge of God's creation (*scientia*) with wisdom (*sapientia*), or knowledge of the eternal truths of God. Science was to be done in the context of one's relationship with God, both for doxological purposes and to bring uniquely Christian wisdom to bear on the scientific endeavor. As science and theology came to operate on separate, parallel tracks, they no longer seemed to need each other. As the scientific disciplines now only referred to Christian theology *after* reaching their conclusions—as a nonintegral afterthought—it made it all the easier for the next generation of academics to simply drop this

---

[47]Francis Wayland, *The Elements of Moral Science* (Boston: Gould, Kendall, and Lincoln, 1844), 136.

[48]Marsden, *Understanding Fundamentalism and Evangelicalism*.

step altogether. By the 1920s, it was no longer in fashion to hold Christian beliefs in the academy. Just as science dropped Christian theology in the early twentieth century, forces were at work that would eventually lead evangelicals to distance from science and intellectual pursuits, leading to what George Marsden called the "academic dark age of conservative evangelicalism" during the 1920s to 1940s.[49] As we will explore further below, this led to a lack of in-depth study of spiritual development, which was one of the major negative consequences of the legacy of the Enlightenment.

The conservative-liberal split. A convergence of trends including urbanization, the social gospel, and the secularization of society and the academy led to a split in North American evangelicalism. Amid the vast changes occurring in society, theological liberalism sought to save some form of Protestantism that could peacefully coexist with the seeming certainty of the rising tide of secular humanism and higher criticism. Many of the leaders in the liberal movement had evangelical upbringings and likely formed an emotional attachment to Christianity. When they came to the universities and the leading theological seminaries, they found that classical evangelical beliefs were not intellectually respectable. The future leaders of the liberal movement were faced with a choice from their perspective: abandon Christianity altogether, or accommodate Christian theology to fit with the new scientific ethos. While some did abandon the faith, others chose the path of accommodation—presumably those with an emotional attachment to Christianity. In order to do this, they had to *liberate* Christianity from its traditional beliefs (hence the term *liberalism*) and align it with the *modern* scientific zeitgeist (hence the movement is also referred to as *modernism*). Three core strategies were involved in this liberating, modernizing process, all of which led to a reaction among conservatives and to a split between these two groups.[50] The significance of the split for our purposes is that it led to the conservative fundamentalist movement, which held on to

---

[49]Marsden, *Understanding Fundamentalism and Evangelicalism*, 183.
[50]Marsden, *Understanding Fundamentalism and Evangelicalism*. See chapter one for a more thorough discussion of the strategies of liberalism.

classical Protestant doctrine, but at the expense of a deep experiential knowledge of God.

First, Darwinism was applied to understanding religion as a move to protect Christianity from historical and scientific criticism. Christianity and the Bible were viewed as products of social evolution. This changed the rules of engagement. The issue was no longer whether the Bible was historically true or not. That was not a meaningful question in the framework of social Darwinism. In the modern view, God reveals himself in human history and social change is a manifestation of the kingdom of God. God works through the natural means of our religious experiences. The Bible was no longer a testimony of factual events about the incarnation of God in Christ. Rather, the Bible was viewed as a record of the religious experience of the Hebrew people. It was a faithful rendering of such religious experiences, and that was its whole point. Understanding such religious experiences would help humanity advance. Christianity, recast according to modernism, was immune to historical criticism, but focused on religious experience untethered from biblical doctrine.

A second way of protecting Christian doctrine from the attack of higher criticism was to identify Christianity solely with how we live, not with what we believe. Liberals argued that Jesus emphasized the ethical dimension of life, and this would surely outlast the onslaught of higher criticism. This led to an emphasis on Sunday school education, since most liberals had become connected to Christianity through nurturing Sunday school experiences rather than through radical conversion experiences.

The third strategy of liberalism was to emphasize religious feelings as central to Christianity. In this strategy, the modern theological movement followed the German theologian Friedrich Schleiermacher (1768–1834) in asserting that religion is based on the subjective experience of absolute dependence. Science and historical criticism could pursue its agenda, but it could not touch the realm of the heart. Christianity once again had been saved from, and put on a parallel track with, modern science, in a way that reminds one of the notion of double truth in the late twelfth century that we highlighted above. However, this was a Christianity re-envisioned to the point that it was no longer recognizable to conservative evangelicals. Part of the profound confusion here is that emotion and the heart play a critical role in spiritual transformation, but because liberalism co-opted religious feelings into a framework that recast the very nature of the gospel, emotion became associated in many evangelical circles with the dismissal of doctrine in general and with the social gospel in particular. As a result, over time some segments of the conservative movement threw the baby out with the bathwater.

As the modern theological movement developed in the early 1900s, it led to the fundamentalist-modernist controversy that broke wide open in the 1920s. In the first decade of the twentieth century, fundamentalism focused on providing a defense of traditional Christian doctrine. As time went on, the movement developed an oppositional and separatist stance. More and more, fundamentalists combated liberal theology, religious experience, and the social gospel, which was substituting personal regeneration through Christ with social reform. Personal regeneration through Christ was a nonnegotiable doctrine of Christianity to fundamentalists, and they did not want this to get lost in the social gospel movement. Hence, they de-emphasized social justice and increasingly emphasized correct doctrine and personal regeneration, which reflected the great reversal of American evangelicalism.

Fundamentalism also gradually shifted from a scholarly strategy to a political one, which centered on opposing the teaching of biological evolution in America's public schools. This came to a head in the famous 1925 Scopes trial, testing the anti-evolution law in Tennessee. Scopes's guilt was quickly established, but the key to the trial was when Clarence Darrow put William Jennings Bryan on the witness stand.[51] Darrow succeeded in demonstrating that Bryan, a leading critic of evolution, did not have extensive knowledge about biological science, making his position appear foolish. Fundamentalists were painted as opposing academic freedom and attempting to force their views on the public through

---

[51]Marsden, *Understanding Fundamentalism and Evangelicalism.*

political means. Consequently, the national influence of fundamentalism waned significantly after 1925. No longer able to influence the culture through politics, they began to retreat from public life.

With this loss of influence in universities, denominations, and public opinion, the conservative fundamentalist branch began to establish its own structures. This, as Mark Noll has argued at length, led to disastrous results for the life of the evangelical mind.[52] Related to the "scandal of the evangelical mind," there are two aspects of fundamentalism that have led to a thin, rationalistic approach to spiritual transformation.

First, reminiscent of the Reformation, fundamentalism led to a focus on doctrine, and because of that, explicit knowledge. The reasons for this are understandable in historical context. In their view, the modern theological movement—including the emphasis on religious experience, ethics, and the social gospel over and against belief and doctrine—was changing the very nature of the gospel and historic, orthodox Christianity. Fundamentalist leaders felt compelled to emphasize correct doctrine—the "fundamentals of the faith" as they were called. Because the boundaries on essential doctrines were being pushed, they felt the need to focus on holding these boundaries. This created an ethos in which (fundamentalist) evangelicalism, and indirectly spiritual growth, became about believing correct doctrine in a narrow rational sense, more than about deep implicit beliefs embodied in love of God and neighbor. Relationality was lost in the fundamentalist fray. We see here a new version of dead orthodoxy. Just as German Lutherans emphasized explicit confessions to contrast themselves from Calvinists in the Second Reformation, fundamentalists emphasized the explicit fundamentals of the faith to differentiate themselves from their liberal counterparts.

Moreover, the fact that the liberal movement emphasized ethics, social justice, and religious feelings meant that fundamentalists had to denounce such things—at least from their perspective. Ethics and social justice were de-emphasized partly because of their connection to liberal theology. We can see difficulty throughout the movement in

---

[52]Noll, *Scandal of the Evangelical Mind.*

holding tensions—in holding experiential knowledge together with explicit knowledge of doctrine. The result was a dead fundamentalist orthodoxy that has hindered the development of relational spirituality in evangelicalism.

Second, as fundamentalists lost control over the major academic institutions, they started their own schools. Bible institutes were started to focus on practical training in evangelism and ministry. Other disciplines were only studied insofar as they directly assisted the cause of evangelism and ministry. Likewise, fundamentalists started autonomous seminaries, separate from colleges and universities, which was a North American creation.[53] Just as theology was becoming split from spirituality as a result of the Enlightenment, it was also, not coincidentally, becoming separated from other disciplines. This had a negative impact on the development of a robust theoretical paradigm for sanctification, to which we will return momentarily. This split was part of the overall professionalization and narrowing of academic disciplines. The problem here is indirectly related to a narrow Enlightenment focus on explicit knowledge to the exclusion of experiential knowledge. Enlightenment science propagated a narrow, truncated epistemology. In this view, the only way of truly knowing something is through rational, explicit means. Over time this view infiltrated our deep beliefs and practices related to spiritual development. The result was that knowing God gradually shifted toward knowing about God. There was certainly good that came out of these academic institutions; however, spiritual growth and maturity received relatively little attention and by default came to be associated with the explicit knowledge gained in the formalized discipline of theology.

It should be acknowledged that this split between faith and reason, reflected in the liberal-fundamentalist split, did not affect all of North American Christianity equally. African American Christianity, in particular, seems to have maintained a tighter connection between faith and reason, between evangelism and social justice concerns, between lived reality and theology. James Evans Jr. writes, "The black religious story is

---

[53]Noll, *Scandal of the Evangelical Mind*.

an attempt to integrate both the inner, personal and the outer, political life of its hearers in the midst of moral chaos."[54] The backdrop of slavery did not allow the luxury of separating out everyday life from theology, and religious experience was a powerful source of comfort to African American Christians. In addition, metaphysical and epistemological commitments reflect the encounter with traditional African concepts, including the view that the whole universe is sacred, as well as reflecting the conversion to Christianity during slavery.[55]

These factors minimized the influence of a Western Enlightenment heritage. Consequently, "reason . . . is not a primary source for African American theology. . . . Reliance on the categories of formal episte-mology or on the 'objective' approach to the faith is not particularly useful to African American theology because those categories cannot always adequately explain African American experience."[56] Instead, the-ology in the context of the African American church has historically brought together theological insights related to freedom, justice, and equality with the sociopolitical and spiritual needs of black people.[57] This kind of context, instead of resulting in a fundamentalist retreat from the social gospel, was able to produce a Martin Luther King Jr. and birth the civil rights movement.

The Split and the Current State of Spiritual Development

Let us pause here to recap what we have learned about the split between faith and reason, and the consequent split between theology as informed by both relational/experiential and explicit knowledge and theology as a purely explicit discipline. From the beginning of the Middle Ages through the final split in the Enlightenment, theology moved slowly away from encom-passing both relational/experiential knowledge and explicit knowledge to becoming more clearly defined as a distinct discipline representing explicit

---

[54]James H. Evans Jr., *We Have Been Believers: An African-American Systematic Theology* (Minne-apolis: Fortress Press, 1992), 25.

[55]C. Eric Lincoln and Lawrence H. Mamiya, *The Black Church in the African American Experience* (Durham, NC: Duke University Press, 1990), 2.

[56]Evans, *We Have Been Believers*, 28-29.

[57]Lincoln and Mamiya, *Black Church*, 7.

knowledge. By the end of the thirteenth century, the scholastic method of dialectic or logic had been embraced as the primary methodological approach, and the content of the discipline of theology had been standardized. Furthermore, philosophy and theology had been distinguished from each other, and theology was relegated to the realm of belief (or opinion) in contrast to knowledge. This line of the original, integrative theology (*theologia*) became associated over time with faith, spirituality, and religious experience. A second line of theology became identified with the explicit study and knowledge of God, and separated from its original context of contemplation of God: the pursuit of a deep experiential knowledge of God.

The impact of the Enlightenment on sanctification within North American evangelicalism was an ironic one-two punch. On the one hand, evangelicalism's love affair with the Enlightenment led to an overly rationalistic approach to the Bible and spirituality that privileged explicit knowledge at the expense of relational/experiential knowledge. This split was captured by Richard Lovelace in his book *Dynamics of Spiritual Life*, in which he labeled it "the sanctification gap."[58] Lovelace lamented a split between many Christians' explicit knowledge about theological doctrine and their sanctification, or actual growth in their relationship with God.

On the other hand, this love affair with science unwittingly led to the separation of science and religion, which paved the way for the secularization of the academy. As Christianity was gradually being removed from the public intellectual arena, anti-Christian polemicists promoted an overstated image of a long-standing war between science and religion. This further polarized the liberal-fundamentalist split. This led to fundamentalists retreating from the social sciences, society, and intellectual life in general. They started their own Bible institutes and seminaries and focused on studying the Bible but gave limited focus to studying other disciplines. All of these trends, ultimately stemming from a staunch commitment to Enlightenment science, have deeply shaped evangelicalism's understanding of sanctification, in both

---

[58]See Richard Lovelace, *Dynamics of Spiritual Life: An Evangelical Theology of Renewal*, expanded ed. (Downers Grove, IL: IVP Academic, 2020) for a discussion of "the sanctification gap."

direct and indirect ways. It has led to a model of spiritual development—permeating the very fabric of many segments of evangelicalism—that is at once overly rational and at the same time underdeveloped in its theory of spiritual experience and development.

This state of affairs suggests that something more is required to grow than explicit knowledge by itself. The early church fathers and mothers would commend to us the singular importance of a deep relational knowing of God, something that has been all but lost in significant sectors of the Protestant and evangelical traditions. This, however, raises two crucial questions. First, what is the role of explicit knowledge in spiritual development? Second, do explicit and relational/experiential knowledge work together somehow, and if so, how? The split and resulting sanctification gap also suggest that we need deeper theories about the process of spiritual development itself.

Fortunately, this split is not the end of the story. As noted in the introduction, we are currently in the midst of a revolution in our understanding of human development, suggesting that human beings are fundamentally relational. Our relationality points the way toward a more holistic understanding of spiritual development by providing the context in which explicit and relational/experiential knowledge function as a unity. In chapter two we will set the foundation for a relational spirituality paradigm by developing a relational view of the concept of the image of God as being-in-relation.

Conclusion

We close this chapter by returning to the reunification of theology and spirituality. As with the great theologians of the early church, we need to recapture the notion that explicit theology, or reflection on God, Scripture, and the spiritual life, is inseparable from our implicit spirituality—that is, our experiential knowing of God in our lived experience. Explicit theology and reflection provide the parameters for pursuing a deeper relationship with God. It anchors our experiential knowledge of God in the pursuit of the love of God and others in the kingdom of God. Explicit theological reflection also helps us process our implicit relational experiences. Implicit spirituality is the living out of the *mystikos*, or "hidden," life in Christ—that is, the unending implications of the gospel for our lives. It is the working out of explicit theological doctrine in our lived experience. We do not need detached doctrine; nor do we need unanchored spiritual experience. We need them both working together— *theologia*, or contemplation of God. What holds them together is the relational goal of loving God and neighbor.

PART 2

The Nature and Goal of Spiritual Transformation

The Image of God

A Theology of Being-in-Relation

FROM THE PATRISTIC ERA to contemporary times, Christian theologians have sought answers to theological anthropology in the biblical concept of the *imago Dei*—the profound notion that every person is created in the image of God. However this is understood, the great Christian thinkers throughout the centuries have agreed that it reveals most fundamentally what it means to be human. The nature, purpose, or activity derived from being created in the image of God, in turn, necessarily informs our understanding of spiritual development—the process of being conformed to the image of Christ, who is the exact image of God. The end goal and means of spiritual development both flow from our human nature, which reflects the nature of God.

If, as we have proposed in chapter one, the split between theology and spirituality and the staunch commitment to Enlightenment science linked to this trend have led to overly rational and theoretically underdeveloped models of spiritual growth, then we must reimagine these models. An appropriate starting point for this project is the image of God. A deeper understanding of how human beings are like God, and what it means to be fully human, will inform a model of spiritual development that holds together theology and spirituality, and explicit and implicit knowledge. We will suggest that, on balance, biblical themes and theological reflection point to a relational view of the *imago Dei* that provides the conceptual foundation for a relational spirituality model.

While a comprehensive review of the major historical views and developments of the *imago Dei* is beyond our scope, we start by briefly orienting the chapter around the two broad historical views and biblical themes of the *imago Dei*. We then discuss resources for a trinitarian-relational view of the *imago Dei*, highlighting the contributions of Augustine, Karl Barth, and Emil Brunner. Building on these foundations, we then turn to contemporary trinitarian themes. We then pull these threads together to present the contours of a trinitarian-relational model of the *imago Dei* referred to as being-in-relation.

Toward a Trinitarian-Relational View of the *Imago Dei*

Although the *imago Dei* has been the central concept in developing a Christian anthropology throughout the history of Christianity, theologians have not agreed on what the concept actually means. There are divided opinions on the meaning of the biblical terms involved, as well as on the taxonomies of the divine image that have been proposed by Christian scholars.[1] However, two broad views that have emerged provide a useful taxonomy to orient us.[2] After providing a brief sketch of these views, we highlight the biblical themes, showing how relationality provides an integrating principle for the *imago Dei*.

---

[1]Stanley J. Grenz, *The Social God and the Relational Self: A Trinitarian Theology of the Imago Dei* (Louisville, KY: Westminster John Knox, 2001).

[2]Scholars group the major views of the *imago Dei* differently. For example, in *Basic Christian Ethics*, Paul Ramsey proposes two primary views of the *imago Dei*, which comprises the highest level of summary of the various views: the substantialist or ontological view and the relational view. Expanding on this classification, James Beck and Bruce Demarest suggest a three-category taxonomy consisting of the substantive/ontological, relational, and functional views, the latter of which is typically encompassed within the substantive view in two-category taxonomies. Stanley Grenz offers a slight variation on the above three-fold taxonomy, categorizing the major views as substantial/structure, relational, and goal/destiny. Bernard McGinn also suggests three major views: the intellectual, volitional, and interpersonal, the first two of which are generally considered aspects of the substantive view, while the interpersonal view corresponds to the relational view. James R. Beck and Bruce Demarest, *The Human Person in Theology and Psychology* (Grand Rapids: Kregel, 2005), 143; Stanley J. Grenz, *The Social God and the Relational Self: A Trinitarian Theology of the Imago Dei* (Louisville, KY: Westminster John Knox, 2001); Bernard McGinn, "Humans as *Imago Dei*: Mystical Anthropology Then and Now," in *Sources of Transformation: Revitalising Christian Spirituality*, ed. Edward Howells and Peter Tyler (New York: Continuum, 2010); Paul Ramsey, *Basic Christian Ethics* (New York: Charles Scribner's Sons, 1950).

***Two broad views of the* imago Dei.** The dominant view of the *imago Dei* until the Reformation was the structural-rational view, which interprets the *imago Dei* as being comprised of certain characteristics or capacities built into the structure of the soul. Sometimes referred to as the substantive view, the emphasis here is on the nature or essence of the human substance (as an individual entity). Because the image is part of our very nature, it remains whether or not a person is in relationship with God and whether or not a person is relating rightly to God.

The capacity most often highlighted as central is that of rationality, and volition has typically been viewed as part of human rationality or reason.[3] Exercising dominion over creation as God's vice regent, derived from the creation mandate in Genesis 1:26-28, has likewise been viewed as an extension of rationality and volition. The human capacity for, and exercise of, dominion over creation is sometimes referred to as a separate functional view of the *imago Dei*, but historically it developed within the broader view that emphasizes rationality.

This view was developed by church fathers who were influenced by ancient Greek thought, and it became the accepted view until the end of the Middle Ages.[4] Augustine, in particular, shaped this view in complex ways. He emphasized structures and capacities of the soul or mind (i.e., the ability to remember, understand, and love God) and proper relationship with God. The structural aspect was certainly present in Augustine's model, but the overall emphasis was on relationship with God, a point to which we will return. However, as medieval scholastic theologians built on his theory, a more intellectual or rationalistic vision of the *imago Dei* emerged, represented most clearly by Thomas Aquinas's view.[5] For Augustine, the powers of the rational soul to know and love God—human reason broadly construed—involved an internal meditative process of discernment that appears to be more of a personal, relational way of knowing than a strictly logical way of knowing. In contrast, for medieval thinkers such as Aquinas, reason (including knowledge of

---

[3]Douglas John Hall, *Imaging God: Dominion as Stewardship* (Grand Rapids, MI: Eerdmans, 1986).
[4]David Cairns, *The Image of God in Man,* 2nd ed. (London: Collins, 1973).
[5]Grenz, *Social God.*

God) involved gaining knowledge through empirical observation in a move from effect, through inductive processes, to knowledge of causes. Thus, the image of God consists in an intellectual grasping of the essence of God. This rationalistic emphasis within the structural view developed in concert with the split between explicit theology and implicit spirituality discussed in chapter one. As such, this structural view of the image of God contributed to the focus on explicit knowledge within theology.

The second broad view is what we might call the dynamic relational view, which understands the divine image as referring to a fundamental relationship between human beings and God. The emphasis on dynamic here is on the actual relating to God as God intended. In this view, the *imago Dei* is an activity or verb rather than a set of capacities that reside in the soul. Hence the image of God exists when we relate rightly to God as intended. When we are cut off from God through various means, the image of God is all but nonexistent.

The initial architect of this shift from the structural-rational view was Martin Luther, whose line of thinking was extended by John Calvin. Both Reformers viewed the image of God in dynamic terms, emphasizing the New Testament sense of the image of God—that is, not static endowments or capacities (e.g., rationality and will) but the proper functioning of those capacities in relation to God. The Reformers initiated a new trajectory of thinking about the image of God, partly as a reaction to the patristic and medieval formulation that human capacities (that were thought to comprise the *imago Dei*) remained untainted by the fall (what is referred to as the "two-story" model of nature and grace).[6] In pointing to original righteousness as the location of the *imago Dei*, Luther was emphasizing the activity—the verb—of imaging God. The emphasis was on righteousness as a dynamic phenomenon in the context of

---

[6]This so-called two-story medieval scholastic model follows Aquinas's principle that "grace perfects nature." In this model, the image was viewed as consisting of natural capacities (e.g., reason and will, which enable a certain natural theological knowledge of God), whereas the likeness was viewed as a divine gift added to human nature through an act of grace. The divine gift was understood to be moral righteousness and the theological virtues. In this model, the fall did not tarnish the natural capacities of reason and will (the first story); rather, it removed supernatural gifts (the second story). See Grenz, *Social God*, 160.

relationship with God, rather than on static capacities. In an analogy originated by Augustine, and later used by Calvin, the dynamic relational view pictures humans as reflecting God as a mirror reflects the image of a person.[7] While the concept of relationality per se is implicit for Luther,[8] a number of theologians in the modern era have developed variations of the dynamic relational view, building on the Reformers' emphasis on the proper functioning of human capacities in relation to God.[9]

While some scholars classify Luther and Calvin in the structural-rational view of the *imago Dei*,[10] others place the Reformers in the relational view because of their emphasis on the dynamic nature of imaging God.[11] Clearly, there is something new emerging with Luther's view that breaks with the historically predominant structural-rational view. Because of this new vision and the emphasis on the dynamic nature of imaging God as an action over and against structural capacities, we suggest the more precise label of the dynamic relational view. We will elaborate below on this general relational view by integrating trinitarian themes and incorporating structural elements of the image of God (i.e., relational capacities), which tend to be de-emphasized in contemporary relational views. Before proceeding to this, we highlight key biblical themes of the *imago Dei* that point toward a relational view.

Biblical themes of the* imago Dei *in relational perspective. Against the backdrop of these two broad views, it is helpful to consider the major biblical themes regarding the *imago Dei* with a lens toward their relational significance. In the three Old Testament passages referencing the *imago Dei* in the early part of the book of Genesis, two Hebrew words are used: *tselem* (translated as "image") and *demut* (translated as "likeness"). The basic meaning appears to be that human beings are a

---

[7]Grenz, *Social God*, 166.

[8]Hall, *Imaging God*, 101.

[9]Among these theologians were Soren Kierkegaard, Dietrich Bonhoeffer, Karl Barth, G. C. Berkouwer, Paul Jewett, and Stanley Grenz.

[10]See, for example, Beck and Demarest, *The Human Person*.

[11]For example, Stanley Grenz and Douglas John Hall both consider Luther and Calvin to hold a relational view of the *imago Dei*. Grenz, *Social God*; Hall, *Imaging God*.

representation of God that is somehow "like" God.[12] Most contemporary biblical scholars see the two terms as synonymous or slight variations on the same meaning.[13] *Demut* may be considered a term that amplifies the meaning of *tselem*, emphasizing that the representation (*tselem*) is similar to the original.

While there are multiple views of the meaning of *tselem* and *demut* in the Old Testament, it is important to note here that the presence of the *imago Dei* at the time of the creation of humans points to the universality of the image of God, and reference to it as the basis for the prohibition of murder (Genesis 9:6) points to the continuation of the image of God after the fall. These basic themes are reinforced and expanded in the New Testament.

While the Old Testament does not clearly delineate the concept of the image of God, biblical scholars have highlighted four conceptual themes in the Hebrew understanding of the *imago Dei*: similarity, counterpart, representation, and dominion.[14] Edward Curtis notes that the way Adam's son resembles his father is analogous to the way in which humans are similar to God, and this seems to be a similarity of function and of acting on behalf of the father.[15] We see here a connection between the themes of *similarity* (in function) and *representation*. In commenting on Genesis 1:26, Hans Walter Wolff highlights the *counterpart* theme, which corroborates a relational view: "The unique nature of man in creation is to be understood in the light of his special relationship with God."[16] Curtis also picks up on this theme in noting that the *imago Dei* "implies that the human was made with the capacity for relationship with God."[17] The third theme of *representation* can be seen in the ideology that kings in the ancient Near East not only functioned as an image of a deity but also as the representative of the god whose image they bore. This view

---

[12]Edward M. Curtis, "Image of God (OT)," *Anchor Bible Dictionary*, ed. David Noel Freedman et al., 6 vols. (New York: Doubleday, 1992), 3:390.

[13]Grenz, *Social God*.

[14]Curtis, "Image of God," 3:390.

[15]Curtis, "Image of God," 3:390.

[16]Cited in Grenz, *Social God*, 195.

[17]Curtis, "Image of God," 3:390.

suggests the very significant idea that human beings are to mediate the presence of God within creation.[18] Dominion or stewardship over creation is also a significant theme, although the emerging scholarly consensus holds that dominion is the result of the image of God, not the image per se.[19]

Each of these themes captures an aspect of the way in which human beings resemble God. As such, it seems likely that they are all facets of one unified idea regarding what it means to be created in the image of God. We would suggest that trinitarian themes of relationality, which we explore more below, can help us reconcile and integrate these views. While they all reflect an important dimension about how humans are like God, each aspect is a facet of our essential relational nature. The core of this nature is found in the centrality of *personal relationships* with God and other human beings, which are necessary for human flourishing, and for growing into the image of Christ, which makes us more fully human.

Integrating the various Hebrew understandings of the *imago Dei*, then, we would suggest the following. Humans are *similar* to God as beings-in-relation (a model we outline below), and because of this essential similarity in relational nature, they are always a direct interpersonal *counterpart* in relation to God and, by extension, in relation to fellow human beings. Moreover, being God's counterpart suggests *representing* God or *mediating* God's presence by being a loving presence to the world. In addition, humans are a loving presence primarily in interpersonal relationships, but also secondarily in relation to the creation by exercising *stewardship* or *dominion* over it. Viewed in this light, then, relationality is at the very center of every aspect of the Hebrew understanding of what it means to be like God.

The New Testament affirms the Old Testament teaching of the image as the universal essence of human nature (James 3:9; 1 Corinthians 11:7). In addition, it develops this foundational idea with the concept that Jesus

---

[18]Curtis, "Image of God," 3:390.
[19]Stanley Grenz notes that there is "near consensus" in recent years on this point. See Grenz, *Social God*, 197.

Christ is the perfect image of God, and believers are being progressively conformed into the image of Christ, who is God's glory.

In three main passages (2 Corinthians 4:4-6; Colossians 1:13-18; Hebrews 1:3), the New Testament develops the concept of Christ as the image of God in two interrelated ways.[20] First, it shows Christ as the perfect image of God in his preeminence, or supremacy, in two intimately connected senses: (1) preeminence above all creation in his *deity* and (2) preeminence in the new creation as the true human.[21] In this life, believers grow toward the perfect humanity exemplified by Christ, as the *imago Dei* is renewed in them by being conformed to the image of Christ. To be conformed to the image and likeness of Christ is to become more fully and truly human. N. T. Wright summarizes well: "Humanity was made as the climax of the first creation (Gen. 1:26-27): the true humanity of Jesus is the climax of the history of creation, and at the same time the starting-point of the new creation."[22] Second, the New Testament demonstrates Christ as the perfect image of God in his radiation of God's glory.

In addition, Christ, as the visible image (*eikōn*) of the invisible God (Colossians 1:15), is pictured as the specific image or reality into which believers are being conformed. This is noted in reference to the past (in God's predestination of believers; Romans 8:29), present (2 Corinthians 3:18), and future (in relation to the resurrection of the body; 1 Corinthians 15:49).[23] Most relevant to our purpose is the present, ongoing transformation of believers into the image of Christ. In 2 Corinthians 3:18, Paul states: "And as the Spirit of the Lord works within us, we become more and more *like him* and *reflect his glory* even more" (emphasis added). This theme of being changed into Christ's likeness leads to an eschatological outcome in the future. Two central passages link the image of God to humanity's future via the concept of glory. First, the future salvation of the Christian is guaranteed, in that the predestination is conformity to the *image* of God's son (Romans 8:29). Human beings will finally achieve

---

[20]Grenz, *Social God.*

[21]Cairns, *Image of God in Man.*

[22]N. T. Wright, *Colossians and Philemon: Tyndale New Testament Commentaries* (Grand Rapids, MI: Eerdmans, 1986), 70.

[23]Cairns, *Image of God in Man,* 49.

the state of likeness to God that was intended for them from the beginning. Second, in his resurrection, Jesus is the "first fruit" of believers, who will also be resurrected in the final victory over death. When this glorious event occurs, Paul tells us, we will "bear the *image* of the heavenly man [i.e., Christ]" (1 Corinthians 15:49 NIV, emphasis added). Jesus' resurrected body serves as the paradigm for all believers who will be conformed to his image.

A synthesis of New Testament themes, then, presents a more precise christological picture of the *imago Dei*. In this synthesis, we find a relational logic for the *imago Dei* that we can depict as follows. Jesus is the exact, perfect image of God, and God's very nature is love (1 John 4). Therefore, the most central characteristic of Jesus is love. We know this because he is God and because he taught love as the greatest of the commandments (Matthew 22). In this vein, Anthony Hoekema writes that looking to Christ to discern the image of God suggests that love should be the focus rather than intelligence or reason.[24] We can suggest, then, that the foundational idea behind being conformed to the image of Christ is this: participating in the divine love of the Trinity and becoming more loving. Love, we might add, is the defining nature and goal of trinitarian relationality. In contending that a christological vision of the *imago Dei* is one of love, we are at the very same time advocating for a relational view of the image of God. With these biblical themes in mind, we turn to trinitarian resources for a relational view of the *imago Dei*.

Resources for a Trinitarian-Relational View of *Imago Dei*

There is a rich trinitarian theme in Christian theology suggesting that relationality is at the core of what it means to be created in the image of God. An explicitly trinitarian-informed view of the *imago Dei* goes back to Augustine, who described the image of God in human beings as an *imago trinitatis*—an image of the Trinity.[25] As noted above, the great Reformers, Luther and Calvin, adopted a generally more relational view of the *imago Dei*, departing from the long-standing view of the *imago Dei*

---

[24]Anthony A. Hoekema, *Created in God's Image* (Grand Rapids, MI: Eerdmans, 1986), 73.

[25]Augustine, *On the Trinity*, trans. E. Hill (Brooklyn, NY: New City Press, 1991).

as rationality.[26] The general shift from the rational to the relational view of the *imago Dei* involved a move from finding the image in an analogy of being (i.e., essence, nature, capacities that reside in a person, such as rationality) to an analogy of relation. However, in moving to an analogy of relation, the notion of a structural aspect to the *imago Dei* was largely lost—a move that is problematic in that it threatens the universality of the image of God and its continuation after the fall.

In this section we review Augustine's view of the image of God, suggesting that, on balance, he maintains a structural view, while contributing to a relational view of the *imago Dei* as well. Augustine is the first theologian to explicitly develop the *imago Dei* in light of the Trinity. As we will see, he does this in a unique and complex way. While he perhaps does not explicate the details of a fully relational view of the *imago Dei*, he certainly moves us toward an explicitly trinitarian-relational view. Following this, we highlight the trinitarian contributions of Karl Barth and the relational-existential model of Emil Brunner, which holds in tension the structural and dynamic-relational aspects of the *imago Dei*. These theories provide foundational resources for more contemporary developments, which pave the way for a synthesis we present.

Augustine's trinitarian participation with God. We noted in chapter one that Augustine followed the handmaiden approach to secular philosophy initiated by Philo and developed more thoroughly by Clement of Alexandria. He held in high regard the role of reason in the spiritual life, although it was always a means to the end of the pursuit of God. He taught his disciples to use reason, and logic ("rational discourse") in particular, to better understand spiritual doctrine and to solve problems encountered in Scripture. His approach to secular philosophy and reason is consistent with his teachings on the image of God as Trinity. This approach, indeed, is a significant reason why Augustine's formulation of the *imago Dei* is difficult to classify in one of the common historical approaches. His theory is often classified as what we are calling the structural-rational view, and yet, for Augustine, the contemplation of God

---

[26]Cairns, *Image of God in Man.*

in the higher capacities of the rational mind should always be accompanied by love for God. As Grenz put it, "The concept of the *imago Dei* that emerged from Augustine's reflections was sufficiently complex and many-sided so as to set the stage both for the triumph of the structural understanding in the Middle Ages and for its demise in the Reformation."[27]

We can certainly see different threads in Augustine's writing that can be used to support both the structural view of rational capacities and a more dynamic relational view. An additional factor adding to the confusion is that Augustine did not conceptualize rationality or what is often translated as "mind" in a narrowly rationalistic sense. Despite his view being most often classified as rationality (as a structure of the soul), it seems that the essence of Augustine's viewpoints more toward relationality than rationality. This line of thinking goes back prior to the split between explicit theology and implicit spirituality (discussed in chapter one), which deepened with the medieval scholastic model and was solidified by the Enlightenment. While contemporary trinitarian scholarship has advanced our thinking, there are rich conceptual resources prior to the split that enlighten our current models and need to be reclaimed. Thus, we draw from Augustine as a representative patristic resource for a relational approach to the image of God.

Augustine's view of the *imago Dei* is grounded in the Trinity. Humankind is not only the image of the one God, according to Augustine, but also of the divine Trinity, for the one God is triune.

> God said, "Let us make man to our image and likeness (Gen 1:26) and a little later on it adds, "And God made man to the image of God" (Gen 1:27). "Our," being plural in number, could not be right in this place if man were made to the image of one person, whether of the Father or the Son or the Holy Spirit; but because in fact he was made in the image of the trinity, it said "to our image." And then in case we should suppose that we have to believe in three gods in the trinity, while this same trinity is in fact one God, it goes on to say, "And God made man to the image of God, which amounts to saying "to his image."[28]

---

[27]Grenz, *Social God*, 152.
[28]Augustine, *On the Trinity* 12.2.6.

Once Augustine establishes this, he proceeds to use the image of the Trinity in humankind as an analogy to help us understand the triune nature of God.

Augustine developed the idea that the image of the trinitarian God is found in a trinity of interrelated relational capacities within the mind or soul: the capacity to remember, understand, and love oneself and God.[29] These are certainly capacities or structures of the soul, and hence we see Grenz's argument that Augustine solidified the structural view. In some sense, all these capacities were broadly understood by Augustine as rationality. However, by *rational* or *intellectual*, Augustine did not mean solely the ability to reason. He used this term to refer to those capacities in the human soul that differentiate it from animals. This includes reason, morality, and self-consciousness, but the highest capacity of the rational soul is using reason—or understanding—to behold God. In discussing Augustine's understanding of reason, TeSelle contends that he is not referring to "the 'verbal' kind of reasoning which manipulates concepts themselves; reasoning is a movement of the mind by which it construes the contents of apprehension, 'discerning' where one thing is really distinct from another, 'connecting' where there is genuine unity."[30] It seems that this aspect of the image of God, for Augustine, refers to acting and knowing reflectively with self-awareness, discerning the underlying nature of things through direct apprehension.

In sum, it is evident that there is a thread within Augustine suggesting that the image of God can be found in humankind's capacity for reason. However, we would suggest that this is a short-sighted and superficial view of Augustine's complex synthesis of the image of God. The thrust of his view emphasizes an intersubjective relationality with self and God.

---

[29] Augustine first developed an interpersonal analogy of the Trinity as love being comprised of the three aspects of the lover (*amans*), that which is loved (*quod amatur*), and the love that flows between the two (*amor*). He then developed two trinities of the mind to which he devoted much more attention. First, he compared the Father, Son, and Holy Spirit to mind, knowledge, and love, within the human mind or psyche. He then arrived at what he thought was a superior analogy of memory, understanding, and love/will. Augustine, *On the Trinity* 12.2.6. See also Metropolitan Kallistos Ware, "The Holy Trinity: Model for Personhood-in-Relation," in *The Trinity and an Entangled World*, ed. J. Polkinghorne (Grand Rapids, MI: Eerdmans, 2010), 118.

[30] Eugene TeSelle, *Augustine the Theologian* (London: Burns and Oates, 1970), 82.

The emphasis of Augustine's trinitarian view of the image of God is that human beings have the capacity to love God and should actualize that capacity by remembering, understanding, and loving God. Augustine's model, then, implicitly holds to the structural view, although the structural capacities (memory, understanding, and will/love) are to be used in the service of relationship with God. In fact, the purpose of having these faculties is to allow humans to be in relationship with the God whose image they bear. The ultimate manifestation of the *imago Dei* is the person using these faculties in proper relation to God. In his development of Augustine's thought, Anselm responded to a query as to how the soul is made to the divine image by stating: "God always remembers, always knows, and always loves himself. And so if you are unceasingly mindful of him, as your model, if you know him, if you love him, you will be to his image."[31]

Augustine sets an example of a relational view that does not negate structural capacities. While he explicitly builds the *imago Dei* on the Trinity, he focuses more on interrelated psychological processes within the person than on relational processes between people.[32] However, the goal is to help us better understand the relationality inherent within the Trinity, and to use these capacities to behold and love God. As such, he moves us toward an explicitly trinitarian-relational view of the *imago Dei*. The stage was set for this framework to develop more fully with the revival in trinitarian theology.

The trinitarian turn in the **imago Dei**: *Karl Barth and Emil Brunner.* With the revival of trinitarian theology during the second half of the twentieth century, the dynamic relational view, first articulated by the Reformers, took on a trinitarian flavor.[33] While Augustine

---

[31] Anselm, *Liber Medit. Et Orat. I, 1* (*Patrologia Latina*, ed. J. P. Migne [Paris, 1841-] 158:710).

[32] These capacities are of the same substance, or "consubstantial" in a way that is analogous to the three persons of the Trinity, who are distinct persons, yet of the same substance. In this way, Augustine argued that the trinitarian nature of God is reflected, or imaged, in the mind/soul of the human person. These capacities are relational, but Augustine's emphasis was on the way in which their interrelation helps us better understand the trinitarian nature of God, yet with the end goal of beholding God. See Augustine, *On the Trinity* 12.2.6.

[33] Roderick Leupp, *The Renewal of Trinitarian Theology: Themes, Patterns & Explorations* (Downers Grove, IL: IVP Academic, 2008).

had first drawn on the Trinity to inform his view of the *imago Dei*, much of this shift was sparked by Karl Barth's "rediscovery" of the doctrine of the Trinity.[34] Writing around the same time, Emil Brunner also developed a relational view of the *imago Dei* that paved the way for more recent developments.

Following the Reformers, Karl Barth initially saw the *imago Dei* as being completely lost in the fall. Later, he revised his view and saw the image of God as continuing to exist after the fall, not in any particular thing that humans are or do, but simply in their existence. He stated, "[Man] is God's image inasmuch as he is man."[35] Barth's exegesis of Genesis 1:26-27 led him to conclude that the image points back to the trinitarian nature of God. Just as the members of the Trinity exist in relationship, so we image God in being created male and female. Barth emphasized here that both in Genesis 1:27 and Genesis 5:2 the statement about being created in God's image is associated with the phrase "male and female he created them." Just as in the Trinity there is an "I" and a "Thou" confronting each other, so also humans confront each other in a kind of parable of the divine nature.

Barth also saw the image reflected in our ability to exist in relationship to God. Unlike the rest of the created order, humans have, from the beginning, the potential to exist in an "I-Thou" relationship with God. This relationship with God is not present in all humanity, but the possibility of it is. The image of God is revealed in Jesus; in Jesus we see that the image is found in being related to God.[36]

Barth was careful to clarify that the image of God is not a capacity per se, but a relation: the man-woman relation and the human-God relation. The image cannot be found in the person alone, but only in the person-in-relationship. The image is universal because the relationship between male and female, and person and friend, is paradigmatic and universal. In fact, Barth has been critiqued for the radical nature of his claim of

---

[34]Grenz, *Social God*, x.

[35]Karl Barth, *Church Dogmatics* III/1, *The Doctrine of Creation* (London: T&T Clark, 1958), 184.

[36]Karl Barth, *Church Dogmatics* III/2, *The Doctrine of Creation*, Part 2 (London: T&T Clark, 1960), 58-60.

universality. In his view, since the essential nature of humans is to be in relationship with God, turning away from God is not a possibility; rather, it is "the ontological impossibility of man's nature."[37] Turning away from God would annihilate human nature, but since God maintains the relation, this is actually impossible.

Emil Brunner followed Augustine in positing that the *imago Dei* involves both a noun and a verb—what he calls "word" (specifically, the word of God) and "answer." Elsewhere, he calls these the "formal" and the "material" senses of the image of God.[38] While Brunner rejected the radical position taken by Karl Barth in his earlier writings, he retained Barth's emphasis on relationality.

Brunner saw the image as consisting of two aspects. One aspect, structural in nature, is comprised of the capabilities that distinguish humans from animals, which are retained after the fall (the formal sense). These structural aspects, however, are highly relational: "responsibility from love, in love, for love."[39] Included in these are the capacity for being addressed by God in love (i.e., the capacity for understanding speech) and being required to respond to God in love (i.e., the capacity for responsibility). A certain knowledge of these capacities remains even in non-Christians, in the form of an awareness of moral responsibility or obligation.

The second aspect consists of the relationship with God. It occurs when a person responds appropriately to God in responsive love. This material aspect of the image is also reflected in loving relationship with other people. Although Brunner does not fully develop this aspect of the image, it is clearly informed by a trinitarian theology. By distinguishing the formal and material aspects of the image of God, Brunner is able to retain a universal image of God after the fall, while also emphasizing the need for relationship with God to restore the full image.

---

[37]Barth, *Church Dogmatics* III.2, 136.
[38]Emil Brunner and Karl Barth, *Natural Theology*, trans. Peter Fraenkel (London: Geoffrey Bles, 1946), 31.
[39]Emil Brunner, *Man in Revolt: A Christian Anthropology*, trans. Oliver Wyon (London: Lutterworth Press, 1939), 99.

Contemporary Trinitarian Themes for a Relational View of *Imago Dei*

We noted above that there has been a revival in trinitarian theology in recent decades. Prompted by the unintended split between doctrine and Christian life, outlined in chapter one, scholars are exploring the implications of a trinitarian framework for theology and Christian life, including the image of God.[40] This has fostered a renewed and more nuanced understanding of God's intrinsic relationality, which informs a trinitarian view of the *imago Dei*.

Sharing in the mutual love of the Trinity. "The being of God," notes John Zizioulas, "is a relational being: without the concept of communion it would not be possible to speak of God."[41] God's relationality can be characterized by a key Greek word used by Saint Basil the Great: *koinōnia*—or what we might call communion, fellowship, or mutual love. God is a tri-unity of persons who: (1) share the same will and attributes, (2) maintain their specific individuality, and (3) reciprocally love one other. Modern psychological theories suggest that healthy relationships require both connection and separateness. With psychological merging, there is no relationship—at least no healthy relationship. This applies to the intersubjective nature of the Trinity as well, even if only in an analogical way. In fact, human relationality reflects God as the model. As Saint John of Damascus noted, the trinitarian God is "united yet not confused, distinct yet not divided."[42] Because communion is intrinsic to God, all our Christian experience is a trinitarian experience—either implicitly or explicitly.[43] Whether we recognize it or not, the Christian life is fundamentally a participation in the divine life of God's mutual love.

When we say God is a relational being, we can further characterize this relationality as divine love or communion. This is revealed to us in

---

[40]Donald Fairbairn, *Life in the Trinity: An Introduction to Theology with the Help of the Church Fathers* (Downers Grove, IL: IVP Academic, 2008), 3-12.

[41]John D. Zizioulas, *Being as Communion: Studies in Personhood and the Church* (Crestwood, NY: St. Vladimir's Seminary Press, 1985), 17.

[42]Quoted in Ware, "The Holy Trinity," 108.

[43]See Fred Sanders, *The Deep Things of God: How the Trinity Changes Everything*, 2nd ed. (Wheaton, IL: Crossway, 2017). See also Ware, "The Holy Trinity," 107.

Scripture and is the foundation for our Christian experience.[44] John declares that "God is love," and that "those who abide in love abide in God, and God abides in them" (1 John 4:16 NRSV; cf. 1 John 4:7-8). The Gospel of John further illuminates the Father's love for the Son. John explains to his disciples, "The Father loves the Son and has placed all things in his hands" (John 3:35 NRSV). We read in Jesus' prayer in John 17 that this love has existed eternally "before the foundation of the world" (John 17:24 NRSV).

The divine love of the Trinity is captured, albeit imperfectly, by the ancient trinitarian teaching of perichōrēsis. This Greek word, translated in Latin as *circumincessio*, means to "permeate" or "interpenetrate." Leonardo Boff implies a connection with koinōnia in describing perichōrēsis as "a permanent process of active reciprocity, a clasping of two hands: the Persons interpenetrate one another and this process of communing forms their very nature."[45] Perichōrēsis pictures each member of the Trinity as dwelling in the other two while maintaining individuality. While all metaphors fall short in fully capturing the reality of the Trinity, a helpful one that has been offered is that of three fountain jets gushing upward, uniting into a single stream of water.[46]

This interpenetration among the Trinity is reflected biblically in the unity of the Father and the Son. Jesus explicitly declares this unity in John 14:11: "I am in the Father and the Father is in me." T. F. Torrance contends that this unity, or perichōrēsis, is true of the Trinity as a whole: "In the mysterious communion of the eternal Persons in the Godhead Father, Son, and Holy Spirit wholly indwell one another as God, without ceasing to be what each personally and distinctively is in relation to the others, so that the fullness of the Godhead applies unrestrictedly to each divine Person as well as to all of them together."[47] An analogy within human relationships that partially captures this concept is a term mentioned above that comes from the field of relational psychoanalysis:

---

[44]Ware, "The Holy Trinity," 113.
[45]Leonardo Boff, *Trinity and Society*, trans. Paul Burns (Maryknoll, NY: Orbis, 1988), 135.
[46]Boff, *Trinity and Society*, 128.
[47]Quoted in Leupp, *Renewal of Trinitarian Theology*, 74.

intersubjectivity. Intersubjectivity refers to the intermingling of two sub-jectivities, or two minds. It reflects a deep mutual knowing between two people, in which each knows the mind of the other without ceasing to maintain the separateness of his or her own mind or personhood.

One might think of a married couple whose subjectivities become united in a very real sense, without either spouse losing his or her indi-viduality. Their minds are fused—two and yet one. In his book *I Am a Strange Loop*, cognitive scientist Douglas Hofstadter describes a moment, just months after his wife Carol died suddenly at the age of forty-two, in which he came across her picture. In his poignant description of the union he experienced with Carol, we catch a glimpse of perichōrēsis:

> I looked so deeply that I felt I was behind her eyes, and all at once, I found myself saying, as tears flowed, "That's me! That's me!" And those simple words brought back many thoughts that I had had before, about the fusion of our souls into one higher-level entity, about the fact that at the core of both our souls lay our identical hopes and dreams for our children, about the notion that those hopes were not separate or distinct hopes but were just one hope, one clear thing that defined us both, that welded us together into a unit, the kind of unit I had but dimly imagined before being married and having children. I realized then that although Carol had died, that core piece of her had not died at all, but that it lived on very determinedly in my brain.[48]

This love among the Father, Son, and Spirit is extended to embrace the community of believers. This may be the reason God created the world in the first place. It has been suggested that God freely chose to create the world so that others might share in the experience of God's love.[49] It is part of God's very nature to desire to share his love. Thus, Jesus says to the disciples, "As the Father has loved me, so I have loved you; abide in my love" (John 15:9 NRSV). This theme is continued in John 17, when Jesus says to the Father, "[You] have loved them even as you have loved me." He goes on to say, "I made your name known to them, and I will make it known, so that the love with which you have loved me may be in them, and I in them" (John 17:23, 26 NRSV). We can see that the

---

[48]Douglas Hofstadter, *I Am a Strange Loop* (New York: Basic Books, 2007), 228.
[49]Ware, "The Holy Trinity," 107-24.

themes of abiding and love are intertwined such that the object of abiding is God's love. God invites us to abide or participate in the divine love among the Trinity.

The church fathers captured this notion of participating in the divine life with the Greek word *theōsis*.[50] This concept refers to the process through which human beings become divine, or like God, in some way. The church fathers were clear that theōsis does not mean that Christians become divine in the same way God is divine. Rather, through adoption as children of God, believers: (1) share in the status of divine children; (2) share in godly qualities, such as those described in 2 Peter 1:5-7; and (3) share in the fellowship or mutual love between the Son and Father, and more broadly the communion among all three persons of the Trinity. While all three strands of theōsis are emphasized by the church fathers, Donald Fairbairn argues that the third strand—sharing in the communion of the Trinity—is the foundational and most biblical way to express the idea of theōsis.[51]

We see this mutual love among the Trinity expressed in concrete ways in the movements of salvation history as well as in our personal and corporate spiritual experience.[52] We see the interflowing love between the Father, Son, and Holy Spirit in creation (Genesis 1:2), in the incarnation (Luke 1:35), in the resurrection of Jesus (Romans 8:11), at Pentecost (Acts 2:1-4), and in baptism (Matthew 28:19) and prayer (Romans 8:26). From this trinitarian perspective, then, salvation, justification, and sanctification are not so much abstract propositions or separate doctrines. Rather, they are all part of a unified experience that flows from participation in the communal love that has eternally existed within the Trinity. This renewed emphasis on the Trinity places relationality at the center of all theology, including conceptualizations of the *imago Dei*, which bears directly on our task of understanding human and spiritual development.

---

[50]Fairbairn, *Life in the Trinity*.
[51]Fairbairn, *Life in the Trinity*, 9.
[52]See Fairbairn, *Life in the Trinity*; see also Ware, "The Holy Trinity," 107-29.

***The social-ecclesial self and the* imago Dei.** This trinitarian line of thought has been carried forward into relational notions of the *imago Dei* by contemporary theologians such as Stanley Grenz and Colin Gunton.[53] Gunton, for example, articulates this analogy of relation in a poignant way:

> We are in certain ways analogous to the persons of the Trinity, in particular in being in mutually constitutive relations to other persons. Who and what we are derives not only from our relations to God, our creator, but to those others who have made and continue to make us what we are. Just as Father, Son and Holy Spirit constitute the being of God, so created persons are those who, insofar as they are authentically personal, . . . are characterized by subsisting in mutually constitutive relations with one another. . . . To be in the image of God is therefore to be in necessary relation to others so made. . . . The doctrine of the image thus places us in a layered network of relationships, first to God the creator, then to one another, and then to the world in its diversity.[54]

For Gunton, to be in relationship with God and others is an essential feature of the *imago Dei*. Relationships with others make us what we are, a notion corroborated by the power of attachment relationships in shaping our soul. God would not be God without the three persons of the Godhead who have always existed in relationship with each other—at least not in any biblical sense that we can imagine. Likewise, we would not be human and would not reflect the image of God without the relationships that comprise the fabric of our being as we internalize them.

Stanley Grenz emphasizes the *imago Dei* as the social self, or the self-in-community. "The image of God," he concludes from his extensive review, "does not lie in the individual per se but in the relationality of persons in community."[55] Grenz further describes the self-in-community as the ecclesial self. In his view, the true self that fully images God as intended is constituted in a foundational way by the relationships among the people of God as they commune with the triune God. The telos of

---

[53]See Grenz, *Social God*; and Colin Gunton, *The Triune Creator: A Historical and Systematic Study* (Grand Rapids, MI: Eerdmans, 1998).

[54]Gunton, *Triune Creator*, 208-11.

[55]Grenz, *Social God*, 305.

salvation history toward the new humanity of God's people orients and informs what the image of God means. It is formed by the relationships among the body of Christ—the church—as the members reflect the love among the Trinity by participating together in that love. Grenz states: "A theological anthropology influenced by the contemporary rebirth of trinitarian theology describes the relational self not merely as persons-in-relationship but as the ecclesial self, the new humanity in communion with the triune God."[56] The ecclesial self, then, is defined by its eschatological trajectory. This suggests that the image of God "is eschatologically oriented, but is nevertheless already actual in principle, and it becomes manifest in the community which is a readable epistle of Christ."[57]

Believers are to love each other in the same way God loves us, thereby manifesting the image of God. This happens through a Spirit-empowered, relational process in which we find our identity by being "in Christ," which means participating in the love among the Trinity. Yet, we do this not in an individually focused way but by participating in the body of Christ, thereby sharing together in the dynamic of God's love. The ecclesial self-in-community images God in this rich, multifaceted love for one another in the new family of God, and by extension, for all humanity. The self-in-community marks the idea that the image of God is only fully expressed corporately through those who are bound together by sharing in the story of Christ and the love of God. Fellow believers are knit together by the process of sharing in the narrative of Christ and by locating our own story in Christ's larger story.[58] In this way, we make sense of our own lives and find our identity together in this shared story. With the goal of creating the new humanity, "the Spirit engages in the work of transforming this ecclesial persons-in-relationship so that as a people imbued with the character of Christ, who is the image of God, they might together reflect God's own character and thus shine as the *imago Dei*."[59]

---

[56]Grenz, *Social God*, 312.
[57]G. C. Berkouwer, *Man: The Image of God,* trans. Dirk W. Jellema (Grand Rapids, MI: Eerdmans, 1962), 111-12.
[58]Grenz, *Social God*, 328.
[59]Grenz, *Social God*, 334.

***Relationality and being in the* imago Dei.** Given that the image of
God is represented in communal fellowship and divine love, Grenz
argues that this calls for a relational ontology of personhood, which also
seems implied in Gunton's view. This notion suggests that the image of
God, and by extension personhood, is not located within the individual
but rather in the relationships among persons in community. In a strict
version of a relational ontology view, persons are reduced to their relationships. This leads to certain conceptual problems, such as "the individual being absorbed into an undifferentiated collective."[60] In light of
this, it is worth noting here that the shift to an analogy of relation in the
last half of the twentieth century has been, almost without exception,
pitted against an analogy of being in the proposal of a relational ontology
as described above. W. Norris Clarke noted that this rich development
of the relational aspect of the person has been "suspicious of, or even
positively hostile towards the notion of person as substance."[61] This represents an understandable but misguided reaction to the classical Aristotelian conceptualization of relations as being accidental to human
nature rather than essential. Essentialism has generally come to refer to
a view of human persons as static beings that are not foundationally
formed through relationships. However, rather than positing the analogy
of being and of relation as mutually exclusive, I would suggest that both
are intricately intertwined in a relational view of the *imago Dei*
as being-in-relation.

More recent theologians have embraced perspectives on the *imago
Dei* that bridge structural and relational views. Douglas John Hall, for
example, contends that just as the triune God is "Being-in-relationship,"
humans are "beings-with-God" and "beings-with-humankind."[62]
Moreover, while Stanley Grenz calls for a relational ontology, or "ontology of communion," he argues against a strict reductionist ontology.
He notes that "the communal nature of the ecclesial self must not be
understood as undermining in any way the importance of the individual."

---

[60]Grenz, *Social God*, 333.
[61]W. Norris Clarke, *Person and Being* (Milwaukee, WI: Marquette University Press, 2008), 4.
[62]Hall, *Imaging God*.

He continues: "The common sharing of the life of Christ through the Holy Spirit in no sense destroys the individuality of its members, who maintain full responsibility and value as the objects of Christ's redeeming love."[63]

Extending the thought of Thomas Aquinas, Clarke developed this line of thought more fully, contending that to be fully human means to be substance-in-relation. He states that "relationality is a primordial dimension of every real being, inseparable from its substantiality, just as action is from existence. . . . It turns out, then, that relationality and substantiality go together as two distinct but inseparable modes of reality."[64] On one side of the being-in-relation coin, human beings, as image bearers, have a nature or essence. Substance is the primary mode that grounds all else, including relationships. A relationship, in itself, is not identical to the people who have that relationship. However, rather than negating human relationality, it turns out that the nature that inheres in the person-as-substance—the in-itself dimension of being—is fundamentally relational. Being-as-substance, in other words, naturally flows into being-as-relational since relationality is intrinsic to the human substance.[65] As Hall puts it, "We cannot cease to be beings whose lives are intended for relationship with God."[66] This leads to the relational model of the *imago Dei* proposed here: being-in-relation.

Being-in-Relation: A Trinitarian-Relational View of the *Imago Dei*

We have reviewed numerous threads of the *imago Dei* in our journey toward a trinitarian-relational view. Here we briefly tie these threads together around an overarching trinitarian theme in a model I will refer to as "being-in-relation." This model has three integral psychological-theological-spiritual organizing principles: (1) the relational nature of humans made in the image of the trinitarian God; (2) the

---

[63]Grenz, *Social God*, 333.
[64]Clarke, *Person and Being*, 14.
[65]Clarke, *Person and Being*, 14.
[66]Hall, *Imaging God*, 144.

relational goal of sanctification as loving presence, which is the result of being renewed in the image of Christ; and (3) a relational process as the means of sanctification. In the remainder of the book, we will draw on contemporary psychology and theology to elaborate on each of these aspects.

Relational nature. Following the trinitarian line of thinking outlined above, the proposal here is that the person is a human substance or soul that has a relational nature. Given that the essential dynamic in the triune God is love, God is intrinsically relational in his very nature. This suggests, as noted above, that human beings also have an intrinsically relational nature. Furthermore, humans reflect God most centrally in our capacity to love God and others. This nature never changes regardless of how loving or unloving one's relationships are. This is the *imago Dei* as a noun.

This view would appear to be the most consistent with the Old Testament passages describing the *imago Dei*, in that it reflects an imaging of God that is universal, describing every human person, and that continues after the fall. While the fall damaged the image, it did not eradicate it. This view also appears to be superior to views emphasizing rationality and volition, in that it focuses on characteristics of God that appear to be more emphasized in the biblical text than are God's rationality and volition: the loving relationships among the Trinity.[67]

Relational goal. The view proposed here is in alignment with theologians who have emphasized New Testament teachings affirming that Christ perfectly demonstrates God's image, and that our goal as humans is the renewing of the image of God as we become more like Christ.[68] This is the actualization and development of our relational nature: knowing and loving God and others in increasingly mature ways throughout our lives, which moves us toward the relational telos or end goal of sanctification.

---

[67]Anthony Hoekema makes this point that looking to Christ to discern the image of God suggests that reason and intelligence are less central than love. See Hoekema, *Created in God's Image*, 73.
[68]Wright, *Colossians and Philemon*, 70.

More specifically, the end goal of sanctification might be described as loving presence. Anthony Hoekema rightly points out that if we are to be conformed to the image of Jesus, then we should not focus on what distinguishes humans from nonhuman creation to discern the flourishing *imago Dei*; rather, we should look to Jesus, and the most striking thing about Jesus was his love, which was an extension of the love between him and the Father, empowered by the Spirit.[69]

We are called to be a "loving presence" in our relationships, families, and communities. This draws on the central idea of love while also integrating the notion of mediating presence, which is a central Hebrew understanding of the image of God.[70] Part of the *imago Dei* is representing God by mediating his loving presence to others; thus, the representational aspect of the image is an extension of love, not a wholly separate aspect. Loving presence is a way of being with God and others, and a way of representing God's likeness, which is most clearly found in the glory of Christ, who is the image of the invisible God (Colossians 1:15). In a foundational sense, sanctification is the renewal of the *imago Dei*, which we believe has been pervasively damaged by the fall. If the image of God signifies being-in-relation as suggested here, then sanctification is the renewal of being-in-relation (to God and others) through love.

While love is primarily described in the New Testament by *agapē*—a steadfast, self-giving disposition most purely expressed in Jesus freely sacrificing his life for sinful humankind—it also contains dimensions of friendship (*philia*), longing (*eros*), and particularly parental affection (*storgē*).[71] As we will argue in chapter six, all of these terms are expressions or forms of love, rather than different kinds of love. God loves us in all these ways highlighted above. He longs for reconciliation and relationship with his creation. Jesus calls his disciples "friends" (John 15:13-15). Moreover, the prototypical expression of God's love may well be that of parental affection, or attachment love. One of the primary metaphors used for salvation is that we are adopted into God's family

---

[69]Hoekema, *Created in God's Image.*
[70]Curtis, "Image of God," 3:390.
[71]Grenz, *Social God*, 317.

(Romans 8:15, 23; Romans 9:4; Galatians 4:5; Ephesians 1:5). This brief overview of love, which we will elaborate on in chapters six and seven, provides a rich vision of God's love for human beings, which is a reflection of the mutual indwelling and love (perichōrēsis) among the Trinity. This, in turn, provides a picture of the love we are to have for the new family of God, and all humanity, which manifests the image of God. Furthermore, as we noted, the goal is not that believers love God and others solely in dyadic relationships, but corporately as the body of Christ shares in God's love together.

Relational process. The third element of our model, relational process, represents the least developed aspect of a theology of the image of God. The relational image of God in us means that we develop, grow, and change primarily and directly through relationships, and more specifically through the mutual love of the Trinity. Being-in-relation can only be renewed through a relational currency. In fact, while we always maintain the image of God in the form of relational capacities, relationships affect our soul throughout our lives for good or for ill. In other words, relational experiences are uniquely and profoundly implicated in the sanctification process through which we are renewed in the image of Christ. Love always develops us toward being more fully human and deeply alive (i.e., more like Christ), and hate and disconnection always damage our souls and move us away from the flourishing life God intended for us. Psychology greatly informs this process, which will be articulated further throughout the book.

In addition to emphasizing the relational nature of the mechanisms of change, it is important to highlight that this renewal of the image of God is a process. The scope of the New Testament paints a picture of sanctification as a relational process of conforming to the image of Christ, which is the renewal of the *imago Dei*. For example, in Colossians 3:9-10, Paul says, "Do not lie to each other, since you have taken off your old self with its practices and have put on the new self, which is being renewed in knowledge in the image of its Creator" (NIV). Paul is saying that we put on the new self at one point in time—salvation—but that the new self is being continually renewed in the image of God. Believers who put their faith in Christ enter into a process of being transformed and re-newed into the image of Christ, who is a pure image of the invisible God.

An emphasis both on relational mechanisms and process is clear in the book of Ephesians, which presents a vision for relational life in the context of the body of Christ. Here we have a picture of the Greek fathers' notion of *theōsis*—the communal process by which believers participate in God's love. Chapter four indicates that Christ provides certain gifts to members of the church "so that the body of Christ may be built up" (Ephesians 4:12 NIV)—an image reflecting a developmental growth process in order to reach maturity: "attaining to the whole measure of the fullness of Christ" (Ephesians 4:13 NIV). Ephesians 4:16 goes on to clarify that in relying relationally on Christ, "the whole body . . . grows and builds itself up in love, as each part does it work" (NIV). This passage reflects a relational growth process in which the growth appears to be dependent, not on individual efforts at self-improvement, nor exclusively through relationship with Christ, but through relationship with Christ mediated by Christ's body, in a number of relational processes. The image of God is fully inhabited and manifested only within the com-munal context of the body of Christ.

Conclusion

In this chapter, we have built on several relational resources in outlining a trinitarian-relational model of the image of God. We suggested that a synthesis of key biblical themes supports a christological-relational view of the image of God. As we are conformed to the image of Christ, we become more loving and more truly human, just as Christ is the para-digmatic true human. Building on these themes, we first looked to Au-gustine as a representative patristic resource, prior to the split between theology and spirituality, for an early trinitarian-relational view of the *imago Dei*. We then highlighted more contemporary trinitarian themes and have built on these to propose a three-part model of being-in-relation: (1) the relational nature of humans made in the image of the trinitarian God, (2) the relational goal of sanctification as loving presence, and (3) a relational process in which we are loved into loving as the means of sanctification. We are designed to participate in and express God's love in the communal context of the body of Christ, in which we individually and corporately manifest the image of God by radiating his love to each other and to the world.

While the *imago Dei* may seem to be an abstract concept far removed from our daily lives, I would suggest that a trinitarian-relational view of the image of God has far-reaching implications for spiritual transformation. If God is a relational, loving being, then we can affirm philosopher John Macmurray's maxim: "'I' need 'You' in order to be myself."[72] If we truly need each other—in individual relationships and in community—to reflect God and become who God intended us to be, then this should inform how we seek to grow in Christ and ultimately how we mediate God's loving presence to the world.

Embracing a trinitarian view of the image of God will impact not only how we engage with the family of God but also how we engage in our broader communities, and how we seek to bring the reality of the kingdom of God into this life.[73] This is particularly important in our present historical moment in which loneliness, racial injustice, and societal division are widespread.[74] Kallistos Ware notes, "Every form of community—the family, the school, the workplace, the local Eucharistic center, the monastery, the city, the nation—has as its vocation to become, each according to its own modality, a living icon of the Holy Trinity."[75] When the body of Christ collectively loves its members, and extends this love by bringing compassion to the world, especially to those who are marginalized, we act in the name of the Trinity and reflect the image of God in which we were made.

---

[72]John Macmurray, *Persons in Relation* (London: Faber & Faber, 1961), 69.

[73]Ware, "The Holy Trinity," 127.

[74]Vivek Murthy, "Work and the Loneliness Epidemic: Reducing Isolation at Work Is Good for Business," *Harvard Business Review*, September 2017, https://hbr.org/cover-story/2017/09/work-and-the-loneliness-epidemic. See also C. Wilson and B. Moulton, "Loneliness Among Older Adults: A National Survey of Adults 45+," prepared by Knowledge Networks and Insight Policy Research (Washington, DC: AARP, 2010).

[75]Ware, "The Holy Trinity," 127-28.

Created to Connect

A Psychology of Being-in-Relation

WE ARE PROFOUNDLY relational beings. The absence of close relationships is a health risk factor more important than smoking, obesity, and physical activity in its effects on mortality rates.[1] Close relationships help us cope with stress and meet our needs for social connection. In addition, they are foundational for physical and mental health, and for meaning and spiritual growth into the likeness of Christ. In this chapter, we will consider the scientific evidence suggesting that God created us as prewired to connect. As we discussed in chapter two, the Bible and trinitarian theology establish a broad framework for this in the concept of the image of God. Likewise, contemporary research from numerous fields is converging on a relational paradigm of human development and fleshing out our biblical understanding of how profoundly relational we are. We are born for loving relationships with God and others.

This prewiring plays out in two ways. First, we are born with the ability to relate. Infant research demonstrates that these capacities for interpersonal engagement are in place from a very young age. Second, early loving relationships are crucial for our development into maturity—emotionally, relationally, and spiritually. Several lines of research are converging in suggesting a new perspective on how the brain functions—namely, that it is dependent on relationships to develop properly and to organize itself.

---

[1]Paula R. Pietromonaco and Nancy L. Collins, "Interpersonal Mechanisms Linking Close Relationships to Health," *American Psychologist* 72 (2017): 531-42.

The evidence from these studies has led to a new paradigm of development indicating that our neural connections synchronize with our relational connections, wiring our relational experiences into our brain circuits.[2] Moreover, when our early relationships are deficient, relationships later in life can lead to significant change in our brains and healing in our souls. We are created for relationships, and relationships remain central to our well-being and spiritual development throughout our lives.

In this chapter we will provide an overview of several interrelated windows into how we are prewired to connect. First, we will turn to infant research suggesting that infants are profoundly relational from day one, and even in utero. Second, we will explore the need for relationships in early development through the lens of attachment theory, which we elaborate on in chapter five. Following this, we will explore some of the biological underpinnings of our relational capacities. The relational spirituality paradigm that has emerged has profound implications for understanding and fostering spiritual development, and the prewired-to-connect nature of our souls is the foundation of this new relational spirituality paradigm.

The Relational Infant and the Origin of Relational Capacities

Donald Winnicott, a British pediatrician and psychoanalyst, was well known for saying "there is no such thing as an infant."[3] What he meant is that we really cannot understand a baby apart from the baby-mother relational matrix. Just as there has been a revolution in our understanding of the brain in recent decades, there has also been a revolution in our understanding of infants. This revolution has borne out Winnicott's maxim.

Developmental scientists used to think that infants are basically passive and nonrelational.[4] However, infant research in the last thirty

---

[2]Daniel J. Siegel, *The Developing Mind*, 2nd ed. (New York: Guilford Press, 2012).

[3]Donald W. Winnicott, "The Theory of the Parent-Infant Relationship," *The International Journal of Psychoanalysis* 41 (1960): 587.

[4]In the early to mid-1970s, Margaret Mahler and her colleagues proposed that infants go through a "normal autistic" phase the first four to five months of life, in which they have no sense of a separate self, or drive for relationship. This view is no longer held by contemporary infant

years has taught us several broad principles that paint a portrait of infants as amazingly relational.[5] First, we have learned that infants are born with the capacity to "catch" the emotions of others. Second, they are capable of influencing, and being influenced by, relational interactions. In other words, what happens inside infants' subjective experience is impacted by what happens between them and their relational partner. In addition, what happens between the dyad affects infants' experience and ability to regulate their own internal states. Third, infants innately anticipate. They are capable of developing incredibly complex implicit models that govern their expectations of how interactions with others will play out. Below we consider each principle in turn.

Emotional responsiveness: catching others' emotions. There is growing evidence that human beings are prewired to respond to others' suffering. Some evidence comes from studies of lab rats and rhesus monkeys, while some comes from infant research and studies of adults using fMRI technology (functional magnetic resonance imaging). For example, when a laboratory rat is suspended in the air by a harness, it screeches and struggles to get free. When one of its fellow lab rats sees the other rat's plight, it also becomes distressed and manages to rescue it by pressing a lever that lowers the victim safely to the ground.[6]

In another study, six rhesus monkeys are trained to pull chains to obtain food. A seventh monkey receives a painful shock whenever one of them pulls the chain for food, and the other six monkeys see this happening. When they see their fellow monkey being shocked, four of the original six monkeys start pulling a different chain that gives them less food but doesn't administer a shock to their friend. The fifth monkey stops pulling the chain for five days, and the sixth monkey stops pulling it for twelve days. These last two monkeys were literally

---

researchers, and a more relational view of infants was articulated by Daniel Stern in his book, *The Interpersonal World of the Infant* (New York: Basic Books, 1985). See also Margaret S. Mahler, Fred Pine, and Anni Bergman, *The Psychological Birth of the Human Infant* (New York: Basic Books, 1975).

[5]For a synthesis of the last thirty years of infant research, see Ed Tronick, *The Neurobehavioral and Social-Emotional Development of Infants and Children* (New York: W. W. Norton & Co., 2007).

[6]See Daniel Goleman, *Social Intelligence* (New York: Bantam Books, 2006), 55.

starving themselves in order to prevent the seventh monkey from being shocked.[7]

Human infants, likewise, show an automatic impulse to attend to others' suffering. From birth, when babies see or hear another baby crying in distress, they start crying as though they were the ones distressed. However, they rarely cry in response to hearing a recording of their own cries. Moreover, after fourteen months of age, babies not only cry when they hear another baby crying, they actually do something to try to relieve the other baby's distress.[8]

Mutual coordination of internal and relational states. If you watch a new mother with her baby for any length of time, you will see her make interesting and contorted faces at her newborn. When a mother shows a look of surprise, her baby will raise her eyebrows in a look of surprise. Most parents, when feeding their babies, open their mouths without realizing it as they move the spoonful of food closer to their mouth. Babies imitate their parents' open-mouth expression, which facilitates the feeding process.

In fact, infants as young as forty-two minutes can imitate an adult's facial expression.[9] Infants are able to sense a match between what they *see* on the adult's face, and what they *feel* in their own faces. This is what infant researchers call "cross-modal matching." This means that infants can translate back and forth between information from the environment (e.g., an adult's facial expression) and information from their own bodies (e.g., the feeling of making a certain facial expression). This is one way in which infants coordinate their inner states with relational states, suggesting that infants are prewired for relationality.

Neuroscience has taught us that certain regions in each hemisphere of the adult brain specialize in processing positive or negative emotions. In neuroscience parlance, these brain circuits are lateralized for

---

[7]Goleman, *Social Intelligence*, 55.

[8]Goleman, *Social Intelligence*, 55.

[9]A. Meltzoff, "Foundations for Developing a Concept of Self: The Role of Imitation in Relating Self to Other and the Value of Social Mirroring, Social Modeling, and Self Practice in Infancy," in *The Self in Transition: Infancy to Childhood*, ed. D. Cicchetti and M. Beeghly (Chicago: University of Chicago Press, 1990), 139-64.

processing positive and negative emotions. It turns out that by ten months, infants' brains are likewise lateralized for positive and negative emotion. For example, in one study, as an infant watched a video of a laughing actor, his brain registered positive emotion (electroencephalogram or EEG activation of the left frontal lobe). As he watched a video of a crying actor, his brain exhibited a pattern of negative emotion (EEG activation of right frontal lobe).[10] In this study, the infants did not have to match the partner's facial expression to be influenced by it. This suggests that simply perceiving emotion in another creates a resonant emotional state in the infant.

We also see mutual coordination in the way infants respond to interactional events with their mothers. Picture a mother playing peekaboo with her twelve-month-old baby. She holds a pillow in front of her face, and then suddenly moves the pillow, exuberantly exclaiming "peekaboo!" as her gaze reunites with her baby's. Her baby breaks into joyous laughter at the sudden appearance of his mother. This is the way most infants respond to some kind of positive interaction with their mothers—with positive emotions. Not only that, but most infants in this scenario respond by showing a "positive emotion" EEG pattern of left frontal lobe activation.[11] However, by ten months of age, infants of depressed mothers show a very different response pattern. The same peekaboo event triggers negative emotions, and a "negative emotion" EEG pattern (right frontal lobe activation) in these infants. These infants' internal states are still coordinated with relational events, but the way the coordination is organized is reversed compared to infants of nondepressed mothers. However, this demonstrates from another vantage point the close linkage between infants' internal states and their dyadic interactions.

If you watch a mother and her baby during a face-to-face interaction, you will notice that the baby will periodically look away for a few seconds and then look back. The mother, on the other hand, will look at her baby

---

[10]R. Davidson and N. Fox, "Asymmetrical Brain Activity Discriminates Between Positive Versus Negative Affective Stimuli in Human Infants," *Science* 218 (1982): 1235-37.

[11]G. Dawson, L. Grofer Klinger, H. Panagiotides, S. Spieker, and K. Frey, "Infants of Mothers with Depressive Symptoms: Electrophysiological and Behavioral Findings Related to Attachment Status," *Development and Psychopathology* 4 (1992): 67-80.

the entire time. This is very parallel to what happens in psychotherapy. When I see a client in psychotherapy, I tend to maintain eye contact throughout the entire session. Clients regulate their sense of connection by regulating their eye contact with the therapist. Infants do the same thing. They have full control over their gazing behavior, which allows for very sophisticated social interactions. Infant researcher Daniel Stern notes, "When watching the gazing patterns of mother and infant . . . one is watching two people with almost equal facility and control over the same social behavior."[12] Infants actually regulate their heart rates by visually disengaging from their mothers for brief periods of time. When their heart rate rises above its normal baseline, they process less information from the environment. In order to regulate themselves and decrease their arousal level, they look away from their mothers. After they look away for five seconds, their heart rate returns to its baseline level, indicating that they can process more information.[13] In addition, by six months, infants of depressed mothers have elevated heart rates and higher levels of the cortisol stress hormone. These infants appear to be in a chronic state of elevated arousal and distress. Thus, we see that infants regulate themselves through their social interactions and that their arousal levels match the quality of their social interactions.

Infant research has also taught us that infants have very sophisticated perceptions of emotion expressed through voice and face. By six months, infants can tell the difference between a rising pitch and a falling pitch, and they show a bias toward the positive, rising pitch.[14] By seven months in utero, infants' facial muscles are almost fully developed. At birth, they are almost on par with adults in their ability to move facial muscles. By six months of age, infants can display the seven basic emotions of interest, joy, disgust, surprise, distress, sadness, and anger. Their perception of facial emotion is so good that neonates can discriminate between expressions of surprise, fear, and sadness on an adult's face. In addition,

[12]Daniel Stern, *The Interpersonal World of the Infant* (New York: Basic Books, 1985), 21.
[13]T. Field, "Infant Gaze Aversion and Heart Rate During Face-to-Face Interactions," *Infant Behavior and Development* 4 (1981): 307-15.
[14]A. Fernald, "Four-Month-Old Infants Prefer to Listen to Motherese," *Infant Behavior and Development* 8 (1987): 181-95.

they mimic these expressions so well on their own faces that, if you were watching, you would be able to guess which face they were mimicking.[15]

By ten months of age, infants actively seek out emotional information from their caregivers to help them understand their environment. In a classic "visual cliff" experiment, an interesting object was placed on the other side of what appeared to the infants to be a cliff (a glass table). It appeared to the infants as though they would fall if they attempted to cross the cliff. If an infant's mother displayed a fearful facial expression, the infant didn't cross. However, if an infant's mother smiled, the infant would cross the visual cliff. We can see that infants naturally look to interpersonal interactions to help them understand their environment and guide their behavior.[16]

One of the fascinating ways that infant research has revealed the "relational infant" is through close-up, frame-by-frame analyses of video clips of face-to-face play between infants and their mothers and fathers. The goal in face-to-face play is for the baby and caregiver to attend to one another and take delight in one another. This situation brings out an infant's strongest communication skills and provides an awe-inspiring window into what Daniel Stern calls the "subtle instant-by-instant regulation of social contact."[17]

In one study, a five-week-old infant, Elliott, is filmed with three different people for two minutes each: his mother, a student, and the principal researcher of the study.[18] In the first interaction with his mother, his mother appears somewhat expressionless and a bit depressed. Elliott is fussy and avoids eye contact. The mother begins to shake Elliott, gently but rapidly. The rapid rhythm upsets Elliott more and he has trouble calming himself down—a normal difficulty for his age. At some point, his mother begins to sing "Happy Birthday" to him, and for whatever reason, this seems to work. The moment she starts singing, you see Elliott's unfocused gaze shift to alert eye contact. This is the first time the

---

[15]Beatrice Beebe and Frank Lachmann, *Infant Research and Adult Treatment: Co-Constructing Interactions* (Hillsdale, NJ: Analytic Press, 2002).

[16]Beebe and Lachmann, *Infant Research.*

[17]Daniel Stern, *The First Relationship* (Cambridge, MA: Harvard University Press, 1977), 502.

[18]See chapter five of Beebe and Lachmann, *Infant Research.*

mother has helped Elliott regulate his emotions. However, eventually he loses interest, and she is not able to find another way to reengage him.

Next the student enters. She is very animated, much more animated than Elliott. She is not tracking with his feelings. She has a wide smile, but Elliott doesn't look happy. He frowns and looks quite sober. The student appears to be out of sync with him. She then picks him up and sways rhythmically, which seems to help perk him up a bit. They briefly engage with each other by making eye contact, but then the interaction falls apart and Elliott begins to cry.

The researcher then enters and vocally matches the rhythm of Elliott's cry. Then she gradually slows down her vocals and lowers the volume, and Elliott immediately calms down. He becomes alert and his gaze focuses. Then Elliott begins to look a bit sleepy, his arousal level dipping too low. So the researcher provides a more animated facial expression but keeps the volume of her voice low in order to increase his arousal slightly but also soothe him. As Elliott begins to slip into a slumber, the researcher speeds up the rhythm with her face, voice, and head. At this, Elliott engages visually with her and becomes more alert.

These three interactions illustrate Winnicott's maxim "there is no such thing as an infant." The infant-partner unit, or system, includes Elliott's ability to regulate his own emotions, the various levels of attunement by each partner, and the dyad's ability to navigate the emotional terrain with whatever abilities Elliott brings to the table (as well as the capacities of the adults). They also illustrate the transformation of the infant's internal state, and that this is achieved in the context of the ongoing, mutually coordinated relational process. The transformation of the infant's state turns out to be very important. It is through these split-second interchanges that the infant learns what to expect in terms of how important interactions will play out. We turn now to evidence that infants develop complex expectations about interactional patterns.

Expectations of interactional patterns. Infants are amazing in their abilities to (1) develop complex expectation models about various aspects of their environment and (2) categorize information. This is not only true of objects but of social interactions as well. Many studies have confirmed that this holds true in a laboratory setting, but there is good reason to believe that what holds true in the lab also holds true in the real-life social world of the infant. First, social information is far more salient, redundant, and capable of providing meaningful feedback than information manipulated in a lab. Second, there is substantial direct evidence that infants generalize relational patterns and develop expectations about relationships based on these generalizations.

If a three-month-old infant watches an event only twice, she will be able to figure out whether it is likely to happen again and develop an implicit set of rules that will shape her expectations regarding that event.[19] Infant researchers call these implicit rule sets "expectancy models," or "schemas," and they believe that expectancy models work in the same way for social interactions as they do for nonsocial events. This process is so foundational that the speed with which three- to five-month-old infants develop expectancy models in general predicts their verbal intelligence at two to five years.[20]

Another foundational component of expectancy models is the ability to categorize. For example, infants can classify faces by gender at six months of age.[21] Infants' ability to categorize in general is the basis for how they categorize expectations about how interactions typically proceed. Relational experiences are classified into categories by the end of the infant's first year. We refer to expectancy models about interactions as "attachment filters" in chapter five.[22]

Another piece of evidence for expectancy models in natural social contexts comes from infants of depressed mothers. By six months, infants of depressed mothers show depressed behavior with a

---

[19]J. Fagen et al., "Expectancies and Memory Retrieval in Three-Month-Old Infants," *Child Development* 55 (1984): 936-43.

[20]Beebe and Lachmann, *Infant Research.*

[21]M. Lewis and J. Brooks, "Infants' Social Perception: A Constructionist View," in *Infant Perception: From Sensation to Cognition*, vol. 2, ed. L. Cohen and P. Salapatek (New York: Wiley-Interscience, 1975), 101-48.

[22]These expectancy models are referred to in numerous theoretical traditions with various names, such as internal objects (object relations theory), internal working models (attachment theory), mental models, and schemas (cognitive and developmental science). These models turn out to powerfully shape our relational experiences in adulthood, a topic to which chapter five will be devoted.

nondepressed, appropriately attuned female.[23] This suggests that the nonnormal pattern these infants display with their mothers is organized enough that infants expect that other interactions with strangers will mirror their interactions with mother. In fact, by ten months, the brains of these infants mirror the depressed brains of their mothers.[24]

In a set of experiments using the still-face paradigm, a mother plays with her baby for two minutes. Then she is instructed to face her baby for two minutes without moving her face or making any sound. Her baby smiles and coos at her, trying to engage her. When she doesn't respond, the baby looks surprised and then seems to disengage, while still intermittently trying to evoke a response from her mother.[25] In a similar experiment, an infant is shown a video of her mother responding to her in an interaction that had taken place several minutes earlier, so the mother's responses do not match the infant's current behavior. Infants showed the same surprise and disengaged response as in the still-face studies. We see from these experiments that because infants are prewired to connect, they expect their partners to respond in a contingent way, and when this doesn't happen, they get upset.

How infants cope with the distress caused by violations of their expectations turns out to be quite revealing. By six months, the way an infant copes with the stress of the still-face experiment is stable and predicts the infant's attachment tendency at one year. Infants who smile and coo at their mothers in an effort to engage her tend to have a secure attachment at one year. However, infants who do not attempt to engage their mothers tend to exhibit an insecure attachment at one year.[26] The stress induced by the still-face paradigm seems to trigger the need for comfort and security (i.e., it activates the

---

[23]T. Field et al., "Infants of Depressed Mothers Show 'Depressed' Behavior Even with Non-Depressed Adults," *Child Development* 59 (1988): 1569-79.

[24]Dawson, "Infants of Mothers with Depressive Symptoms," 117.

[25]E. Tronick et al., "The Infant's Response to Entrapment Between Contradictory Messages in Face-to-Face Interaction," *Journal of the American Academy of Child and Adolescent Psychiatry* 17 (1978): 1-13.

[26]J. Cohn, S. Campbell, and S. Ross, "Infant Response in the Still-Face Paradigm at 6 months Predicts Avoidant and Secure Attachments at 12 months," *Development and Psychopathology* 3 (1991): 367-76.

attachment system, which we will discuss in chapter five), and the way infants cope with the distress reveals a particular expectancy model that has already developed.

Finally, there are a number of longitudinal studies that provide evidence for the development of expectancy models in infancy. For example, patterns of mother-infant vocal rhythm coordination at four months predict attachment status and cognition at one year.[27] In addition, many studies show that social interactions in the first six months predict a variety of social and cognitive outcomes in the second and third year.[28]

In sum, we have learned from infant research that mother and infant jointly construct interaction patterns that are linked to their internal processes. These internal processes are gradually internalized through an implicit form of memory (see chapter four), which then shape future interactions, forming a feedback loop. The dyadic interaction and the infant's own self-regulation influence each other on a continuous, moment-by-moment basis. Infants are prewired to develop complex models of expectation in terms of how an interactive sequence will unfold. That infants are so profoundly, immediately, and automatically relational suggests that relationality is part of God's design for human nature and spiritual development.

The Invisible Bond of Attachment

In our review of infant research above, we mentioned the concept of attachment to parents. An attachment relationship is a particular kind of relationship—a deep connection between a caregiver (or attachment figure, such as a parent) and someone on the receiving end of that care, such as a child. When a child becomes attached to her parent, usually by six months of age, something happens inside of each one and between the two of them. An invisible bond develops that is supported by a literal brain-to-brain linkup between parent and child. This invisible bond

---

[27]J. Jaffe et al., "Rhythms of Dialogue in Early Infancy," *Monographs of the Society for Research in Child Development* 66, no. 2, serial no. 264 (2001): 1-32.

[28]Beebe and Lachmann, *Infant Research*; Tronick, *Neurobehavioral and Social-Emotional Development*.

manifests itself in three characteristics. First, infants seek to stay close to their attachment figures (physical proximity), and—the flip side of this coin—they become distressed when they are separated from their attachment figures (separation distress). In infancy, connection is regulated primarily through physical proximity, but as we get older emotional connection relies less on physical proximity. Second, attachment figures provide—to varying degrees—a haven of safety in times of distress and a secure base from which to explore the world. Overall, they provide children a sense of felt security about themselves and their worlds. When distressed, the child seeks out her attachment figure for safety and emotional comfort and regulation. When this happens consistently, it creates a secure base for the child to play and explore her world because she knows her attachment figure will be there for her if needed. Third, attachment figures provide the relational context for intersubjectivity, or a sense of mutual knowing, influence, and belonging. Intersubjectivity is a concept that was developed independently in the fields of infant research and adult psychoanalysis.[29] In essence, it refers to the subjective space created by the interaction of two minds and reciprocally influenced by both minds. Our sense of felt security comes primarily from the specific people to whom we are attached.

When young children get hurt physically or emotionally, they don't run to any random adult for comfort. They run to mommy or daddy, or some other attachment figure. No one else will do. To be attached means that you are "spoken for" by your attachment figure(s). Secure attachment means someone in this world has signed up to look out for you, to always be *for* you.

Attachment relationships remain significant throughout life and serve the same two functions: secure base and safe haven. We continue to need

---

[29]In the field of adult psychoanalysis, Robert Stolorow and George Atwood proposed the concept of intersubjectivity, or the "intersubjective field," as "the larger system created by the mutual interplay between the subjective worlds of patient and analyst." Their overarching thesis is that this system of reciprocal mutual influence is a new paradigm that calls for a radical revision of all aspects of psychoanalytic theory because it thoroughly impacts how the psychoanalyst knows, and therefore how he or she should conduct psychoanalysis. Robert D. Stolorow and George E. Atwood, *Contexts of Being: The Intersubjective Foundations of Psychological Life* (Hillsdale, NJ: Analytic Press, 1992).

others for safety and for exploration throughout life, though this might look different as adults. When we can rely on close others as secure bases, we are willing to engage in challenging, growth-enhancing pursuits, knowing that we can depend on our relationships to get us through the rough spots. We also weather difficult life events better, making it more likely that we will grow and change as a result of those events. When we experience others as a safe haven, we can explore new directions, set goals for ourselves and pursue them, and thus develop and grow.[30]

For example, one study of marriages found that availability, encouragement, and noninterference of the spouse—the three characteristics of a secure base in adulthood—enabled progress toward goals.[31] Goals give us a sense of purpose and are a crucial component of meaning. In this way, attachment relationships are necessary for personal growth and for living meaningful lives. Because of their connection to growth and meaning, these attachment functions have important implications for spiritual development, a point to which we will return later in the book.

Attachment Relationships and the Expression of Genes

You are probably familiar with the nature-nurture debate that poses two competing factors that determine our development. One view holds that nature, or our genetic makeup, largely determines how our brains develop, and consequently, how every aspect of our personhood develops. The other view, nurture, holds that our life experiences play the major role in determining who we will become. In recent years, this debate has completely imploded. Contemporary scientists consider this dichotomy to be an unhelpful way to think about our development. The Commission on Children at Risk put it this way: "The old 'nature versus nurture' debate—focusing on whether heredity or environment is the main determinant of human conduct—is no longer relevant to serious

---

[30]Brooke C. Feeney and Nancy L. Collins, "A New Look at Social Support: A Theoretical Perspective on Thriving Through Relationships," *Personality and Social Psychology Review* 19 (2015): 113-47.

[31]Brittany K. Jacubiak and Brooke C. Feeney, "Daily Goal Progress Is Facilitated by Spousal Support and Promotes Psychological, Physical and Relational Well-Being Throughout Adulthood," *Journal of Personality and Social Psychology* 111 (2016): 317-40.

discussions of child well-being and youth programming."[32] Part of the reason for this is that our relational connections shape the brain circuits that process emotions, meaning, and relationships. This means we cannot neatly separate nature from nurture as we once thought we could.

There is now convincing scientific evidence that development results from the product of experience and our unfolding genetic potential, which sheds more light on our relational nature.[33] Genes have two main functions: (1) they provide a filter for information that is to be passed down to the next generation, and (2) they have a transcription function that determines when genes are expressed through the process of protein synthesis, based on the information encoded within their DNA. Transcription is influenced by relational experiences, which means that relationships impact how neurons connect with one another forming the neural networks, or circuits, that make up our brains. Relational connections, then, directly influence the formation of new synaptic connections in the brain, changes in the strength of neural connections, and the dissolution of neural connections.[34]

The *Hardwired to Connect* report by the Commission on Children at Risk explains this concept using a helpful analogy. If you think of genes as an alphabet from which "words" are produced that represent the biochemical messages of our nervous system, relational experiences influence *which* letters are transcribed, *how often* they are transcribed, and in *what order* they are transcribed, all of which determine the content of the biochemical messages in our nervous system.[35] In other words, relational connections influence the way our genes are expressed, and the expression of our genes in turn changes the neural networks in our brains. The physical structure of neural networks is how our brains record or remember information.

---

[32]Commission on Children at Risk, *Hardwired to Connect: The New Scientific Case for Authoritative Communities* (New York: Institute for American Values, 2003).

[33]Siegel, *Developing Mind*, 30-33; Commission on Children at Risk, *Hardwired to Connect.*

[34]Siegel, *Developing Mind*, 33-35; Michael J. Meaney, "Maternal Care, Gene Expression, and the Transmission of Individual Differences in Stress Reactivity Across Generations," *Annual Review of Neuroscience* 24 (2001): 1161-92.

[35]Commission on Children at Risk, *Hardwired to Connect.*

A more specific window into this general concept is provided by research on rhesus monkeys. These studies have shown that the way in which genes affect behavioral outcomes depends significantly on social contexts. One study found that about 15 to 20 percent of rhesus monkeys inherited a disposition toward anxiety. In situations most monkeys would experience as novel and interesting, these monkeys became very anxious. In addition, they produced significantly higher levels of the stress hormone called cortisol. However, when these genetically at-risk, anxious monkeys were placed under the care of highly nurturing female monkeys, their anxiety disappeared. The improved social environment seems to have buffered or removed the genetic vulnerability to anxiety.[36]

Other studies have shown even more robust interactions between social context and genetic vulnerability. For example, in some rhesus monkeys, variation in a gene associated with the neurotransmitter serotonin seems to create a predisposition toward aggression and poor impulse control. When these monkeys are raised in nurturing environments, not only does their aggressive behavior disappear, but they actually thrive and climb near to the top of the rhesus monkey social ladder.[37] This is an even more powerful nature-nurture interaction, in which social experience overcomes a genetic vulnerability and produces a positive outcome.

We also see the impact of relationships on gene expression in newly emerging treatments for a disorder that has a significant genetic component—schizophrenia. More than two million people in the United States have been diagnosed with schizophrenia. Because it is believed to have a strong genetic component, the standard treatment for many years has been strong doses of antipsychotic medications that reduce hallucinations and delusions but often cause debilitating side effects, such as

---

[36]Stephen J. Suomi, "Developmental Trajectories, Early Experiences, and Community Consequences," in *Developmental Health and the Wealth of Nations: Social Biological and Educational Dynamics*, ed. D. P. Keating and C. Hertzman (New York: Guilford Press, 1999), 189-200.

[37]Stephen J. Suomi, "How Mother Nurture Helps Mother Nature: Scientific Evidence for the Protective Effect of Good Nurturing on Genetic Propensity Toward Anxiety and Alcohol Abuse," in *Commission on Children at Risk*, Working Paper 14 (New York: Institute for American Values, 2002), 18-19.

tremors and weight gain. The predominant thinking, until relatively recently, has been that genes are the main culprit in this disorder, so relationships and talk therapy don't really help schizophrenia. This thinking is changing as we learn more about the power of relationships to foster health and healing.

For example, a recent study compared a comprehensive treatment approach to first-episode psychosis that emphasized relational connection (i.e., talk therapy and family support) to a usual community care approach that emphasized medication.[38] Results showed that the comprehensive relational approach, as a whole, led to better outcomes. Participants in this program (1) stayed in treatment longer, (2) experienced greater improvement in quality of life and symptoms, and (3) displayed higher levels of involvement in work and school. This is just one area beginning to show the power of relationships to transform genetic vulnerabilities. The impact of our attachment relationships on brain development and genetic expression point to the fundamental importance of the neurochemistry of attachment and the social circuitry of the brain.

The Neuroscience of Connection

Neuroscience has taught us that the physical brain structures that process our relational experiences are dependent on certain relational experiences with attachment figures in order to grow and develop in a healthy manner. Because of this, neuroscientists refer to these parts of the brain as "experience-dependent." For example, when a mother and baby gaze at each other, or engage in mutually attuned facial interactions and soothing vocalizations, it promotes psychobiological regulation in the infant, and the mechanism for this is the development of the orbital frontal cortex (OFC) circuit, which is known to integrate the circuits responsible for attachment, social relationships, and emotion regulation.[39]

---

[38]J. M. Kane et al., "Comprehensive Versus Usual Community Care for First-Episode Psychosis: 2-Year Outcomes from the NIMH RAISE Early Treatment Program," *The American Journal of Psychiatry* 173, no. 4 (October 2015): 362-72.

[39]Louis Cozolino, *The Neuroscience of Human Relationships* (New York: W. W. Norton & Co., 2006), 72.

It turns out that these early relational experiences with caregivers (or lack thereof) are literally imprinted into infants' brain circuits. Below we will examine research on three interrelated aspects of the relational brain: the neurochemistry of connection, the orbital frontal cortex, and the vagus nerve.

Oxytocin: the neurochemistry of connection. The warm and tender feelings a child and her mother or father experience in a moment of connection, the pain of separation, and the joy of reuniting all have neurochemical processes that make these experiences possible. This is not to say that if we understand the neurochemical processes, we know all there is to know. We contend that human beings are not reducible to brain events. Nonetheless, we are embodied beings, and understanding the neurochemistry that underlies attachment bonds gives us deeper insight and appreciation into our relational nature.

Through a series of biochemical processes, the interactions between mother and child cause the release of oxytocin, prolactin, endorphins, and dopamine, which create positive feelings. In addition, these neurochemicals stimulate the growth of the orbital frontal cortex (OFC), which is responsible for processing social-emotional information, as noted above.[40]

Recent animal studies give us insight into the role of various neurochemicals, such as the neuropeptides oxytocin and vasopressin, in attachment bonding. In fact, there is evidence that these neuropeptides play important roles in social behavior across the lifespan—not just in infancy. They shape the brain during fetal development, are present in increased quantities in women giving birth and breastfeeding, are involved in parenting behaviors, regulate social interactions such as play behaviors in adolescence, and are present in cooperative behaviors in adulthood, including pair bonding in romantic relationships.[41] In fact, lack of regulation in oxytocin and vasopressin is found in individuals

---

[40]Jakk Panksepp, *Affective Neuroscience: The Foundation of Human and Animal Emotions* (New York: Oxford University Press, 1998).

[41]Heather K. Caldwell, "Oxytocin and Vasopressin: Powerful Regulators of Social Behavior," *The Neuroscientist* 23 (2017): 517-28.

who have disorders characterized by impaired social cognition, such as autism related disorders, personality disorders, and schizophrenia.[42]

Of particular interest to us in examining the neurochemistry of attachment are studies that indicate that oxytocin is essential to the establishment and ongoing quality of parent-child attachment.[43] Oxytocin is present in high levels during the crucial bonding period between the mother and the newborn, increasing the mother's responsiveness to cues from her own child in contrast to cues from other children. Oxytocin is involved equally in parental sensitivity in mothers and fathers, stimulating behaviors such as affectionate touch, social gaze, and tactile stimulation. Oxytocin seems to enhance the reward system in parents, encouraging them to attend to their child's social cues and engage in responsive parenting behaviors. For example, one fMRI study found that on viewing their own infants' faces (as opposed to the faces of other infants), fathers showed greater activation of brain reward regions, including those associated with oxytocin. Oxytocin also seems to be involved in the synchrony of parent and child hormonal, physiological, and behavioral cues, such as those described in the studies above. In other words, the release of oxytocin promotes behaviors that stimulate further connection, in a positive feedback loop of coregulation.[44] Children who receive less attuned parenting will experience less of an increase in oxytocin during this critical period of brain development, and this appears to have long-term effects on their oxytocin system.[45]

The orbital frontal cortex: the capacity to catch emotions. I remember walking out of my office one afternoon to get a client in the waiting room. We walked back to my office. In our usual routine, Angie glanced at me as she walked by me to sit down, while I stood by the door waiting to close it. When our eyes met in that momentary glance and I

---

[42]Caldwell, "Oxytocin and Vasopressin," 524.

[43]Monika Szymanska et al., "Psychophysiological Effects of Oxytocin on Parent-Child Interactions: A Literature Review on Oxytocin and Parent-Child Interactions," *Psychiatry and Clinical Neurosciences* 71 (2017): 690-705.

[44]Bert N. Uchino and Baldwin M. Way, "Integrative Pathways Linking Close Family Ties to Health: A Neurochemical Perspective," *American Psychologist* 72 (2017), 590-600.

[45]Uchino and Way, "Integrative Pathways," 595.

saw the look on her face, my stomach tightened. A deep feeling of uneasiness hit me like a lightning bolt. As I sat down, tuning into my experience while looking at her, a strong feeling of sadness came over me. I would find out moments later that her relationship with her boyfriend had ended, reverberating a deep loss she had experienced in childhood.

When I saw my client's face in that first moment, the expression on her face traveled through my thalamus, where all sensory information enters the brain, and through one pathway known as the "low road," straight to my amygdala, which is responsible for extracting the emotional meaning of a nonverbal message. This direct thalamo-amygdala pathway mimicked my client's emotions in my own body.[46] This "low road" brain circuit does not communicate initially with the higher (cortical) processing systems of the brain such as the sensory cortex and the hippocampus that are believed to be involved in thinking, reasoning, and consciousness (the "high road").[47] The way we register what someone else is feeling is that our brains create a similar feeling in us. In this way, we "catch" others' feelings. This is how I knew what my client was feeling from a mere momentary glance. I didn't logically deduce it based on higher-level cortical processing. I felt it in my body and subjective experience. Scientists refer to this as "emotional contagion." The fact that we can catch others' emotions so easily suggests that our brains are prewired to connect us to others in a direct brain-to-brain, emotion-to-emotion way.

This direct connection happens largely through what we see on others' faces. It is said that the eyes are the window to the soul. It turns out that the eyes contain nerve projections that lead directly to the central brain structure responsible for empathy and discerning emotions—the orbital

---

[46]Joseph LeDoux, *The Emotional Brain* (New York: Touchstone, 1996), 161.

[47]Joseph LeDoux labeled this latter pathway as the "high road," in which information travels from the sensory thalamus to the sensory cortex and then to the amygdala, and in another high-road pathway to the hippocampus and then to the amygdala. The amygdala is like the hub of a wheel because it integrates lower-level inputs with higher-level information from the sensory cortex, and with still higher sensory-independent information about context from the hippocampus. It links all this information in order to appraise the emotional meaning of events. The low road is a "quick and dirty processing system" and is about twice as fast as the high-road pathway. See LeDoux, *Emotional Brain*, 161-63.

frontal cortex (OFC). When two people's eyes meet, as in the example with my client, their orbital frontal areas, which are especially sensitive to facial cues such as eye contact, become linked. These pathways are how we recognize others' emotional states.

The OFC, which is located behind the orbits of the eyes, enjoys strategic real estate within the brain. It is located at the crossroads of the uppermost part of the emotion centers of the brain and the lowest part of the analytic thinking centers. The OFC has direct, neuron-to-neuron connections to three major regions of the brain: the top part of the brain, or cortex (responsible for analytic thinking); the amygdala (responsible for many of our emotional reactions); and the brain stem (responsible for automatic responses).[48] The design and connections of the OFC, then, suggest that it coordinates thoughts, feelings, and actions.[49]

The OFC helps us make sense of our worlds, and it does this on the basis of social-emotional meaning. The OFC contains neurons that specialize in detecting emotions on someone's face and in their voice, and in connecting these social messages with one's visceral, bodily experience. The circuits in the OFC track affective significance; that is, they track what someone or something means to us in terms of our well-being. Thus, the OFC uses social-emotional information in evaluating what events in our lives mean to us, and this affective significance in turn plays a major role in determining the responses that are needed and in rallying and coordinating the various brain regions to respond appropriately. A significant research literature is emerging that demonstrates how our brains process social-emotional meaning and how we catch others' emotions.

When mothers look at their own infants, their brains immediately respond with a message of emotional significance. In one study, mothers looked at pictures of their own infants and unfamiliar infants. When they looked at pictures of their own infants, fMRI readings showed that their OFC lit up. In contrast, their OFC did not light up in response to pictures

---

[48]Siegel, *Developing Mind*, 312.
[49]Cozolino, *Neuroscience of Human Relationships*, 54.

of unfamiliar infants. In fact, more activity in the mothers' OFC was associated with stronger feelings of love and warmth.[50]

Whenever we look at a photograph of a face that displays a strong emotion, our facial muscles automatically mirror the expression of the face in the photograph. For example, in a clever study, people were shown angry and happy faces while their facial expressions were monitored by miniature electrodes. The angry and happy faces were shown very rapidly (thirty milliseconds) and in between a set of neutral faces, so the participants had no idea that they had seen the angry and happy faces. Despite this lack of awareness, they displayed distinct facial muscle reactions corresponding to the angry and happy faces.[51] This facial mirroring happens below the radar of our awareness. When we automatically imitate others' expressions, it stimulates in us the feelings we display on our faces, connecting us to the other person whom we are imitating. Recreating the inner psychophysiological state of another person helps us to participate in their subjective experience, and is the basis for empathy.

When people look at a face displaying a strong emotion, they not only imitate the facial expression, but their brains imitate the same neural firing pattern. For example, when people looked at a photograph of a frightened face while being monitored by an fMRI, their brains acted like *they* were afraid.[52] Likewise, when you watch a movie, your brain acts like you are experiencing what you are watching. This sense of reality is what draws us into movies, and it is orchestrated by our brains. These are examples of how we catch others' emotions, and this process operates across the entire spectrum of feelings.

We also catch others' emotions through interpersonal synchrony. Louis Sander describes a beautiful example of interpersonal synchrony between an infant and her father, captured in still frames:

---

[50]Jack B. Nitschke et al., "Orbitofrontal Cortex Tracks Positive Mood in Mothers Viewing Pictures of Their Newborn Infants," *NeuroImage* 21 (2004): 583-92.

[51]U. Dimburg, M. Thunberg, and K. Elmehed, "Unconscious Facial Reactions to Emotional Facial Expressions," *American Psychological Society* 11 (2000): 86-89.

[52]Paul J. Whalen et al., "A Functional MRI Study of Human Amygdala Responses to Facial Expressions of Fear Versus Anger," *Emotion* 1 (2001): 70-83.

One sees the father glance down momentarily at the baby's face. Strangely enough, in the same frames, the infant looks up at the father's face. Then the infant's left arm, which had been hanging down over the father's left arm, begins to move upward. Miraculously, in the same frame, the father's right arm, which had been hanging down at his side, begins to move upward. Frame by frame, the baby's hand and the father's hand move upward simultaneously. Finally, just as they meet over the baby's tummy, the baby's left hand grasps the little finger of the father's right hand. At that moment, the infant's eyes close and she falls asleep, while the father continues talking, apparently totally unaware of the little miracle of specificity in time, place, and movement that had taken place in his arms.[53]

When we catch others' feelings like this, it creates a brain-to-brain bridge, a "neural Wi-Fi" connection.[54] The two brains become functionally linked—or coupled—crossing the barrier of skin and skull. Each brain is then online with respect to the other as they actively communicate and mutually influence each other. In a very real sense, two brains become wirelessly united, forming a feedback loop in which the output of one brain becomes the input of the other, and vice versa. In neural Wi-Fi, two brains function as one, each having access to the resources of the other—the information it processes, and the way it processes information. In short, this brain linkup creates a functional brain circuit across two brains. Our brains, then, are designed to literally connect with other brains, and this connection is what helps us to respond to others' suffering with empathy and compassion.

Mirror neurons: the capacity for empathy. Mirror neurons are, as their name suggests, neurons with mirrorlike properties and functions that become active both when we execute an action and when we observe someone else executing the same action. This allows us to recognize, from the inside, others' intentions and subjective states. Giacomo Rizzolatti, the Italian neuroscientist who discovered mirror neurons, explains that they "allow us to grasp the minds of others not through

---

[53]Louis Sander, "Thinking Differently: Principles of Process in Living Systems and the Specificity of Being Known," *Psychoanalytic Dialogues* 12, no. 1 (2002): 11-42.
[54]Daniel Goleman, *Social Intelligence* (New York: Bantam Books, 2006), 38.

conceptual reasoning, but through direct simulation; by feeling, not by thinking."[55]

In order to act with compassion on someone's behalf, we need to have empathy, or some sense of their experience. Mirror neurons underlie the ability to empathize, triggering the same brain activation patterns when we observe the emotions of others as when we feel our own emotions; we feel the emotions of others as if they were our own.[56] Mirror neurons, as one neuroscientist explains, "give you the richness of empathy, the fundamental mechanism that makes seeing someone hurt really hurt you."[57] Brain imaging studies suggest that if you answer the questions "How are you feeling?" and "How is he feeling?" virtually the same neural circuitry lights up in both cases.[58] In other words, our brains do almost the same thing when we reflect on our own feelings and the feelings of others. In addition to empathy, our central nervous system supports the ability to coregulate emotions and social functioning through a very specialized nerve that connects our heart and brain.

The vagus nerve: the capacity for coregulation. The vagus nerve is part of our central nervous system; it emerges from the brain stem and connects the heart to the brain. More specifically, it connects the heart to the brain pathways that regulate the muscles of the face, head, and neck, creating the "face-heart connection."[59] When the vagus nerve is functioning properly, it helps us to function socially. Stephen Porges has demonstrated that the vagus nerve forms a social engagement system that helps us to navigate relationships well.[60] It controls the muscles in the face that allow us to listen well to others, accurately read emotions in

---

[55]Giacomo Rizzolatti, quoted in Goleman, *Social Intelligence*, 43.

[56]Ryszard Praszkier, "Empathy, Mirror Neurons and SYNC," *Mind & Society* 15 (2016): 1-25.

[57]Christian Keysers, quoted in Greg Miller, "New Neurons Strive to Fit In," *Science* 311 (2005): 938-40.

[58]Kevin Ochsner et al., "Reflecting upon Feelings: An fMRI Study of Neural Systems Supporting the Attribution of Emotion to Self and Others," *Journal of Cognitive Neuroscience* 16 (2004): 1746-72.

[59]Stephen W. Porges and Senta A. Furman, "The Early Development of the Autonomic Nervous System Provides a Neural Platform for Social Behavior: A Polyvagal Perspective," *Infant and Child Development* 20 (2011): 106-18.

[60]Stephen W. Porges, *The Polyvagal Theory: Neurophysiological Foundations of Emotions, Attachment, Communication, and Self-Regulation* (New York: Norton, 2011).

their facial expressions, and respond physically in order to engage socially with others. The better our vagus nerve is working, the more adaptive our social behavior.

Because the vagus nerve connects our face to our heart, it is an important link between our social behavior and our ability to regulate our reactions to stress. When it is functioning well, it regulates our heart rate, allowing us to calm down. When the vagus nerve is not functioning well, we use more primitive, unregulated ways of dealing with stressors, such as fight or flight, tantrums, and shutting down. Due to its key roles in relationships and managing stress, the vagus nerve has strong links to psychological well-being.[61]

The key point here is that the vagus nerve connects our ability to relate to others with our ability to deal with life. It wires us for connection, allowing us to engage with others and to be soothed by others. Like other relational parts of our brain, the vagus nerve develops rapidly in the first few months of life, and requires positive social interactions in order to develop normally. Neglect or trauma can result in deficits in the ability to engage in normal social interactions, and can make it difficult for people to self-soothe and calm down. It should come as no surprise that there is an established connection between secure attachment and a healthy vagus nerve.[62]

Fortunately, the biological story doesn't end here. Positive interactions can strengthen the vagus nerve. Feeling connected to others can lead to healthier vagus nerve activity, suggesting that relationships are a powerful mechanism of healing.[63] Positive psychologist Barbara Fredrickson speaks of this healing connection as "micro-moments" in which we connect briefly with another person over a shared positive emotion.[64] In these so-called micro-moments, a synchrony occurs between our

[61]Bethany E. Kok and Barbara L. Fredrickson, "Upward Spirals of the Heart: Autonomic Flexibility, as Indexed by Vagal Tone, Reciprocally and Prospectively Predicts Positive Emotions and Social Connectedness," *Biological Psychology* 85 (2010): 432-36.

[62]L. M. Diamond and A. M. Hicks, "Attachment Style, Current Relationship Security, and Negative Emotions: The Mediating Role of Physiological Regulation," *Journal of Social and Personal Relationships* 22 (2005): 499-518.

[63]Kok and Fredrickson, "Upward Spirals."

[64]Barbara L. Fredrickson, *Love 2.0* (New York: Hudson Street Press, 2013), 15-22.

biochemistry and behaviors; we mirror each other as we smile, lean in, and express connection verbally and nonverbally. These experiences produce a change within us, including positive changes in the functioning of our vagus nerve. These micro-moments only happen when two conditions are met: (1) when we feel safe (which brings us back to the importance of secure attachment), and (2) when we are in physical proximity with another. Eye contact is crucial; the vagus nerve helps us interpret and navigate the meaning of what we see in each other's faces, allowing for this synchronicity.[65]

Conclusion

We have seen that we are born with the capacity to relate to others, including the capacity to respond to the emotions of others and to engage in complex social interchanges. Infants also have the capacity to internalize patterns of interactions, forming expectations for future interactions. We have introduced attachment theory, which suggests that attachment relationships serve as a secure base in times of stress and as a safe haven from which to explore the world. We have also seen how attachment relationships with caregivers are capable of significantly influencing the expression of genes.

The bottom line is that we are profoundly relational from cradle to grave. We rely on loving relationships to develop normally in the early years, and we depend on loving interactions with others to thrive throughout life. Specifically, one of the ways we benefit from loving relationships is through the coordination of interpersonal processes between two people, this dance of coregulation that is clear in attachment relationships and in which oxytocin, the OFC, mirror neurons, and the vagus nerve all play roles. We coregulate each other. We coordinate gaze, speech, and movements, and this causes us to strengthen the bond between us.[66] Whether we call this coregulation, synchrony, attunement, or interpersonal emotion regulation, the idea is the same. Moreover,

---

[65]Oxytocin may play a role here, as it may affect brainstem nuclei controlling the vagus nerve. Uchino and Way, "Integrative Pathways," 595.
[66]Uchino and Way, "Integrative Pathways."

when we are in these loving relationships, the result is a spiral of growth into greater well-being,[67] and an increased ability to live life meaningfully and to love others well.[68] We are loved into loving, and as this occurs, we grow into the image of God as exemplified in Christ.

---

[67]Kok and Fredrickson, "Upward Spirals."
[68]Pietromonaco and Collins, "Interpersonal Mechanisms," 534.

Relational Knowledge

We Know More Than We Can Say

WE ARE CREATED FOR THE PURPOSE OF LOVING relational connections with God and other people, and we are designed such that we grow and develop through relational connections. Building on this foundational concept, we turn now to different types of knowledge and how they inform our understanding of spiritual development from a relational perspective.

In this chapter, we present evidence for the notion that there are two fundamentally distinct ways of knowing: what scientists refer to as implicit (gut-level, intuitive) knowledge and explicit (analytic, propositional) knowledge. This idea becomes crucial in light of the rationalistic Enlightenment paradigm that has influenced many evangelical models of knowing, sanctification, and the image of God. As the title of the chapter suggests, there are things we know at some level that we do not, or cannot, formulate in words. The British psychoanalyst Christopher Bollas called these "unthought knowns."[1] They represent a deeper, more personal kind of knowing than the rational knowledge emphasized in the Enlightenment.

We will ultimately argue that both forms of knowing are important and mutually reinforce one another in the sanctification process. In so doing, we will emphasize both ways of knowing and the integration of

---

[1]Christopher Bollas, *The Shadow of the Object: Psychoanalysis of the Unthought Known* (New York: Columbia University Press, 1987).

the two as being especially important. This harkens back to a more unified model of knowing that existed prior to the split between explicit theology and implicit spirituality that we reviewed in chapter one. Our goal is to reclaim this more holistic way of knowing God (and others) while advancing this model with contemporary scientific research on ways of knowing.

While both ways of knowing are important, implicit knowledge—especially implicit *relational* knowledge—is particularly important for two reasons. First, it is foundational for spiritual transformation. Second, it is a necessary corrective to the vestiges of rationalism left over from the Enlightenment in much of evangelicalism today. In emphasizing implicit relational knowledge, it is important to note that there are certain traditions that overemphasize experience and seem to lose the parameters and meaning of experiences brought by doctrine and explicit knowledge of God. Ultimately, relationally derived meaning holds both ways of knowing together, and differences in the way the sanctification process is understood in different Christian traditions can be explained, at least partially, in light of the degree to which a tradition emphasizes one way of knowing to the exclusion of the other.

In this chapter, we review scientific evidence for implicit relational knowledge. Emotion is an integral part of implicit knowledge, and so we start by looking at the new view of emotion that has emerged in recent decades, followed by an overview of the four components of emotion. We then explore implicit knowledge in more depth, including how it is qualitatively different from explicit knowledge, how the two ways of knowing can work together, and how implicit relational knowledge is foundational to our relationship with God. We close by examining the concept of relational knowledge in Scripture, suggesting that the Bible sees this personal way of knowing as foundational for our faith. Ultimately, we hope to show that implicit relational knowledge drives the quality of our relationships with God and others, which means that it has to be transformed if we are to experience deep growth.

The Emotion Revolution

Just as the Enlightenment led to a rationalistic approach to knowledge, theology, and the spiritual life, in neuroscience it led to a view that disparaged emotions. This view grew out of a movement known as the cognitive revolution, or the "new science of mind," which emerged in the middle of the twentieth century.[2] The cognitive revolution focused on unconscious processes such as attention and perception (all viewed as *logical* reasoning processes), while intentionally excluding emotion.[3] Part of the reason emotion was excluded from study is that it was viewed as an illogical force that disrupts the flow of information processing and therefore is inferior to cognitive processes.

It is interesting to note here the parallels between cognitive science and the predominant view of persons and knowing that grew out of scholasticism and the Enlightenment, discussed in chapter one. The focus on rational, explicit knowledge that grew out of this paradigm set the tone for the new science, out of which the cognitive revolution developed. While cognitive science is not taught in most seminaries, it seems likely that general notions from the cognitive revolution influenced implicit views of change in the sanctification process. The notion that emotion is a disrupting force, and not an organizing way of knowing our personal meaning, continues to have significant influence in many segments of Protestant Christianity, particularly within evangelicalism. The breadth of current neuroscience research, however, no longer supports this view of emotion.

In more recent decades, a new view of emotion has emerged—what has been called the emotion revolution. This has come about from the convergence of object relations theory, relational psychoanalytic theories, attachment theory, infant research, and affective neuroscience, among other theoretical traditions, as noted in the introduction. In addition, cognitive science has developed more sophisticated theories of how information is represented in the brain, which has contributed to a broader

---

[2]Howard Gardner, *The Mind's New Science: A History of the Cognitive Revolution* (New York: Basic Books, 1987).
[3]Gardner, *Mind's New Science.*

psychological (as opposed to a strict neurobiological) theory of infor-mation processing. Contrary to earlier cognitive science theories of emotion as a *disrupting* force, emotion is now understood to be a broad, *organizing* force in human functioning. It increasingly seems that emotion provides the broad context of meaning that organizes and influ-ences all information processing.

One theory that describes emotion as an organizing influence is mul-tiple code theory. Multiple code theory, developed by Wilma Bucci, sug-gests that there are at least two, and likely more, forms or "codes" by which the brain represents information.[4] Multiple code theory con-tributes evidence to the view that emotion is an organizing way of knowing ourselves and the world. *As such, emotion can be thought of as an implicit form of knowledge about ourselves and our environment as we perceive it.* It also sheds light on the different levels of complexity of meaning captured in emotion, a topic to which we will turn shortly.

The research coming from multiple code theory has moved us away from a narrow model of cognitive information processing and simulta-neously contributed to a deeper understanding of emotion. Bucci's theory involves three levels or codes of information processing. Two of these codes process information in the language (or "code") of emotion, and are referred to as "emotional information processing" (EIP). The key distinction between EIP and cognitive information processing (the third level or code) is that EIP has to do with appraising the meaning of in-ternal and external events *for our well-being*.[5]

After reviewing what we can learn about emotions from neuroscience, we will turn to the components of emotion, levels of complexity of emotion (which will take us back to multiple code theory), and the in-fluence of emotion as a global state system. Finally, we will consider

---

[4]Wilma Bucci, *Psychoanalysis and Cognitive Science* (New York: Guilford Press, 1997). This model of the architecture of cognition is referred to variously as subsymbolic, connectionist, or parallel distributed processing (PDP).

[5]Bucci's work shares features with Daniel Kahneman's description of two systems of thinking, "fast" thinking and "slow" thinking, although Kahneman's work focuses more on cognitive as-pects such as heuristics and biases. See Daniel Kahneman, *Thinking, Fast and Slow* (New York: Farrar, Straus and Giroux, 2011).

some fascinating research that illustrates emotion as a form of implicit knowledge, and how this applies to our relationship with God.

The Brain and Emotion

In order to understand emotion, which is central to relational knowledge, we have to understand some foundational concepts about the brain. The brain is connected to two "worlds," or two sources of information: the world *inside* our bodies, or its internal milieu, and the world *outside* our bodies, or the external environment. Neuroscientists suggest that the main task of the brain is to manage what the body needs from the external world—in other words, to bridge the divide between our internal and external worlds.[6] Antonio Damasio, a leading neuroscientist, was the first to meaningfully track the brain's role in connecting the inner and outer worlds.[7] He concluded that our brain simultaneously represents and monitors the external environment, and the internal environment inside our bodies.

A first major point to help us understand emotion and implicit knowledge is that, at the juncture of the internal and external worlds, the brain is inherently evaluative. It tells us whether something in the external environment is good or bad by making that thing *feel* good or bad (or somewhere on the spectrum from good to bad). Thus, we constantly experience a nonverbal, nonreflective evaluation of how we are doing with respect to our body and the outside world.[8] We might say that evaluation is what emotion is *for*, and emotion is, in turn, what our bodies are *for*.[9]

To illustrate, a client of mine, Jane, suffers from posttraumatic stress disorder and dissociative symptoms due to severe trauma and abuse. One of the recurring themes in therapy is that she perceives me to be

---

[6]Mark Solms and Oliver Turnbull, *The Brain and the Inner World* (New York: Other Press, 2002).
[7]Antonio Damasio, *The Feeling of What Happens* (San Diego: Harcourt, 1999).
[8]These brain structures are located in the middle and upper portions of the brainstem, and include the hypothalamus, ventral tegmental area, parabrachial nuclei, periaqueductal gray, raphe nuclei, nucleus locus coeruleus complex, and reticular formation. Solms and Turnbull, *The Brain and the Inner World*, 107-8.
[9]For an exploration of the function of embodiment that draws a similar conclusion that bodies are for the purpose of emotion and relationships, see M. Elizabeth Lewis Hall, "What Are Bodies For? An Integrative Examination of Embodiment," *Christian Scholar's Review* 39 (2010): 159-76.

dangerous or untrustworthy at times, much like her father was. This might stem from a general state of mind that has been triggered by other events outside of therapy, or from some communication (often non-verbal) in a session that triggers a memory, or some combination of both. Toward the end of one session, Jane said to me, "I am having some issues come up related to you, and I need to talk about them, but I don't really know how to explain them." As I asked her more about this, she said she felt alone, afraid, and like she couldn't trust me, but she wasn't sure why. When she started describing this, I could sense the quality of her voice and overall emotional state change.

What I sensed were changes in her viscera that were then reflected in her nonverbal communication. Her brain[10] evaluated the situation with me to be potentially threatening, and this evaluation took place by means of certain changes in her body, such as increased heart rate, more shallow and rapid breathing, and redirection of blood from the gut to the skeletal muscles. This produced a certain *quality* in her state of consciousness that we might call fear. The background feeling of her state of consciousness was evaluating the external situation (sitting in a room with me) by producing visceral responses and telling her that danger might be close at hand. The amygdala communicates with the periaqueductal gray (PAG) in the brainstem where the sense of fear is generated. These changes in the body are then communicated to the somatic monitoring structures in the brainstem, forming a feedback loop. The subjective quality of her state of consciousness is what she felt, and what she felt was an evaluation of the situation: fear. Thus, our brain tells us what we feel, but not merely what we feel; it also tells us what we feel *about* something.

The state of the environment inside the body, and our brain's representation of that state, can be broadly understood as emotion. A second major point is that emotion can be thought of as a sensory modality that provides information about the internal milieu inside the body as it interprets and responds to internal and external events. *Emotion, then, is*

---

[10]The lateral and central nuclei of the amygdala process this evaluation.

the nonverbal and automatic way we evaluate the meaning of our experiences on the basis of visceral changes. However, emotion operates differently than other sensory modalities in several ways. First, it is internally directed. That is, only you can *directly* experience your emotions. Other people do not have direct access to them. As we discussed in chapter three, we do catch others' emotions, but this is one step removed. Only you can directly, subjectively experience your viscera's responses to the outside world.

Second, it is not just the experience, or perception, of emotion that is subjective. *What* your emotion systems perceive in any given situation is also subjective, and based in part on implicit (bodily) memory of past experiences. When you experience an emotion, what you experience is your own subjective (visceral) *response* to an event, not the direct event itself. To state it differently, you experience the unique subjective meaning of an event to you, which is the evaluation inherent in the state of your internal milieu. For example, when someone hears a loud popping noise outside, and her arousal heightens a little bit, she is emotionally perceiving her own subjective, bodily response to the noise, not the noise itself. She hears the noise aurally, but does not emotionally perceive it directly. The response to the very same noise could be very different for another person due to implicit memories of similar noises.

A former client, Frank, was in World War II and was a prisoner of war in Korea. Many years later, he told me that when he would hear a sudden, loud noise, he would respond with full-blown posttraumatic stress symptoms because, to him, the noise *meant* something. Any noise remotely similar to a gunshot got encoded in the low-road circuit of the fear system in his brain in order to automatically alert him to danger. When he experienced extreme anxiety and terror due to a noise like this, and corresponding visceral changes, he was emotionally perceiving his subjective response to the noise, which was determined by the meaning assigned to it by his brain.

The third major point that is crucial to understand about emotion is that it is a "state-dependent system" that has a global influence on brain functioning. This means that the brain systems that process information from the internal milieu of the body, as well as those that process the representational maps of the body, broadcast information to widely distributed parts of the brain.[11] The implication that is critical for our purposes is that emotion systems influence explicit thought processes. As Michael Rousell puts it, "Emotion is the rule, rationality is the tool."[12] Depression, for example, demonstrates the global influence of emotions on conscious memory and explicit thought. When people wake up depressed, they report that everything seems worse than the day before, even though they know, intellectually or explicitly, that their life situation has not changed. Their explicit thoughts become depressive and negative because the lens through which they see the world is their emotional state. The rapid, nonconscious networks of emotion shape the way we think about the world before we become aware of our perceptions and thoughts.[13]

Emotions, then, provide a powerful source of information. Because they are processed automatically and outside of our direct control, our emotional responses provide the clearest window into the deepest level of our soul—the meanings we connect to relationships and events in our lives. We cannot manipulate the emotional meaning we assign to events, so they reveal what we really believe at a gut level about ourselves and others in our relational world. This does not mean we encourage people to do whatever they feel like doing if it is something that clearly goes against God's design. However, it does mean that if we want to be transformed at the very core of our being, we must start with our emotional responses because they comprise an implicit form of relational knowledge that guides our sense of self

---

[11]These systems are referred to as "state-dependent systems" (or "parallel distributed processing") in contrast to the "channel-dependent systems" that process information from the external world. For example, the neurons from one brainstem nuclei in this system project onto a very large number of other neurons. In this way, a nucleus in the brainstem can influence all lobes of the forebrain at the same time. In addition, forebrain neurons influenced by one state-dependent nucleus can be simultaneously influenced by others. Solms and Turnbull, *The Brain and the Inner World*.

[12]Michael A. Rousell, *Sudden Influence: How Spontaneous Events Shape Our Lives* (Westport: Praeger, 2007), 67.

[13]Louis Cozolino, *The Neuroscience of Psychotherapy: Building and Rebuilding the Human Brain* (New York: W. W. Norton & Co., 2002).

and how we relate to God and others. We turn now to the interrelated components of emotion.

Four Components of Emotion

Scholars use the words *emotion* and *feeling* in different ways, which can be confusing. Some use the terms synonymously, while others use them to refer to different phenomena. This state of affairs is partly due to the fact that emotion is a very broad concept. In general, as we have noted, emotion is the way we evaluate the meaning of our experiences with respect to our well-being. However, neuroscientists and psychologists who study emotion generally include four components under the rubric of emotion.[14] To further complicate matters, there are different levels of emotion that reflect the complexity of the meaning assigned to an experience and build on the most basic components of emotion. In this section we will address the basic components of emotion, and return to levels of complexity in the next section. We will address some of the terminology issues as we discuss the different aspects of emotion.

As we noted, the triggering of evaluative emotion systems leads to a cascade of changes in the brain and body that are manifested in four highly related components: (a) changes in the viscera; (b) the motor and behavioral expression of emotion, including the readiness for responses that flow from these changes; (c) the subjective experience that arises from all of these changes; and (d) cognitive appraisal of stimuli and situations. When Frank heard loud noises that signified danger to him, he experienced all four of these aspects of emotion.

What visceral changes did he experience? When he perceived danger, the fear system (one of four basic emotion command systems in the brain) was triggered.[15] When danger is computed, the brain circuits that

---

[14]Bucci, *Psychoanalysis and Cognitive Science.*

[15]The core processing unit of this system is the amygdala. Upon determining that potential danger is present, the amygdala sends information through its projections in the hypothalamus to the periaqueductal gray (PAG) in the brainstem. The PAG is one of the most important structures in the middle and upper zones of the brainstem that monitor and regulate information about the viscera, or the homeostatic physiology of the body, by generating a map of the functions of the body. In addition to the PAG, these structures include the hypothalamus, ventral tegmental area, parabrachial nuclei, raphe nuclei, nucleus locus coeruleus complex, and the reticular

process this cause changes in the viscera through two mechanisms: neurotransmitter systems and hormones released in the bloodstream that exert their own effect on the viscera. When Frank's fear system was activated, he experienced a number of visceral changes, including increased heart rate, more shallow and rapid breathing, and redistribution of blood from his gut to his skeletal muscles. All this took place automatically without him having to think about it, in order to prepare him to deal with the potential danger. This reminds us that *emotion is inherently evaluative*, and that *the evaluation is always with reference to our well-being*. We will come back to this, but I want to note here that the way our emotion systems determine well-being is highly influenced by our primary environment, including our relational environment.

The second component of emotion consists of the behavioral or motor expression of emotion. The *emotion*-generating part of the brain has direct access through its projections to one of its *action*-generating mechanisms.[16] The integrated sensorimotor map[17] generates primitive action tendencies such as approach and avoidance, which are closely associated with psychological pleasure and unpleasure. Emotion, then, is not just a perceptual modality directed toward the viscera; it also involves motor expression or discharge. Emotions cause us to want to *do* something. They give us an urge to act in certain ways. Externally, emotion is manifested in several ways, such as through changes in facial expressions, crying, blushing, and in more complex behaviors like lashing out or isolating oneself. In response to sudden, loud noises, Frank expressed fear on his face and had the urge to either fight or run and hide.

Frank not only experienced rapid physiological changes in his viscera and motor expressions, he also had a subjective experience of the entire ordeal. He subjectively felt fear. Part of the evaluative process our brains constantly engage in is the experience of a certain subjective quality that

---

formation. Right next door, in the upper brainstem, the tectum and dorsal tegmentum regulate the movements of the body via a map of the musculoskeletal system. Solms and Turnbull, *The Brain and the Inner World*, 107-8. For an extensive review of the fear system, see Joseph LeDoux, *The Emotional Brain* (New York: Touchstone, 1996).

[16]Solms and Turnbull, *The Brain and the Inner World*.

[17]This map is processed in the tectum and dorsal tegmentum.

reflects the evaluation—the third component of emotion. The brain circuits that process the subjective experience of emotion generate pleasurable and unpleasurable sensations.[18] This sets the qualitative range of the subjective experience of emotion. *Unpleasure* is different from *pain* as we typically use the latter term. Pain refers to a somatic sensation, whereas unpleasure is a psychological (subjective) experience based on the state of the viscera and urges to act in certain ways. But it is more than just the physiological changes in our bodies, and there are many complex nuances to the experience of pleasure and unpleasure. There is an infinite variety of background emotions, reflected in basic shifts in brain states.[19] And while there are a limited number of basic or categorical emotions (approximately six or seven), there are many nuanced combinations of these, which comprise secondary and the so-called social emotions.

Finally, there is also a cognitive appraisal component to Frank's emotion in response to a loud, sudden noise. Frank's initial reaction may include the changes described above, which are a quick-and-dirty processing of the stimulus information—a first rough take processed by the "low road" in which information is input into the thalamus and sent straight to the amygdala.[20] Simultaneously, but more slowly, the stimulus information is processed in a more precise way via the high road. In this pathway, information is sent from the thalamus to the sensory cortex and hippocampus, and then to the amygdala, where it processes the meaning of the stimuli, already computed via the low road. Thus, after Frank's initial reaction, his brain may process that his neighbor has a truck that often backfires and that the noise he heard sounded very similar to previous instances of the truck backfiring. He may also process information about his current life situation—that the war is over and that

---

[18]Of the numerous structures in the middle and upper regions of the brainstem responsible for core consciousness and emotion, the periaqueductal gray (PAG) is of particular importance for subjective experience. This gray matter located deep within the brainstem is organized into lower (ventral) and upper (dorsal) columns. The lower PAG columns generate pleasurable sensations, and the upper PAG columns generate unpleasurable sensations. Solms and Turnbull, *The Brain and the Inner World*.

[19]Daniel Siegel, *The Developing Mind*, 2nd ed. (New York: Guilford Press, 2012).

[20]LeDoux, *Emotional Brain*.

he is in a safe place. All this information then gets processed in the amygdala, causing a reduction in physiological arousal, the urge to run, and the subjective experience of fear.

Recent research suggests that positive (e.g., joy, interest, contentment) and negative (e.g., sadness, fear, anger) emotions may function somewhat differently with respect to the first two components of emotions. Barbara Fredrickson's broaden-and-build theory contrasts how these two groups of emotions function. Negative emotions aid us in survival by facilitating a narrow range of specific actions, such as fight or flight. In order to do this, negative emotions evoke very specific visceral responses, which facilitate actions that are helpful for our survival. For example, fear causes increased cardiovascular activity in order to pump blood to the muscles necessary for flight. In contrast, positive emotions broaden the available action possibilities, enabling greater behavioral flexibility in ways that enhance personal resources in the long term. Rather than being associated with specific cardiovascular patterns, positive emotions help to undo cardiovascular reactivity, returning the body to neutral levels of activation consistent with a broad range of behavioral responses.[21] Put another way, negative emotions help us in the short term, whereas positive emotions help us in the long term.

To return to the terminology issue, some neuroscientists, such as Joseph LeDoux, propose the use of the word *feeling* to refer to conscious awareness of the activity of the emotion system in the brain—that is, to the third component of emotions, which is subjective experience.[22] This fits well with the way the term is used in common parlance. When we say, "I feel sad," we are typically referring to the quality of our subjective experience, although the deep interconnection between these aspects of emotion can be seen in that our subjective experience includes the state

---

[21]Barbara L. Fredrickson, "The Role of Positive Emotions in Positive Psychology: The Broaden-and-Build Theory of Positive Emotions," *American Psychologist* 56 (2001): 218-26; Eric L. Garland et al., "Upward Spirals of Positive Emotions Counter Downward Spirals of Negativity: Insights from the Broaden-and-Build Theory and Affective Neuroscience on the Treatment of Emotion Dysfunctions and Deficits in Psychopathology," *Clinical Psychology Review* 30 (2010): 849-64.

[22]Joseph LeDoux, "Feelings: What Are They and How Does the Brain Make Them?" *Daedalus, The Journal of the American Academy of Arts & Sciences* 144 (2015): 96-111.

of our viscera. Feeling, as we are using the term here, is one important component of emotion, but the concept of emotion in scientific research is much broader than feeling as we have noted. To add one more clarification, the term *affect* is commonly used in ways that overlap with the term *emotion*. However, its technical usage comes from clinical psychology and psychiatry, in which it is used in mental status exams to reference the facial and motor expression of emotion.

The cognitive appraisal dimension of emotion, mentioned above, suggests that cognition is intrinsic to emotion and that it is an oversimplification to neatly separate cognition from emotion. Richard Lane outlined a hierarchical and developmental model of emotional awareness within the field of cognitive science. In the context of this model, he states, "There is nothing about emotion that is not cognitive if one equates cognition with information processing."[23] Along the same lines, philosopher Robert Solomon contends that emotions are ways of apprehending the world, and consequently, emotions are always *about* something—that is, they have an "intentional structure."[24] The intentional structure is the formal object by which an emotion type can be defined. The formal object of fear, for example, is something dangerous. Moreover, emotions are subjective ways of engaging the world, of "cognitively grappling with the world."[25] It is misleading, therefore, to separate cognition from emotion by holding that a cognitive appraisal triggers an emotional response that is distinct from the appraisal. Cognitive appraisals are an integral aspect of emotion given that emotions are dynamic processes in which the situational referent of the emotion, and the emotion itself, are continually reappraised.[26]

[23]Richard Lane, "Neural Substrates of Implicit and Explicit Emotional Processes: A Unifying Framework for Psychosomatic Medicine," *Psychosomatic Medicine* 70 (2008): 214-31.

[24]Robert Solomon, *True to Our Feelings: What Our Emotions Are Really Telling Us* (New York: Oxford University Press, 2007).

[25]Robert Solomon, "Emotions, Thoughts and Feelings: Emotions as Engagements with the World," in *Thinking About Feeling: Contemporary Philosophers on Emotions*, ed. R. C. Solomon (New York: Oxford University Press, 2004), 77.

[26]Jon G. Allen, Peter Fonagy, and Anthony W. Bateman, *Mentalizing in Clinical Practice* (Washington, DC: American Psychiatric Publishing, 2008).

Emotion and Implicit Knowledge

As a multifaceted, dynamic appraisal system, emotion is the basis for what we are referring to as implicit knowledge as opposed to explicit knowledge, which we will elaborate on below.[27] As noted earlier in this chapter, Wilma Bucci developed a broad conceptual framework for implicit and explicit knowledge in her multiple code theory.[28] Bucci proposed that there are three general levels, or "codes," of emotional information processing: (a) subsymbolic emotional processing, (b) nonverbal symbolic emotional processing, and (c) verbal symbolic processing. The first two levels are implicit forms of processing, meaning they are nonverbal codes and not under our direct control. The third code is an explicit form of processing, over which we have more direct control. There is a significant research literature documenting that these implicit and explicit forms of processing and memory involve different neural mechanisms.[29] After outlining these first two levels of implicit processing, we will describe implicit relational knowledge, which is a key concept for understanding spiritual development. We will then turn to Bucci's third level, explicit processing.

Subsymbolic processing includes primary emotions,[30] or what Antonio Damasio calls "background emotions," such as when we have a

---

[27]Portions of the rest of this chapter are adapted with permission from Todd W. Hall and Steven L. Porter, "Referential Integration: An Emotional Information Processing Perspective on the Process of Integration," *Journal of Psychology and Theology* 32, no. 3 (2004): 167-80.

[28]Wilma Bucci, *Psychoanalysis and Cognitive Science*. See also Wilma Bucci, Bernard Maskit, and Sean Murphy, "Connecting Emotions and Words: The Referential Process," *Phenomenology and the Cognitive Sciences* 15 (2016): 359-83.

[29]Daniel Schacter, "Implicit Memory: A New Frontier for Cognitive Neuroscience," in *The Cognitive Neurosciences*, ed. M. Gazzaniga (Cambridge, MA: MIT Press, 1995), 815-24.

[30]This term is used by Siegel to describe the initial level of emotional information processing, or "shifts in brain state [that] result from the initial orientation and elaborative appraisal-arousal processes." In these state shifts, the brain evaluates information from the body and stimuli from the external environment, and regulates the state of mind by activating certain brain circuits and deactivating others. Elaborative appraisal processes determine whether a stimulus is "good" or "bad," and arousal processes prepare the body to act accordingly by directing the flow of energy throughout the body. This sets off a wave of increasingly complex appraisal processes that take into account a host of factors, such as relevant past experiences, emotional and representational components of memory, current internal physiological state, the current social context, and initial appraisals of this information. Siegel, *Developing Mind*, 151; Bucci, *Psychoanalysis and Cognitive Science*.

sense of well-being, malaise, or unsettledness.[31] This most basic form of emotion involves shifts in basic brain states. In other words, this is information processed in a system that does not use symbols like words or images. This foundational form of information processing relies on parallel distributed processing (PDP), which is the way the brain processes a massive amount of information, in different formats and systems, all at the same time.[32] This information—such as the sensation of your stomach tightening—exists in a code, or language, *below* symbols. This type of emotion is so diffuse that it cannot be given a label like *anger* or *sadness*. It is more direct and immediate than symbolic knowledge and is always operating in the background of our consciousness. This system does not exist in the code of verbal reflection, so we are not easily able to articulate the basis for how we know things in this way. In other words, we can think of this type of knowing as "unthought knowns." It involves things we know in this particular way, but which we do not think in words. Indeed, we know much more than we can say.

Examples can be seen in many domains of functioning. For example, it is difficult for the professional soccer player to break down the sequence of body movements involved in kicking a soccer ball at a particular speed, angle, and height into distinct units and to translate this into words. Similarly, we rely on this type of information to infer the emotional states of others in emotionally significant relationships, just as therapists rely on this type of information in inferring the emotional states of clients.

In the next level of complexity, the brain assigns more elaborate meanings to initial appraisals by chunking them into a category such as sadness, anger, happiness, or surprise. There are a number of these basic or categorical emotions that have been found to be universal across all cultures; there is basic agreement on six universal emotions. Damasio identifies these as happiness, sadness, fear, anger, surprise, and disgust.[33]

---

[31]Damasio, *The Feeling of What Happens.*
[32]Bucci, *Psychoanalysis and Cognitive Science.*
[33]Damasio, *The Feeling of What Happens.*

These categories represent the second level of implicit knowledge referred to as "nonverbal *symbolic* knowledge." The brain can assign further meaning beyond the categorical emotions to produce a vast variety of meanings. This represents the next step in chunking information, such that knowledge remains nonverbal and nonconceptual, but it becomes symbolized in the sense that the meaning becomes more differentiated. This is what Daniel Siegel refers to as "nonconceptual knowing."[34] This kind of knowing is experienced in a very direct way. There is an immediacy to the quality of it, and it does not move along by logic. Rather, it moves along by virtue of a nonlinear process.

The primary medium of this code is imagery. Images can be processed sequentially, as in the verbal symbolic code, or in a parallel, continuous manner as with subsymbolic processes. Bucci notes that images, which operate in the nonverbal system outside of language, mediate the organizing and symbolizing of subsymbolic experience and provide the basis for connecting this nonverbal experience to words, a process she has conceptualized as "referential activity."[35] We will return to referential activity later. However, we now turn to a specific kind of implicit knowledge that is particularly relevant to spiritual development: implicit *relational* knowledge.

Implicit Relational Knowledge

Bucci notes that we store important emotional information in the form of "emotion schemas." Emotion schemas include subsymbolic information such as sensory, bodily, and motoric information, as well as

---

[34]Daniel Siegel, *The Mindful Brain: Reflection and Attunement in the Cultivation of Well-Being* (New York: W. W. Norton & Co., 2007).

[35]Bucci, *Psychoanalysis and Cognitive Science*. These two forms of implicit processing have also been discussed in depth by Seymour Epstein in his cognitive experiential self theory (CEST). He postulated two distinct processing systems: the experiential and the cognitive or rational. Epstein's experiential system parallels Bucci's subsymbolic and nonverbal symbolic processing levels. Epstein contends that the processing of the experiential system is preconscious, automatic, holistic, nonverbal, rapid, affect driven, and based on implicit memory. Bucci's and Epstein's implicit processing systems both parallel Daniel Kahneman's System 1, which operates automatically and rapidly (as opposed to System 2, which requires conscious attention, concentration, and choice). Seymour Epstein, "Integration of the Cognitive and Psychodynamic Unconscious," *American Psychologist* 49 (1994): 709-24; Daniel Kahneman, *Thinking Fast and Slow* (New York: Farrar, Straus and Giroux, 2011).

higher-level symbolic information such as imagery. Later, explicit verbal content may be added to the emotion schemas. These emotion schemas are the fundamental organizers of emotional life in humans. They are represented through memories, fantasies, dreams, and the narratives and metaphors of our lives.[36]

In the relational domain, emotional experiences are associated with certain people, clustering into a kind of emotional/relational schema. For example, the infant experiences constantly changing presentations of the primary caregiver (e.g., mother), which are initially processed subsymbolically. This information is then chunked into functionally equivalent classes (i.e., the information is put into nonverbal symbols), which enables the infant to recognize mother, predict her behavior,[37] and maximize emotional communication.[38] This processing is broad and incorporates actions, sensations, and affects that are experienced in a relational context. These functionally equivalent classes then form implicit relational schemas, which are formed by repetitions of relational experiences that share a common affective core.[39] These implicit relational schemas form a sort of filter for processing emotional information in a relational context. For example, there is evidence to suggest that they shape individuals' cognitive, emotional, and behavioral responses to others,[40] presumably by directing the initial orientation and elaborative appraisal-arousal processes.

As with all implicit knowledge, these implicit relational schemas operate outside of conscious awareness, and are based on behaviors, emotions, and images. When implicit memory is retrieved, an individual

---

[36]Wilma Bucci, "The Role of Embodied Communication in Therapeutic Change: A Multiple Code Perspective," in *The Implications of Embodiment: Cognition and Communication*, ed. Wolfgang Tschacher and Claudia Bergomi (Exeter, UK: Imprint Academic, 2011), 209-28.

[37]John Bowlby, *Attachment and Loss* (New York: Basic Books, 1969).

[38]Daniel Siegel, *The Developing Mind*, 2nd ed. (New York: Guilford Press, 2012).

[39]In an earlier article, I refer to these relational schemas as nonpropositional meaning structures. Todd W. Hall, "Christian Spirituality and Mental Health: A Relational Spirituality Framework for Empirical Research," *Journal of Psychology and Christianity* 23, no. 1 (2004): 71.

[40]N. Collins and S. Read, "Cognitive Representations of Attachment: The Content and Function of Working Models," in *Advances in Personal Relationships*, vol. 5, ed. K. Bartholomew and D. Perlman (London: Jessica Kingsley, 1994), 53-90; Judith A. Feeney, "Adult Attachment, Emotional Control, and Marital Satisfaction," *Personal Relationships* 6 (1999): 169-85.

does not have the experience or sense that something is being remembered.[41] This type of knowledge tells us how to be with someone and integrates affect, cognition, and behavioral dimensions. As with more general emotional schemas, these relational schemas are implicit, but can be represented verbally and consciously (although not fully) through the verbal code in the process that Bucci refers to as referential activity.[42] Hence, referential activity results in the articulation in the verbal domain of implicit relational knowledge.

Significant for our purposes of understanding the processes involved in psychospiritual growth, implicit relational knowing is evidenced not only in infants, but continues throughout life in our out-of-awareness experience of how relationships work for us.[43] Moreover, while verbal, conceptual processing is critical to psychospiritual growth, implicit relational knowledge forms the foundation of our knowledge of self and others because it is processed automatically and is not under the direct control of knowledge in the form of words and concepts.

A brief clinical example will help illustrate this. A client, Amy, clearly demonstrated her implicit relational knowledge of emotionally significant relationships in a series of sessions. Several devastating experiences of rejection reinforced Amy's implicit relational knowledge that her need for comfort eventually overwhelms others, leading them to abandon her. She subsequently shut down and withdrew from the therapeutic relationship, behavior that accompanied a certain affectively laden meaning, namely, her implicit relational expectation that I, too, would be overwhelmed by her needs for comfort and would abandon her. She was not aware of this experience until we discussed it; however, she eventually put into words her implicit relational knowledge by stating that she felt that I, of course, was consumed with my own life and had no room for her needs.

A growing body of research illustrates the power of implicit relational knowledge. In one study, Patient X, as doctors call him, suffered two

---

[41]Siegel, *Developing Mind.*
[42]Bucci, *Psychoanalysis and Cognitive Science.*
[43]Siegel, *Developing Mind.*

strokes that severed the connections between his eyes and the rest of the visual system in the visual cortex. His eyes could take in signals, but his brain didn't know the signals were there and couldn't decode them. It seemed Patient X was completely blind. When he was shown shapes or photos, he had no idea what was in front of him. But when he was shown pictures of people expressing emotion, like an angry face, he was able to guess the emotion on the face at a rate far better than chance. Brain scans conducted while Patient X was guessing the emotions showed that his brain used a different pathway than the normal pathway for seeing. Normally, visual input travels from the eyes to the thalamus, which processes sensory data, and then to the visual cortex. In Patient X's case, his brain sent information from the thalamus straight to the amygdala, which computes the emotional meaning of the nonverbal message. Thus, Patient X was *feeling* the emotion on the faces that he could not see—a condition known as *affective blindsight*.[44] He knew the emotions on the faces through this gut-level (implicit) knowledge, not through conscious, verbal knowledge.

In another dramatic illustration of implicit relational knowledge, fifty-nine patients who had attempted suicide in the previous three days were interviewed by the same psychiatrist. The faces of the patients and psychiatrist were recorded during the interviews. One year later, ten of the fifty-nine patients had made another suicide attempt (the reattempter group). The researchers tried to predict which patients would reattempt suicide using two types of information: the psychiatrist's predictions written immediately after the interviews, and the nonverbal communications between the psychiatrist and patients. The psychiatrist's written predictions correctly identified whether or not a patient would reattempt for 29 percent of the patients, whereas the nonverbal analysis correctly classified 81 percent of the patients assessed.[45] In addition, the real predictive power

---

[44]See Daniel Goleman, *Social Intelligence* (New York: Bantam Books, 2006), 15. This condition has been found in other patients as well. For an example of "Patient G.Y.", see J. S. Morris et al., "Differential Extrageniculostriate and Amygdala Responses to Presentation of Emotional Faces in a Cortically Blind Field," *Brain: A Journal of Neurology* 124, no. 6 (June 2001): 1241-52.

[45]M. Heller and V. Haynal, "The Doctor's Face: A Mirror of His Patient's Suicidal Projects," in *The Body in Psychotherapy*, ed. J. Guimon (Basel, Switzerland: Karger, 1997), 46-51.

came not from the patients' facial behavior but from the psychiatrist's facial behavior. With patients who ended up reattempting suicide, the psychiatrist frowned more and showed more animated facial expressions and a higher level of speech.

The researchers suggested that the psychiatrist's negative expressions and increased facial activity were serving two purposes: regulating his own internal state and communicating with his patient. It appears that the patients created a synchronized emotional state in the psychiatrist, which in turn influenced the psychiatrist's own nonverbal behavior. This is how the psychiatrist knew that a particular patient would reattempt. He didn't know this in words (explicit knowledge); he knew this in his body, facial expressions, and subjective experience—literally in his gut.

I had an experience reminiscent of this early in my career when I was practicing psychology in the Army. One evening, I was called into the emergency room to evaluate a woman who was suicidal. I decided that her suicidality was serious enough to admit her to the hospital. I went back to check on her a few days later, to evaluate whether she was ready to be discharged and seen on an outpatient basis. She assured me that her suicidal thoughts were fleeting and that she had no intention of harming herself. After talking with her for about forty-five minutes, I decided to discharge her. As I was walking from the hospital back to my office in a separate building, I noticed a nagging feeling of uneasiness growing in my gut. It just wouldn't go away, so I decided to go back and talk to her again. I turned around, went back to the hospital, and went straight to her room. She was still there, waiting for the discharge papers to be finalized. I sat down, looked her right in the eyes, and said in a gentle but direct tone, "Are you going to kill yourself?" She immediately burst into tears and admitted that she had lied to me and that she was planning on killing herself after she was discharged. Somehow I knew that this woman was dangerously suicidal, and what gave me this information was the feeling in my gut during our conversation.

As outlined in chapter three, infants possess far more knowledge— implicit relational knowledge—than we once thought they did. Much of the infant research literature demonstrates not only that infants are innately relational from day one, but also that they have a powerful implicit, or gut-level, knowing system. Infant researchers call this "presymbolic" knowledge. The parts of the brain that process this gut-level way of knowing (the "right brain implicit self") are online at birth and fully developed by about fifteen months of age.[46] For example, there is evidence that, in utero, infants remember nonverbal aspects of their mothers' communication (i.e., the reading of a particular story), thus showing that they come to know their mother's voice.[47]

While this implicit, gut-level way of knowing is critical in infancy, it is not uncommon for people to assume that we graduate out of this way of knowing once we start talking. Especially in Western societies, we tend to believe verbal, analytic ways of knowing are superior. However, implicit knowing actually continues throughout life and turns out to be very important in relationships.

An interesting phenomenon that illustrates this is speed dating. A group of single men and women gather in the back room of a restaurant. They are paired off with each other, sitting in a circle. They converse for six minutes with each other. When the time is up, they play musical chairs and the men all get up and rotate to sit across from the next woman in the circle. They talk for six minutes. And so it continues. The goal is to decide if they want to spend more time with each person. At the end of each brief conversation, if the person liked their conversation partner, they check a box indicating they want their email to be given to the other person. If both people check each other's boxes, each person is supplied with the other's email. Speed dating has become quite popular, and it suggests that we know in a matter of minutes whether or not we are attracted to someone.

One of the interesting things about speed dating is that when you compare what people say they want in a mate to what they are actually

---

[46]Allan N. Schore, *The Science of the Art of Psychotherapy* (New York: W. W. Norton & Co., 2012).

[47]In one study, at birth, infants preferred a tape recording of *The Cat in the Hat*, heard in utero, to hearing their mothers read a different Dr. Seuss story. Cited in Beatrice Beebe and Frank Lachmann, *Infant Research and Adult Treatment: Co-Constructing Interactions* (Hillsdale, NJ: Analytic Press, 2002).

attracted to in the moment, they often do not match up. Our conscious, verbalized ideal doesn't always match our implicit knowledge. Kim came to see me for therapy due to difficulties in romantic relationships. She was very anxious and feared rejection and abandonment, and yet was involved with a man who was quite rejecting. When she needed contact, he would push her away. She would become more drawn to him and seek him out, despite the fact that this was not what she wanted in a relationship and that she knew this was not good for her.

We might ask, which is the real Kim—the one who wants a caring man or the one who is instantly drawn to a rejecting man? Both aspects are part of her in some sense, but the point is that our implicit relational knowledge wins out when it comes to how we actually relate to others. Although it may not be consistent with our explicit knowledge, our implicit knowledge reveals how we construct the meaning of our relational worlds. This is the starting point for any deep level of transformation. In short, *implicit relational knowledge is the foundational way of knowing in relationships. It is this way of knowing, not explicit knowledge, that drives how we actually relate to others and our capacity to love.* The reason is that this way of knowing is automatic and not under our direct control. These implicit relational schemas have been studied extensively in attachment theory, where they are referred to as "internal working models." Given their importance to our spiritual lives, we will examine them in detail in the next chapter, where I refer to them as "attachment filters." As we will see below, explicit knowledge is important, but it must be integrated with implicit knowledge in order to affect our ability to love God and others.

Explicit Knowledge

The format or code of language is different than it is for images and categorical emotions. The information carried by words is not typically associated with a particular sensory modality, as are images.[48] For example, a group of words has the same syntax and meaning regardless of whether it is heard, read, or processed by touch through braille.

---

[48]Bucci, *Psychoanalysis and Cognitive Science.*

The dominant information processing mode of language is through a sequential, single-channel symbolic format, sending or receiving one message at a time. We cannot process two messages simultaneously, or listen and speak at the same time. The most central feature of language, according to Bucci, is that it is the processing channel over which we have the most direct intentional control.[49]

Richard came to see me for therapy struggling to make it day to day—life as he knew it was falling apart. His wife had recently left him, one of his children had cut off contact with him, and he was not performing well at his job. Understandably, he was very depressed. It seemed only a matter of time until he lost his job, and then, I feared, things would get even worse. Richard was a Christian. He believed that God is sovereign over everything. Logically, of course, this would include his circumstances. Richard believed that God is good. If we follow this truth to its logical conclusion, it means that there was no reason for Richard to be anxious or depressed over his situation. Somehow God would bring good out of this situation. Somehow God was with Richard in this mess. But Richard was very depressed and very anxious. He was barely functioning on a day-to-day basis, sleeping about two to three hours a night, eating almost nothing. At work, he would sit and stare at his computer. Why? Richard's knowledge that God is good was predominantly explicit knowledge, not integrated into his implicit relational knowledge or his "heart."

Explicit knowledge is an analytic way of knowing that is linear, logical, language based, and conscious. It is *linear*, meaning that one piece of knowledge follows from another in a sequential line, and each piece of information is processed in our brains one at a time. Explicit knowledge is *logical*, meaning that certain premises necessarily lead to certain conclusions and we can articulate how we arrive at these conclusions. It is also *language based*, meaning that it is processed primarily in words. Finally, this form of knowing is *conscious*, meaning that it requires

---

[49]This point is echoed by Daniel Kahneman in reference to his System 2 and Seymour Epstein regarding the cognitive system in his cognitive experiential self theory. Epstein, "Integration of the Cognitive and Psychodynamic Unconscious," 709-24; Kahneman, *Thinking Fast and Slow*.

conscious attention and effort to be processed in the brain. This way of knowing is processed in a particular circuit in the brain, primarily in the left hemisphere and the cortex of the brain, referred to as the brain's "high road."[50]

Damasio has noted that the brain sends information from its emotion centers, which evaluate meaning and process our relational experiences, to the prefrontal cortex, the brain's executive center. Interestingly, the prefrontal cortex sends comparatively little input to the emotion centers of the brain.[51] It is largely a one-way road. We are aware of the high road and we can direct it, but we cannot directly influence the low road.

The cortex in each hemisphere of the brain is composed of columns of neurons, each of which is responsible for a certain type of processing. The left hemisphere primarily mediates explicit knowledge, and the nature of how these columns work helps us understand explicit knowledge.[52] The cortical columns in the left hemisphere work more on their own than in the right hemisphere. There are few connections between the columns relative to the right hemisphere. This enables an in-depth and linear analysis that is highly focused and precise. This type of knowledge has an important role, but, as noted above, it does not receive much input from the emotion centers of the brain, which means the personal meaning and contextual information are not included in this type of processing.

Returning to Richard, why is it, then, that he did not have peace in the truth of God's sovereignty? A big part of the reason is that there are different ways of knowing, and knowing this truth *about God* is not the same thing as *knowing God* at an implicit, relational level. Moreover, knowing about God conceptually (in a propositional code) can be completely disconnected, as it was for Richard at this point,

---

[50]As noted previously, in this pathway, information is sent from the thalamus to the sensory cortex, where higher-level analytical processing occurs, and then to the amygdala, which uses this information to modulate its appraisal of meaning that has already occurred based on information that has already arrived directly from the thalamus via the "low road" pathway. LeDoux, *Emotional Brain*.

[51]Damasio, *The Feeling of What Happens*.

[52]Siegel, *Mindful Brain*.

from a more experiential, implicit knowledge of God. This brings us to the importance of bringing the two ways of knowing together as much as possible.

The Knowledge Spiral: Linking Implicit and Explicit Knowledge

Referential activity is essentially the process of linking feelings and words.[53] It is the process of connecting the subsymbolic and symbolic processing systems, which are very different in nature. This referential process (in which each way of knowing references the other), or knowledge spiral, is necessary to integrate functions, organize goal-directed behavior, and establish a unified sense of self. On a basic level, these separate processing systems must be linked in order to talk about our experiences, and to make sense of others' words in terms of our own experiences. Daniel Siegel describes a process similar to referential activity, which he calls "response flexibility."[54] This process appears to be mediated by the orbitofrontal cortex and involves the coordination of sensory, perceptual, and appraisal mechanisms. Siegel proposes that this integrating function results in approaching relationships, life decisions, and narrative responses with self-reflection and a sense of perspective. Response flexibility as conceptualized by Siegel is clearly related to the process of referential activity. The self-reflection underlying response flexibility involves tuning in to one's subsymbolic experiences and drawing out the underlying emotional meaning in ways that can be verbalized.

Referential activity is central to healthy functioning. Yet how do the nonverbal bodily and sensory processes get connected to the symbolic verbal code? Three major phases of the referential process have been identified: an *arousal* phase in which emotion schemas (including implicit relational schemas) are activated, a *symbolizing* phase that includes descriptions of imagery and events, and a *reorganization/reflection* phase.[55]

---

[53]Bucci, Maskit, and Murphy, "Connecting Emotions and Words," 359-83.
[54]Siegel, *Developing Mind.*
[55]Bucci, Maskit, and Murphy, "Connecting Emotions and Words," 369.

In the *arousal* phase, we initially encounter an experience that invokes a set of bodily processes in us: the subsymbolic bodily and sensory processes. For example, after receiving a low grade and critical comments on a paper, a student we'll call John may feel tense and uneasy. At this point, these experiences remain subsymbolic; they have not yet been organized into either nonverbal or verbal symbols. However, they may manifest in physical ways through bodily movements or facial expressions. Because of these physical manifestations, our subsymbolic experiences can be indirectly communicated to others through the nonverbal mechanisms. John may display his underlying tension in a way that his friends can sense it.

Next, these subsymbolic bodily and sensory processes activate our emotion schemas, some of which are the implicit relational schemas described earlier in this chapter. In this way, the continuous subsymbolic information is chunked into more discrete, though still nonverbal, units. In other words, the subsymbolic information is organized by categorizing it into emotion schemas formed by similar events in our past. John's experience of getting a low grade may get incorporated into an emotion schema with the meaning of "being a failure." This is a more discrete representation of his originally very diffuse experience. These schematized experiences often get linked to an image or a specific set of emotions that stem from a prototypical experience. For example, John may find himself picturing and re-experiencing a time when his father was critical of his performance and made similar comments as his professor.

These images exist as a link between the subsymbolic and the symbolic codes and are the basis for what allows us to connect these two separate systems. This linking is finalized in the next step, the *symbolizing* phase, in which these prototypic images are put into verbal form. For example, John might capture his initial tense, uneasy experience by verbalizing, "I always disappoint important people in my life. I'm just a failure."

Once the experience is put into words, operations that depend on the verbal system can be conducted, such as verbal elaborations of images and episodes, the development of abstract ideas based on the images, the application of logic, and the examination of concepts in dialogue with others.[56] In other words, the person can enter into a more reflective, analytical process involving making connections, forming distinctions, and bringing one's broader body of knowledge and experience to bear on the initial experience. Most importantly, the experiences can be brought into relationships with others. John, for example, can now think about his feelings, reflect on other more positive experiences, and gain a sense of perspective that comes from a more rational way of knowing that performance on this one paper does not define his identity. He can share his feelings with a trusted friend and have that friend respond in ways that make him feel affirmed instead of shamed. In this way, over time John's initial experience, and even his implicit relational schemas, can be transformed. As we will see, referential activity is crucial for understanding the processes involved in psychospiritual growth. When people access their internal worlds in this way, it enables a gradual transformation of their sense of self: what they expect in relationships, how they feel about themselves, and how they go about finding meaning in life.

It is important here to link this discussion to the more holistic notion of *theologia* that existed prior to the split between implicit spirituality and explicit theology. When we talk about the knowledge spiral and integrating both types of knowledge, we are attempting to reclaim some of the rich resources of the patristic era, but with new wisdom from modern science. While there were certainly limitations in the patristic formulations, the unified process of knowing God through reflection that was conducted in a contemplative, relational context captures something essential to the process of spiritual development. Contemporary science helps us formulate this integrative knowledge spiral in more precise terms, informed by its neurobiological underpinnings.

Implicit Knowledge of God

In *The Knowledge of the Holy*, A. W. Tozer stated: "Our real idea of God may lie buried under the rubbish of conventional religious notions and

---

[56]Bucci, *Psychoanalysis and Cognitive Science.*

may require an intelligent and vigorous search before it is finally unearthed and exposed for what it is. Only after an ordeal of painful self-probing are we likely to discover what we actually believe about God."[57] We know God in two ways: what we say we believe about God (explicit knowledge) and, in Tozer's words, what we "actually believe about God" (implicit knowledge).

In some segments of Christianity there is a tendency to discount implicit knowledge of God, especially when it is negative. This is partly due to the split between implicit spirituality and explicit theology in the shaping of the Enlightenment, as we discussed in chapter one. We focus on what we know *about* God and what the Bible says *about* God. This is understandable—our explicit knowledge about God is linear and predictable. It is also amenable to change; we know how to change people's ideas about God. People's implicit knowledge of God is more difficult to change; it often does not seem to respond to explicit teaching.

People's implicit relational knowledge of God is inevitably similar to their implicit relational knowledge of their attachment figures. There is not necessarily a one-to-one correspondence, but the parallels are typically striking. For example, I had been seeing Mark in therapy for about two years when he began to withdraw from his relationship with God and gradually pulled out of his spiritual community. At first, he was unaware of the meaning of this behavior and avoided discussing it with me. When we did process the issue, he felt extremely sad and became aware of a sense of abandonment by God. Part of what contributed to Mark's implicit experience of God was years of experiences of his mother being inconsistent in her care, and ultimately abandoning him.

As we talked more about his withdrawal from his church, Mark experienced a stronger sense of abandonment by God. I suggested that this could be linked to a series of recent rejections he had experienced in close relationships, and ultimately to his experience of abandonment by his mother. This resonated with him, and he was gradually able to put words to his gut-level experiences, further articulating the meaning of

---

[57]A. W. Tozer, *The Knowledge of the Holy* (New York: HarperOne, 1961), 9-10.

his sense of abandonment by God. As a result of this referential activity, Mark's implicit knowledge of God was brought into the realm of his explicit knowledge of God, where we could more directly address it.

Implicit knowledge of God was studied in the 1970s by Ana-Maria Rizzuto, an Argentinean psychoanalyst, who was one of the first to develop a comprehensive theory of what she called a person's "God representation."[58] Rizzuto collected extensive case histories on people in order to systematically study the relationship between how people develop psychologically and how their representations of God develop. Our current scientific understanding about the two ways of knowing, Rizzuto's pioneering research, and numerous studies that have followed in this tradition allow us to begin to paint a general picture of implicit relational schemas of God.

Our implicit knowledge of God develops in the earliest periods of our lives, within the context of relationships with attachment figures. As demonstrated in the infant research reviewed in chapter three, infants are profoundly in tune with, and affected by, their earliest relational experiences. Their internal experiences synchronize with their relational experiences, and their brains literally develop a brain-to-brain connection with their attachment figures. This brain-to-brain linkup then produces a physiological state in the infant that mirrors the caregiver's state. In addition, these experiences, and the corresponding neural connections, then lay down synchronized brain circuits in the infant that create stable patterns of interaction with the attachment figure. In the moment-to-moment mutual coordination that goes on in these interactions, the infant develops a gut-level sense of who he or she is to the important people in his or her life. It is here that the infant experiences "the birth of the living God," as Rizzuto so eloquently put it. Thus, our current understanding of relational development would suggest that our implicit relational schemas of God are shaped by our primary attachment figures—mother, father, grandparents—anyone who played a special role in our lives that caused us to develop an attachment bond with them. A number of studies have supported this idea.

---

[58]Ana-Marie Rizzuto, *The Birth of the Living God* (Chicago: University of Chicago Press, 1979).

For example, one study explored the influence of parents on God image.[59] These researchers found that if a person idealized a particular parent, their image of the idealized parent was a better predictor of their God image (or representation) than the nonidealized parent image. When these researchers created a composite score to represent a participant's overall parent image, these composite parent scores matched the God image scores more closely than scores for mother or father did by themselves. A number of studies have shown a link between people's experiences of attachment figures and their experiences of God. For example, one study found that people who have more mature relationships in general are more likely to experience God as loving and benevolent.[60] In addition, these researchers found that people with less mature relationships were more likely to experience God as wrathful, controlling, and irrelevant. Another study found similar results but also showed that people who used more mature defenses, or ways of coping with psychological pain, were more likely to experience God as loving.[61] Likewise, those who used less mature defenses were more likely to experience God as wrathful.

Spiritual mentors in our lives, who function as a type of authority figure, also influence our implicit knowledge or representations of God. John Bowlby, the founder of attachment theory, observed that people become attached to groups and institutions, such as schools, colleges, work groups, and religious groups.[62] People can actually become attached to a spiritual community, and this often occurs through a spiritual leader or mentor. This can be a secondary attachment, but people can also develop a primary attachment to a spiritual mentor or pastoral figure with whom they develop a close relationship. This can be a formal spiritual mentor or an informal spiritual mentor. In either case, a spiritual mentor represents God to the person to a certain extent. In

---

[59]I. T. Birky and S. Ball, "Parental Trait Influence on God as an Object Representation," *Journal of Psychology* 122 (1988): 133-37.

[60]Beth Fletcher Brokaw and Keith J. Edwards, "The Relationship of God Image to Level of Object Relations Development," *Journal of Psychology and Theology* 22, no. 4 (1994): 352-71.

[61]Raymond J. Wootton, "God-Representation and its Relation to Object Relations and Defensive Functioning" (PhD diss., Boston University, 1991), Dissertation Abstracts International (51:5600).

[62]John Bowlby, *Attachment and Loss, Volume 1: Attachment,* 2nd ed. (New York: Basic Books, 1982).

other words, they act on behalf of God because of the nature of the relationship. We look to them in a special way to help us figure out who God is and how God might feel toward us. In this way, such spiritual mentors influence our experiences of God.

Part of the way spiritual mentors influence our experiences of God is by modeling their own relationship with God and spiritual life. There is some fascinating evidence to suggest this. For example, attachment research suggests that parents' attachment to their own parents, as measured by a narrative interview assessment (the Adult Attachment Interview), predicts their children's attachment to them more strongly than their current parenting.[63] This would suggest that a spiritual mentor's attachment to God may predict the mentee's attachment to God. This is speculation at this point, but it suggests a potentially powerful role that spiritual mentors may play in influencing others' experiences of God. This likely happens through modeling. Seeing up close how a spiritual mentor experiences, relates to, and responds to God profoundly shapes the experiences of others.

Finally, as we engage in relationship with God, God himself influences our implicit relational knowledge of God. This is not the God of propositions in the Bible. In other words, our explicit knowledge of God does not *directly* contribute to our implicit knowledge of God. However, explicit knowledge can indirectly impact our implicit knowledge of God through connections we can make between the two ways of knowing. Relational experiences with God through prayer, Scripture, people, and circumstances can all directly shape or help influence our implicit experiences of God.

As noted in the quote by Tozer, people can have large discrepancies between explicit and implicit knowledge of God. How does the degree of synchronization between the two affect us? First, we can presume that the more consistency there is between the two, the more we are growing. If you observe mature Christians, you will see that their experiences of

---

[63]M. H. van Ijzendoorn, "Adult Attachment Representations, Parental Responsiveness, and Infant Attachment: A Meta-Analysis on the Predictive Validity of the Adult Attachment Interview," *Psychological Bulletin* 117 (1995): 387-403.

God tend to correspond to what they explicitly believe about God's goodness and love. When these two ways of knowing God correspond, it creates a sense of resonance and well-being in our experience. This, in turn, fosters our ability to respond flexibly to others in love—to be open to others' needs. This may serve an integrating function, resulting in approaching life decisions and experiences with self-reflection and a sense of perspective.

Second, when we experience disconnection between our implicit and explicit knowledge of God, it creates a sense of dissonance. Some people explicitly know, more or less, what the Bible teaches about God, and how they should live their lives. But their implicit knowledge— their gut-level experiences and relationships—do not match this. Sometimes, this becomes unbearable and people leave the church or disengage from their faith. The chronic sense of distance from God, or anger at God, continually grinds against their explicit knowledge. If someone in their community doesn't help them process their implicit experiences (by articulating feelings and reflecting on them), sometimes the only way they can cope is to cut off the grinding dissonance. We will return to this in later chapters (eight and nine), but bringing our implicit and explicit experiences of God together involves telling our stories to others, which requires linking the two ways of knowing. Sometimes we need someone to listen to our implicit experiences to help us gain access to them. This is one of the primary roles of spiritual community.

Finally, a general way our implicit experiences of God affect us stems from the fact that they are a function of the low-road brain circuit. Like all implicit relational schemas, our implicit experiences of God function as a type of attachment filter that shapes our feelings, beliefs, expectations, wishes, and fears in our relationship with God. Our gut-level knowledge of God—the stories we tell about our relationship with God— biases our experiences of God in ways that shape how we relate to God and our spiritual communities. Now that we've explored implicit relational knowledge from a scientific perspective, and how it contrasts with explicit knowledge, we next highlight how this very same relational knowledge is emphasized throughout Scripture.

Relational Knowledge in Scripture

A few years back, I was giving a talk on spiritual development to a group of Christian college administrators and faculty in which I emphasized the importance of relational knowledge. At one point, one of the attendees raised his hand and asked, "If this kind of knowledge (i.e., implicit relational knowledge) is so important, why don't we see it in Scripture?" It is easy to fall into the habit of focusing on Scripture and doctrine as explicit knowledge in this way. We often use the word *faith* to refer to the content of our beliefs. We often emphasize an intellectual understanding of the content of our faith rather than trust in the person of Jesus who is our salvation.

The short answer to this question is that while implicit relational knowledge is not systematically or overtly addressed in Scripture, it is assumed, demonstrated, and referred to within its pages. We often overlook this because of the rationalistic interpretive lens we bring to the Bible. We've been socialized in our culture to think that the only thing that counts as knowledge is science, and what is meant by *science* is logical reasoning and quantification. Yet there is a deeper, personal kind of knowledge, and we see it in several ways throughout the Bible.

First, if we look at the genres of Scripture, we see the importance of relational knowledge of God. Much of the Bible is comprised of stories. Story is a form of implicit knowledge. The meaning of a story is expressed through its emotionally charged climax, in which you feel the main idea of the story—what Robert McKee calls "aesthetic emotion."[64] Story does not communicate its main idea through propositions.

In fact, the entirety of Scripture tells the grand story of God's relationship with humanity. It traces the story of human beings severing relationship with God at the fall, and God's quest to restore that relationship and renew all things. The story takes many twists and turns, but

---

[64]Robert McKee, *Story: Substance, Structure, Style, and the Principles of Screenwriting* (New York: HarperCollins, 1997).

ultimately God sends his Son Jesus to sacrifice his life for the sins of the world so that through faith in Christ we may enter into the love among the Trinity that has existed for all eternity. Jesus' death and resurrection is the crisis and climax of the greatest story in history. In the structure of a story, the crisis is a choice in the face of a true dilemma, and the climax is the decision or choice the protagonist makes. In the face of the fall, God must remain holy and separated from sin, and yet his character is such that he desires to reconcile relationship with human beings. From a human standpoint, this choice is a true dilemma. How can God remain holy and still be in relationship with sinful humanity? As we know, God chose to sacrifice his Son to pay the penalty for our sin, which made a way for holiness and relationship with sinful humanity. A crucial layer of the story, of course, is that when Jesus was wrongfully accused and sentenced to death by crucifixion, he chose to follow his Father's will and experience a horrifying death and separation from his Father. When we read the climax of the gospel story, we experience the depth of God's love in a way that cannot be grasped solely through propositions.

Likewise, Jesus often taught using parables rather than lectures. Through story, Jesus taught principles in a way that we feel and experience them. For example, in Matthew 20:1-16, Jesus told the story of a vineyard owner who hires day laborers to work in his vineyard. As we read that the vineyard owner pays the eleventh-hour workers the same as those who started at the beginning of the day, we feel the idea: *God is gracious far beyond what we can imagine. God's economy is not ours. God's way of dealing with us is not ours—it is infinitely more gracious.* Jesus' parables are designed to change our heart, not just inform our mind.

Finally, beyond the fact that we see stories throughout Scripture, the Bible refers to two types of knowledge, roughly parallel to implicit and explicit knowledge. The Hebrew word for truth has two basic meanings. There is a propositional aspect to truth (translated as "truth") and a personal, relational aspect (translated as "faith"), and they are intricately related. In Psalm 51 David says, "You desire truth in the inward being."[65]

---

[65]Psalm 51:6 NRSV.

The Hebrew word translated here as "truth" is rendered in other translations as "faithfulness" (New International Version) and "honesty" (New Living Translation), showing the interconnection between the two ways of knowing. While propositional truth may be partly what is in view here, clearly he is referring to holding truth in a way that is deeper and more personal than mere assent to propositions.

In a similar vein, the Hebrew concept of *believe* is holistic; it does not separate propositional beliefs from a deeper, personal holding of a belief. To do so would have been foreign to the Hebrew mindset and to the early Christians. To believe something in the Hebraic sense means not only that you consider something to be true but also that you hold a deep, gut-level knowledge of that truth and live your life according to it. Anything less is not true belief. Dietrich Bonhoeffer captured this well in his classic book *The Cost of Discipleship*: "Only the obedient believe, and those who believe are obedient."[66]

We see a similar distinction in the Greek with two concepts of knowledge: *epignōsis*, a more analytic form of knowing similar to explicit knowledge, and *gnōsis*, a more personal kind of knowing. In the early church, *gnōsis* referred to a more mystical or spiritual knowledge of God that was more direct. *Gnōsis* has some parallels to the contemporary notion of implicit relational knowledge. This is an intuitive knowledge, similar to how we know how to relate to others in a healthy and loving way. This is the kind of knowledge Paul is referring to in Philippians 3:8 when he says, "Everything else is worthless when compared with the infinite value of knowing Christ Jesus my Lord." The word translated "knowing" here is the noun *gnōsis* in Greek, which corresponds to the Hebrew verb *yada*, which also refers to a personal or relational kind of knowledge. In discussing this passage, Ralph Martin notes, "The Pauline expression 'to know Christ' is intimate (my Lord), and glows with the warmth of a direct relationship; it may therefore be taken as equivalent to 'fellowship with Christ' to which Paul was introduced on the day of

---

[66]Dietrich Bonhoeffer, *The Cost of Discipleship*, 1st Touchstone ed. (New York: Simon and Schuster, 1995), 69.

his conversion."[67] Knowing Christ is a relational kind of knowledge that grows throughout our lives because relationships grow and evolve over time. In addition, relational knowledge of Christ will grow throughout life because it is a deep well. The love of the Christ is so great that we will never fully understand it. We will spend the rest of our lives deepening our grasp of Christ's love for us.

This same kind of relational knowing is emphasized in Jesus' teaching on discipleship in Matthew. Discipleship is pictured, first and foremost, as a call to follow Jesus, as we see when Jesus called Peter and Andrew: "Come, follow me" (Matthew 4:19). Discipleship is fundamentally a relationship with Jesus, which is based on relational knowledge of him. Michael Wilkins notes that discipleship, at its core, involves allegiance to Jesus, which is a relational commitment.[68] Duvall and Hays, likewise, state, "It's impossible to even imagine discipleship or righteousness, as Jesus conceives it, apart from relational presence."[69]

This emphasis on relational knowledge and presence is most clearly seen in Matthew in the Sermon on the Mount. The center of the Sermon on the Mount is Jesus' model prayer, in which he invites his disciples into an affectionate communion with the Father (Matthew 6:9-13). His prayer paints a picture of the presence and provision of a loving Father. Jesus concludes the sermon with a profound and sobering teaching: it is not those who merely call out "Lord! Lord!" who will enter the kingdom of heaven, but rather those who do the Father's will (Matthew 7:21). Obedience is characterized not as performing religious acts but as being *known* by Jesus (Matthew 7:22-23). Duvall and Hays conclude, "Jesus's knowledge of his genuine disciples is a *relational knowledge*, and those not known by him are sent away from his presence."[70] In Jesus' core teachings on discipleship, then, we see that the foundational kind of

---

[67]Ralph P. Martin, *Philippians*, rev. ed., Tyndale New Testament Commentaries (Grand Rapids, MI: Eerdmans, 1987), 149.

[68]Michael Wilkins, *Matthew*, The NIV Application Commentary (Grand Rapids, MI: Zondervan Academic, 2004), 179.

[69]J. Scott Duvall and J. Daniel Hays, *God's Relational Presence: The Cohesive Center of Biblical Theology* (Grand Rapids, MI: Baker Academic, 2019), 181.

[70]Duvall and Hays, *God's Relational Presence*, 183; emphasis added.

knowledge for the Christian life is relational knowledge, which consists of a deep abiding relationship with Christ.

Another way we see relational knowledge referenced is in Paul's writings about growth in community. In describing the knowledge involved in this growth through community, Paul uses numerous words to get across the idea and feeling of a full-orbed knowledge that transcends our intellectual assent and transforms our souls. Paul says that spiritual growth takes place within the Christian community as its members are "increased with," "enriched by," "renewed through," and "filled with" knowledge.[71] While Paul definitely emphasized the importance of intellectual understanding (e.g., Paul instructs believers to "demolish arguments and every pretension that sets itself up against the knowledge of God" [2 Corinthians 10:5 NIV]; to "fix your thoughts on what is true, and honorable, and right" [Philippians 4:8]; and to not be "childish in your understanding of these things" but to be "mature in understanding matters of this kind" [1 Corinthians 14:20]), he used many different terms for the general idea of knowledge in order to present a holistic picture of the knowledge that transforms our faith.

For example, Paul used the following Greek terms among others: *nous* (mind), *gnōsis* (personal knowledge), *epignōsis* (intellectual knowledge), *sophia* (wisdom), *synesis* (understanding), *alētheia* (truth), *phronein* (to think), *logizein* (to consider), *anakrinein* (to discern), *peithein* (to persuade), and *dokimazein* (to test).[72] He sometimes used several of these terms in one place to paint the concept of knowledge with broad strokes. We see this in his letter to the Colossians. His goal for his readers is that they will experience "the full riches of complete understanding (*synesis*), in order that they may know (*epignōsis*) the mystery of God, namely, Christ, in whom are hidden all the treasures of wisdom (*sophia*) and knowledge (*gnōsis*)" (Colossians 2:2-3 NIV). According to Paul, then, we grow in faith not just through an intellectual understanding of God but

---

[71]See, for example, Philippians 1:9; Colossians 1:9-10; Colossians 3:10. See Robert J. Banks, *Paul's Idea of Community: The Early House Churches in Their Cultural Setting*, rev. ed. (Grand Rapids, MI: Baker Academic, 1994), 70.

[72]Robert J. Banks, *Paul's Idea of Community: The Early House Churches in Their Cultural Setting*, rev. ed. (Grand Rapids, MI: Baker Academic, 1994), 71.

also through an experiential knowing of the gospel, which is relationship with Christ himself.

Likewise, throughout Paul's writings, he emphasizes that believers are to live out their beliefs or knowledge. Only knowledge that is translated into action and tested through suffering has the mark of genuine Christian knowledge. This stems from his belief that we are embodied, relational beings as opposed to spirits imprisoned by bodies as taught in ancient Greek thought. If this is true, then it makes sense that we grow in the Christian life not only through thinking and reasoning, but also through enacting our beliefs through action and in relationship. We must inhabit and actualize our beliefs, primarily in the realm of relationships, and this is what relational or experiential knowledge does. This is the very nature of implicit relational knowledge. We see this in the numerous ways Paul instructs believers to put their faith into action and live life together. Let's take a look at two examples to illustrate this idea: baptism and the Lord's Supper, or Communion.

Baptism provides a visible expression of an internal change from an old way of life to a new way of life. *The Message* captures this beautifully in Romans 6:3-5: "When we are lowered into the water, it is like the burial of Jesus; when we are raised up out of the water, it is like the resurrection of Jesus." Paul highlights the importance of baptism in several places throughout his letters (see Romans 6:3-4; 1 Corinthians 12:13; 1 Corinthians 15:29; Galatians 3:27; Ephesians 4:5; Colossians 2:11-12). Baptism is a way that the entire person, and not merely the inner self, is involved in one's commitment to God. The knowledge of the gospel becomes relational in the act of putting one's trust in Christ and in the physical expression of this commitment and trust evidenced in baptism. Baptism, then, is a whole-person expression of one's relational knowledge of Christ. When we truly know Christ, we express this knowledge through baptism because to know Christ is to obey him and show our devotion to him.

On the evening before his crucifixion, Jesus instituted with his disciples the ceremony we refer to as the Lord's Supper, or Communion. Those who know and follow Christ are instructed to imbue new meaning in a shared meal together—now they are to do it in remembrance of Jesus. A common Christian practice prior to the establishment of Paul's churches, these shared meals seem to have been full, normal meals, but the Lord's Supper now took on a new significance. Paul addresses the spirit and significance of the Lord's Supper to the Corinthian church, which seems to have lost sight of its meaning (1 Corinthians 11:17-34). The meal is a visible proclamation of Christ's death and the new covenant, or new relationship with God and fellow believers. Paul recounts Jesus' words, indicating that Jesus' body refers to his death, and Jesus' blood refers to the new covenant between God and his people, and the relationships among believers.

These meals were customarily kicked off by the breaking and distribution of the bread and brought to an end with the taking of a cup.[73] These bookends become all the more significant now because between them lies the experience of the new relationships among believers as the family of God. As the members ate and drank together, they visibly expressed their unity and their relational knowledge of Christ. Participating in a shared meal together reminded the believers of their relationship with Christ and each other, and deepened these relationships.

Paul's emphasis in his letter to the Corinthians is on their relationships with each other—the unity of the community. Paul is saying here that those who claim to know Christ and yet allow others to go hungry at the Lord's Supper are lacking something in their knowledge of Christ. Assent to the belief in Christ's death and resurrection must be embodied in the way we treat our brothers and sisters in Christ in general and in the Lord's Supper in particular. If you believe in the resurrection of Jesus, if you know the Father and the Son whom he sent, then you are in relationship with God. You have experiential knowledge of the love among the Trinity and you participate in this very love, which will manifest itself in how you treat fellow believers in the Lord's Supper. This is the kind of knowledge Scripture emphasizes as ultimately important, rather than propositional knowledge by itself.

---

[73]Banks, *Paul's Idea of Community*, 81.

Relational knowledge is also illustrated, perhaps most powerfully, in John 17 where Jesus describes eternal life. We often think of eternal life as a place called heaven or as living forever. Yet this is not how Jesus describes it in this passage. Scripture teaches that all people will live forever—either with God or separated from God. To live forever does not capture the essence of eternal life. In this poignant prayer, Jesus says, "Now this is eternal life: that they know you, the only true God, and Jesus Christ, whom you have sent" (John 17:3 NIV). The phrase translated as "eternal life" means something along the lines of "life of the age."[74] It is referring to the new kind of life that followers of Christ enter into now but will only fully experience at the end of history—in the next age. Much more than merely living forever, eternal life is a quality of life made possible by knowing the Father, and Jesus Christ, whom God has sent.

Notice that Jesus is not saying that eternal life is a thing we possess. It is not a thing, and it is not a state of the soul per se. Eternal life is a relationship with the Father through the Son, empowered by the Holy Spirit. It is a sharing or participation in the love among the three persons of the Trinity. This is consistent with what Jesus told his disciples in the upper room discourse when he invites them to share in the love between the Father and the Son (John 15:9-15). At the very heart of the gospel message—the good news—is the invitation to a deep personal knowledge that comes from a relationship with God.

As an expression of our personal-relational knowledge of Christ, we employ our mind—logic and reason—to gain a deeper understanding of doctrine and the spiritual life. This is what Augustine referred to as "faith seeking understanding" (in Latin: *fides quaerens intellectum*).[75] Faith comes first, and this allows us to gain true knowledge of God. With Paul, we can come to know Christ so intimately that we consider everything else worthless by comparison.

---

[74]Donald Fairbairn, *Life in the Trinity: An Introduction to Theology with the Help of the Church Fathers* (Downers Grove, IL: IVP Academic, 2008), 29.

[75]Augustine, *On Christian Doctrine*, in *The Works of Saint Augustine, A Translation for the 21st Century, Vol. II: Teaching Christianity*, ed. John E. Rotelle, OSA (Hyde Park, NY: New City Press, 1996).

Conclusion

In this chapter, we have reviewed two distinct ways of knowing—explicit knowledge and implicit knowledge—and suggested that it is our implicit relational knowledge that drives the quality of our relationships with both God and others. While contemporary science has advanced our understanding of emotion as a source of implicit knowledge, particularly in relationships, Scripture likewise emphasizes a personal, relational way of knowing Christ. As with the holistic notion of *theologia*, true knowledge of God unites intellectual belief, theological reflection, obedience to Christ, and love. Indeed, this relational knowledge of Christ is eternal life. We truly know much more than we can say when it comes to our relationships, and it is these "unthought knowns" at the core of our souls that must be transformed into the likeness of Christ.

Attachment Filters

How Relationships Shape Our Capacity to Love

THERE ARE CERTAIN RELATIONSHIPS in our lives that shape us far more than others. These attachment relationships with caregivers form our very sense of self, before we can speak, for good or ill. We remember how these important people in our lives feel about us not in words, but in our emotions, bodies, and images—in our implicit, relational way of knowing. In fact, we remember all of our relational experiences from early infancy in implicit memory, and these memories shape us without our conscious awareness.

How does this happen? Over time, experiences in our attachment relationships that are similar, in terms of their subjective sense of meaning, get chunked together and function as "attachment filters" (referred to as internal working models in attachment theory). Attachment filters are the implicit relational schemas, or "expectancy models," we develop in infancy by the end of our first year, as we discussed in chapter three. As the brain continuously looks for patterns in our experiences, the meaning it tags to our experiences gets run through these relational filters. In other words, our attachment filters bias or shape how we experience relationships automatically and without our even knowing it. In short, *memories of relational experiences with emotionally significant people are etched in our souls and become filters that shape how we feel about ourselves, God, and others, and how we determine the meaning of events in our lives.*

We all have unique attachment filters because we all have unique relational histories. However, research in the area of attachment relationships has identified four general patterns or tendencies of attachment. These attachment filters are formed in emotionally significant attachment relationships, but they influence our implicit processing in all our relationships to some extent, including our relationship with God. In this chapter, we take a closer look at the attachment system, attachment to God, and the four specific attachment filters. We'll close with a clinical example illustrating why attachment filters are difficult to change.

The Attachment System

The attachment system influences and organizes our memory, motivations, and emotions with respect to important caregivers.[1] God designed this system to motivate infants to stay physically close to their caregivers, and to establish communication with them. This system operates throughout our lives, but the manner in which overall emotional connection is sought, experienced, and communicated transitions from physical closeness in infancy to emotional intimacy or "felt security" as we become adults.[2] Physical touch remains an important aspect of intimacy, or felt security, in adulthood, but it is less important than in infancy.

Attachment relationships are relationships in which a child looks to a caregiver to provide a *haven of safety* in times of distress, and a *secure base* from which to explore the world. Attachment relationships also continue throughout adulthood. These two functions work together in a mutually reinforcing way, creating a virtuous cycle of security. For example, emotional attunement and comfort when a child is distressed builds a haven of safety. She experiences increased safety, comfort, and relief from distress and learns through such repeated experiences that she can count on her mother (or other attachment figures) to provide this if she encounters distress. The presence of this haven of safety in

---

[1]Daniel J. Siegel, *The Developing Mind*, 2nd ed. (New York: Guilford Press, 2012).

[2]The notion of felt security was introduced by Sroufe and Waters in a key article in 1977, which advanced our understanding of attachment and moved it more toward relationality. See L. Alan Sroufe and Everett Waters, "Attachment as an Organizational Construct," *Child Development* 48 (1977): 1184-99.

combination with encouragement to explore creates a secure base for the child to venture forth into the world. Her mother encourages exploration and is available for support when needed. However, the secure base could not exist without the haven of safety—the experience of being comforted when distressed. Part of what gives the child the feeling of safety to explore is the implicit knowledge that mother will be there to comfort her if she becomes distressed. We can see, then, that the two major functions of a secure attachment relationship work hand in hand.

While the notion of a secure base has been somewhat vague, recent theory and research has further elaborated the characteristics of a secure base. In general terms, a secure base refers to support of the other's exploration, goals, and personal growth. Building on the foundation provided by attachment theory, Brooke Feeney and Roxanne Thrush proposed three main characteristics of a secure base that support exploration.[3] First, a secure base is available when needed to provide emotional and practical support (*availability*). Second, a secure base does not unnecessarily interfere with exploration (*noninterference*). Third, a secure base encourages and accepts exploration (*encouragement*). In testing their theory, they found that for married couples, the three characteristics strongly predicted exploration behavior. Moreover, the provision and receipt of these secure base behaviors was associated with predictable differences in attachment. In other words, spouses with more secure attachment tendencies were more likely to exhibit and accept secure base behaviors. These secure base behaviors, along with the safe haven, are what led to the development of a secure attachment bond.

Most infants respond differently to their mothers in comparison to other people by three months of age. This is the beginning of the development of an attachment bond. By six to nine months of age, most infants become attached to a primary caregiver.[4] This means that they have

---

[3]Brooke C. Feeney and Roxanne Thrush, "Relationship Influences on Exploration in Adulthood: The Characteristics and Function of a Secure Base," *Journal of Personality and Social Psychology* 98, no. 1 (2010): 57-76.

[4]John Bowlby, *Attachment and Loss, Volume 1: Attachment,* 2nd ed. (New York: Basic Book, 1982), 200.

developed a *specific* bond with a caregiver and no one else will do for providing a haven of safety and secure base. When a child has become attached to a caregiver, people are not interchangeable in providing emotional security. Some children never become attached, but the vast majority becomes attached to someone. Attachments develop only with emotionally significant people, and there are degrees of attachment, but they have a profound impact on our ability to relate and function in many ways.

One of the main functions of the attachment system is to establish a relationship in which an infant's immature brain literally uses the mature functions of the parent's brain to help organize and regulate her own functioning.[5] In a secure relational environment, this leads to attuned, or contingent, communication. In a secure attachment relationship, the parent will respond to the infant in a way that is sensitive to the child's emotional communication, which can expand positive emotions and soothe negative emotions.

Sensitivity to emotional signals is a hallmark of secure attachment. The essence of this kind of attunement is the capacity to read signals (mostly nonverbal) that indicate the need for connection and, at times, separateness. In this way, the attachment figure's brain activity directly influences the brain activity of the other. The amazing thing about this is that contingent emotional communication literally creates brain circuits in the child that foster healthy patterns of communication and emotional well-being.[6] We pass down our brain circuitry to our children through our emotional communication. However, emotional communication in the attachment system is a double-edged sword. Noncontingent emotional communication will also lead to the development of brain circuits that are associated with certain dysfunctional patterns of communication and connection. These are different forms of insecure attachment that we will review below.

---

[5]Daniel J. Siegel, *The Developing Mind*, 2nd ed. (New York: Guilford Press, 2012).
[6]Rosemarie E. Perry, Clancy Blair, and Regina M. Sullivan, "Neurobiology of Infant Attachment: Attachment Despite Adversity and Parental Programming of Emotionality," *Current Opinion in Psychology* 17 (2017): 1-6.

As noted in chapter four, implicit relational knowledge (such as our attachment filters) continues to affect us throughout life and is the foundational way of knowing in relationships. Likewise, our need for nonverbal attunement, or contingent communication, continues throughout life. As adults, we use a lot of words in our communication, and this is an important part of our connection to others, but the core of our connection to God and others is a deeper form of emotional communication. Attachment relationships can have different patterns, different attachment filters, which we review in more detail below. These patterns or tendencies are composed of enduring ways in which we access memory, regulate our emotions, relate to others, reflect on ourselves, and tell our stories.

These attachment filters are organized strategies for maintaining relational connections with attachment figures, and to some extent this always occurs in the context of less than ideal relational circumstances with which we need to cope. Within each of these organized strategies, an attachment filter is comprised of an implicit feeling about the self and a corresponding set of implicit expectations about how important people feel toward us. These two aspects of a filter usually fit together, such as a feeling of yourself as unimportant and an expectation of others as being indifferent toward you. However, there can still be quite a bit of variability within the four common attachment filters.

These attachment patterns, or filters, appear to be passed down from generation to generation. Dozens of studies have demonstrated that parents' attachment classification, measured by a semi-structured interview about their attachment history, predicts their infants' attachment classification.[7] These results have been replicated even when parents' attachment is measured prior to the birth of their infant, ruling out the possibility that the association could be due to some influence of the child's interactions with the mother.[8] Other research has traced the transmission

---

[7]Early research in this area used the Adult Attachment Interview to measure parents' attachment classification. Marije L. Verhage et al., "Narrowing the Transmission Gap: A Synthesis of Three Decades of Research on Intergenerational Transmission of Attachment," *Psychological Bulletin* 142 (2016): 337-66.

[8]Peter Fonagy, Howard Steele, and Miriam Steele, "Maternal Representations of Attachment

of attachment across three generations, showing remarkable stability in familial attachment filters over time.[9]

The intergenerational transmission of attachment filters appears to be due to caregiver sensitivity.[10] In other words, parents who experience sensitivity deficits in the ways they were parented tend to also be less emotionally sensitive to their own children. In short, there is clear evidence that we pass our attachment filters—engrained patterns of emotional communication—down to our children. This happens through our relationship with our children, and specifically through our implicit emotional communication that relies heavily on nonverbal channels.

In addition to being passed down through the generations, attachment filters are also fairly stable across many years, although they can change. A number of longitudinal studies have been conducted linking infants' attachment classification with their attachment classification fifteen to twenty-one years later.[11] In about two-thirds of the cases, individuals' attachment filters remained the same up to twenty years later. However, some studies have shown less continuity over time, but in most cases the lack of continuity is referred to as "lawful discontinuity" because there were clearly identifiable events, situations, or relationships that changed the person's attachment filter for better or worse.

In chapter four, we suggested that implicit relational knowledge applies to our relationship with God and highlighted some early research supporting this. A substantial research literature has developed within attachment theory that specifically addresses the question of God as an attachment figure, and the relationship between our attachment to

During Pregnancy Predict the Organization of Infant-Mother Attachment at One Year of Age," *Child Development* 62 (1991): 891-905.

[9]Rosalinda Cassibba et al., "The Transmission of Attachment Across Three Generations: A Study in Adulthood," *Developmental Psychology* 53 (2017): 396-405.

[10]Kazuko Y. Behrens, John D. Haltigan, and Naomi I. Gribneau Bahm, "Infant Attachment, Adult Attachment, and Maternal Sensitivity: Revisiting the Intergenerational Transmission Gap," *Attachment & Human Development* 18 (2016): 337-53.

[11]Erik Hesse, "The Adult Attachment Interview: Historical and Current Perspectives," in *Handbook of Attachment: Theory, Research, and Clinical Applications*, ed. J. Cassidy and P. R. Shaver (New York: Guilford Press, 1999), 395-433. See also Erik Hesse, "The Adult Attachment Interview: Protocol, Method of Analysis, and Empirical Studies," in *Handbook of Attachment: Theory, Research, and Clinical Applications*, 2nd ed., ed. J. Cassidy and P. R. Shaver (New York: Guilford Press, 2008), 552-98.

humans and attachment to God. Before turning to descriptions of each of the four primary attachment filters, we will explore the question of whether and how God acts as an attachment figure in our lives.

God as an Attachment Figure

Do Christians experience God as an attachment figure? In chapter two, we proposed that God is a fundamentally relational being, and this informs our understanding of what it means for human beings to be created in God's image. The parallel question we focus on here is whether Christians *experience* God as an attachment figure.

As we mentioned previously, the role attachment figures play can be characterized by their relative degree of accessibility and responsiveness. They provide physical and psychological protection, support, and comfort. Secure attachment figures provide a secure base from which the individual can explore the world. They also provide a haven of safety for the individual during distress or threat. When we get upset, hurt, or otherwise distressed, we seek out an attachment figure. The question at hand is whether, as Christians, we experience God as a spiritual attachment figure. Does our relationship with God function this way for us psychologically?

There is significant evidence that most Christians do become attached to God and experience God as an attachment figure. Just as with parents or other attachment figures, we turn to God for comfort and safety when we are distressed. As the saying goes, "There are no atheists in foxholes." Attachment researchers note that God clearly fits the definition of an attachment figure.

There is a substantial body of research that supports this idea. Quantitative research on concepts of God going back to the 1960s reveals that the dominant cluster of adjectives by which individuals describe their experience of God include words such as considerate, comforting, helpful, warm, patient, and loving. The second cluster of adjectives includes words such as damning, punishing, jealous, stern, and critical.[12]

---

[12]B. Spilka, P. Armatas, and J. Nussbaum, "The Concept of God: A Factor-Analytic Approach," *Review of Religious Research* 6, no. 1 (1964): 28-36.

While the emotional tone is opposite in the two clusters, they both describe God in very personal and relational terms that are laden with emotion. Data on images of God from the 1983 General Social Survey demonstrate that the most frequently mentioned images could be characterized as supportive as opposed to instrumental.[13]

We tend to turn to God when we experience loss through death or divorce, emotional crises, and relational difficulties.[14] In trials like these, our most likely spiritual response is to pray. It seems, then, that prayer represents an attachment behavior with respect to God, providing a window into the nature of our attachment to God. In addition to providing a safe haven, God provides a secure base for us to not only explore the world but to be salt and light—to co-labor with God in doing kingdom work. On the flip side of this coin, people who go through an experience of losing their religious commitment show the very same separation anxiety symptoms that follow from separation in human attachment relationships.[15] In short, a large body of quantitative research indicates that people tend to experience God in relational terms—terms that map well onto attachment concepts.

There is a growing body of qualitative research corroborating the experience of God as an attachment figure. For example, in a thorough interview study, Marie-Therese Proctor found that people described God in ways analogous to an attachment figure.[16] Their descriptions of God suggested that they could turn to God when distressed, and that God was available to provide comfort. Proctor also reported that actual experiences of God, in addition to descriptions, fit well within an attachment perspective. Individuals' relationship adjectives were

---

[13]H. M. Nelson, N. H. Cheek, and P. Au, "Gender Differences in Images of God," *Journal for the Scientific Study of Religion* 24, no. 4 (1985): 396-402.

[14]See Ralph W. Hood, Peter C. Hill, and Bernie Spilka, *The Psychology of Religion: An Empirical Approach*, 2nd ed. (New York: Guilford Press, 2009); W. James, *The Varieties of Religious Experience* (New York: Collier, 1902/1961).

[15]L. A. Kirkpatrick, "Attachment and Religious Representations and Behavior," in *Handbook of Attachment: Theory, Research, and Clinical Applications*, ed. J. Cassidy and P. R. Shaver (New York: Guilford Press, 1999), 803-22.

[16]Marie-Therese Proctor, "The God Attachment Interview Schedule: Implicit and Explicit Assessment of Attachment to God" (unpublished PhD diss., University of Western Sydney, 2006).

classified along two dimensions: (1) personal to nonpersonal, and (2) positive to negative. In general terms, Proctor found that people experienced God in predominantly personal and positive terms. The specific experiences reported were clearly related to attachment concepts. For example, individuals reported that God was present, dependable, fulfilling, secure, special, or disappointing.

If our relationship with God is an attachment relationship, then does it follow that we experience God similarly to the way we experience our primary human attachment figures? Or do we experience God as a secure attachment figure even when our human attachment figures are substantially unhealthy? Does God fill in the gaps in our attachment needs? The answer to both questions appears to be a qualified yes. The key to reconciling the two possibilities is to understand the *way* God fills in the gaps.

One way attachment researchers have explored this question is by examining the patterns in people's relationships with humans and with God to see if the pattern in one domain (humans) corresponds to the other (God). Researchers have tested whether: (1) individuals' attachment patterns with people *correspond* to their attachment patterns with God, or (2) whether, for those who have insecure attachment relationships with humans, God *compensates* for these insecurities by functioning as a substitute attachment figure for them. Attachment researchers call these "compensation" and "correspondence" models, and they have often been pitted against each other as mutually exclusive. The research on this question provides an important lens into our implicit knowledge of God.[17]

On the surface, the results of the research in this area present a rather inconsistent picture. On the one hand, a number of studies suggest correspondence—that the dynamics of our relationships with God are similar to the dynamics of our human attachment relationships.[18] On the

---

[17]This conceptual framework was introduced by Lee Kirkpatrick in 1992 in a key article that stimulated a subfield of research in this area. Lee A. Kirkpatrick, "An Attachment Theory Approach to the Psychology of Religion," *The International Journal for the Psychology of Religion* 2 (1992): 3-28.

[18]Steven J. Sandage et al., "Attachment to God, Adult Attachment, and Spiritual Pathology: Mediator and Moderator Effects," *Mental Health, Religion & Culture* 18 (2015): 795-808; Beth Fletcher

other hand, several studies have provided partial support for some form of compensation—the idea that God functions as a substitute attachment figure for those with insecure attachments with humans.[19] How do we make sense of these seemingly contrasting findings?

In order to address this question, my colleagues and I conducted a study in which we measured attachment categories in the human domain using a measure of romantic attachment.[20] The basic idea is that human attachment predicts implicit aspects of spirituality that tap into implicit experiences but does not predict explicit aspects of spirituality. The implicit content measures we used were forgiveness, spiritual community, anxious attachment to God, and avoidant attachment to God. The explicit measures tapped into religious commitment and frequency of spiritual practices. We defined these as explicit because we have more control over these aspects of our spirituality than we do over our implicit experiences.

Brokaw and Keith J. Edwards, "The Relationship of God Image to Level of Object Relations Development," *Journal of Psychology and Theology* 22, no. 4 (1994): 352-71; Todd W. Hall et al., "An Empirical Exploration of Psychoanalysis and Religion: Spiritual Maturity and Object Relations Development," *Journal for the Scientific Study of Religion* 37, no. 2 (1998): 303-13; Todd W. Hall and Keith J. Edwards, "The Spiritual Assessment Inventory: A Theistic Model and Measure for Assessing Spiritual Development," *Journal for the Scientific Study of Religion* 41, no. 2 (2002): 341-57; R. A. Merck and R. W. Johnson, "Attachment Theory and Religious Belief," (paper, 103rd Annual Convention of the American Psychological Association, New York, August 1995); Richard Beck and Angie McDonald, "Attachment to God: The Attachment to God Inventory, Tests of Working Model Correspondence, and an Exploration of Faith Group Differences," *Journal of Psychology and Theology* 32 (2004): 92-103; Wade C. Rowatt and Lee A. Kirkpatrick, "Two Dimensions of Attachment to God and Their Relation to Affect, Religiosity, and Personality Constructs," *Journal for the Scientific Study of Religion* 41, no. 4 (2002): 637-51.

[19]Pehr Granqvist, "Religiousness and Perceived Childhood Attachment: On the Question of Compensation or Correspondence," *Journal for the Scientific Study of Religion* 37, no. 2 (1998): 350-67; P. Granqvist and B. Hagekull, "Religiousness and Perceived Childhood Attachment: Profiling Socialized Correspondence and Emotional Compensation," *Journal for the Scientific Study of Religion* 38, no. 2 (1999): 254-73; L. A. Kirkpatrick, "God as a Substitute Attachment Figure: A Longitudinal Study of Adult Attachment Style and Religious Change in College Students," *Personality & Social Psychology Bulletin* 24, no. 9 (1998): 961-97; L. A. Kirkpatrick and P. R. Shaver, "Attachment Theory and Religion: Childhood Attachments, Religious Beliefs, and Conversion," *Journal for the Scientific Study of Religion* 29, no. 3 (1990): 315-34; L. A. Kirkpatrick, "A Longitudinal Study of Changes in Religious Belief and Behavior as a Function of Individual Differences in Adult Attachment Style," *Journal for the Scientific Study of Religion* 36, no. 2 (1997): 207-17; Pehr Granqvist, "Attachment and Religiosity in Adolescence: Cross-Sectional and Longitudinal Evaluations," *Personality & Social Psychology Bulletin* 28, no. 2 (2002): 260-70.

[20]Todd W. Hall et al., "Attachment to God and Implicit Spirituality: Clarifying Correspondence and Compensation Models," *Journal of Psychology and Theology* 37, no 4 (2009): 227-42.

Our results supported our predictions. We found predicted differences between the attachment groups on three of the four implicit measures of spirituality, but no differences on the explicit measures of spirituality. People with secure and dismissing human attachment patterns reported higher levels of forgiveness than those with preoccupied and fearful patterns.[21] Secure individuals reported higher levels of spiritual community than the other three attachment groups. In addition, we found that preoccupied and fearful individuals reported higher levels of anxiety in their relationships with God. In contrast, as we predicted, there were no differences among any of the four attachment groups on their level of explicit spirituality.

A clever series of experiments has also supported this idea more directly by engaging the emotion centers or low-road brain circuits that process attachment-related information implicitly.[22] These researchers used two different subliminal stimulations having to do with separation to activate individuals' attachment systems unconsciously. Participants in the study viewed a stimulus phrase for five milliseconds—long enough for the low-road brain circuits to compute the emotional meaning of the phrase, but not long enough for explicit processing (cortical or high-road circuits) to make the person consciously aware of the phrase. None of the participants reported having seen anything remotely similar to the stimulus phrase.

One of the stimuli was specific to God ("God has forsaken me") and the other was specific to human attachments ("mother is gone"). This allowed the researchers to test whether implicit knowledge of parental attachment figures (i.e., attachment history with parents) overlaps with implicit knowledge of God, such that both affect a person's relational dynamics with God. This is exactly what they found. For both the God and mother stimuli, individuals with an insecure attachment history

---

[21]We suspected and correctly predicted that on a self-report measure, dismissing individuals would report relatively high levels of forgiveness, and we believe this is most likely a form of "pseudo-forgiveness."

[22]A. Birgegard and P. Granqvist, "The Correspondence Between Attachment to Parents and God: Three Experiments Using Subliminal Separation Cues," *Personality and Social Psychology Bulletin* 30 (2004): 1122-35.

showed a decrease in seeking support from God after viewing the subliminal stimulation, whereas those with secure attachment histories showed an increase in seeking support from God. This suggests that individuals with secure attachment tendencies experience God as a reliable source of comfort and seek God out when they become distressed. In contrast, people with more insecure attachments tend to turn away from God when they become distressed.

While our study noted above used all self-report measures, and the subliminal priming study used a self-report measure of attachment, my colleagues and I conducted a study using an interview-based implicit measure of both adult and God attachment.[23] This addressed the methodological concerns that self-report measures cannot fully tap into implicit attachment processes. The interview measuring God attachment was modeled after the Adult Attachment Interview (AAI) and was coded using the AAI coding system. This allowed for statistical analyses of the association between adult and God attachment (both being implicit measures) on two types of measures: (1) a continuous measure of attachment security[24] and (2) a categorical attachment classification. We found significant, moderate correlations between adult attachment and God attachment on three continuous scales: idealization, coherent transcript, and coherent mind.[25] In addition, we found a 68 percent continuity between secure, dismissing, and preoccupied attachment classifications across human and God attachment interviews, and a correlation of .50, indicating a strong association between attachment state of mind with respect to humans and God.[26] Thus, when using measures designed to access implicit processes, we see correspondence between human and God attachment.

---

[23]Annie Fujikawa et al., "The Relationship Between Adult and God Attachment" (unpublished manuscript, Biola University, 2010). See also Todd W. Hall and Annie Fujikawa, "God Images and the Sacred," in *APA Handbooks in Psychology: APA Handbook of Psychology, Religion, and Spirituality*, vol. 1, ed. Kenneth Pargament, Julie Exline, and Jim Jones, (Washington, DC: American Psychological Association, 2013), 277-92.

[24]The interviews were coded on a 1-9 scale for several aspects of attachment, such as idealization, coherent transcript, and coherent mind.

[25]The average correlation across these three scales was .45.

[26]We conducted a Cramér's *V* correlation, which is a type of correlation designed to assess the association between two sets of categorical data, such as attachment classifications.

These findings taken together suggest that when we look at the level of the experiential dynamics of our attachment relationships, or our implicit relational knowledge, our patterns with God parallel those with human attachment figures. This supports the correspondence idea mentioned above. However, our attachment dynamics do not generally predict more explicit dimensions of our spirituality that have more to do with our explicit knowledge system. We have more intentional control over this and over our commitments. This is good, because, as we will see, it allows us to actively participate in facilitating the conditions we need to grow. However, we must understand that the realm of our explicit knowledge system does not *directly* change, or predict, our implicit dynamics with God.

Some people, when they hear this idea, assume that this suggests that their relationship with God can never grow beyond the maturity of their early human relationships. I do not believe this to be the case. I would contend that our relationship with God can change or grow beyond whatever relational shortcomings we inevitably experienced in childhood. Rather, what this means is that transformation in our relationship with God comes about directly through the implicit knowledge system rather than the explicit knowledge system. Furthermore, because our soul, or heart, is unified, it means that this kind of change happens at the core of our soul and flows out into all our relationships. Changes in our relationship with God tend to coincide with changes in our human relationships, and vice versa, because they reflect deep, implicit changes at the very center of our soul.

In sum, a neuroscience perspective suggests, and research supports, the view that we all have two views of God: (1) an explicit view, based on our explicit knowledge about God, and (2) an implicit view, based on our attachment filters. As we suggested in chapter four, our implicit knowledge system applies to our relationships with God and our spirituality as much as it does to human relationships. Just as our attachment filters are organized strategies for maintaining relational connections with human attachment figures, they are also organized strategies for maintaining connection with God. We turn now to descriptions of each of the four primary attachment filters and how they manifest in our relationship with God.

The Four Attachment Filters

We have touched above on various attachment patterns, or filters. While everyone's attachment filter is unique, and we can have different attachment tendencies with different people, most people have a dominant or default attachment filter. Research has identified four main attachment categories: secure, preoccupied, dismissing, and fearful. After reviewing these filters, we will come back to a caveat about these categories and address why attachment filters are difficult to change.

Secure attachment filter. A secure attachment filter means that a person believes, *at a gut level*, that emotionally significant others will be available and responsive when needed. Others will be reliable and can be counted on when support is needed. People with a secure filter have experienced this enough in the past that they expect it of attachment figures without consciously thinking about it. They are typically open to their own need for others and to others' needs. Expecting that emotionally significant people will be there for them when they need them provides a secure base from which to focus on the needs of others. From a spiritual perspective, this secure base is what frees us up to love God and others. Let's take a look at what research has shown about secure attachment.

People with a secure attachment filter develop particular ways to regulate their own emotions: they consciously acknowledge emotional distress, display their distress to others in close relationships, tend to solve problems actively and effectively, and actively seek support from others when they need it. These are hallmark characteristics of people with a secure attachment filter in terms of how they manage and use their emotions. They do not have to think about this. It happens automatically because their relational experiences are processed through the secure attachment filter at an implicit or gut level.

Securely attached individuals can easily access painful emotional memories and have high distress tolerance.[27] They are able to access negative emotional memories without experiencing high levels of

---

[27]Hesse, "The Adult Attachment Interview: Historical and Current Perspectives."

distress.[28] In addition, secure individuals do not generally experience the triggering of other secondary negative emotions when they recall a negative memory. This combination of findings is very significant because it suggests that secure individuals can bring painful emotions online without this triggering a cascade of other negative emotions.[29] For example, they can process sadness over a specific situation without that triggering anxiety. This allows them to work through painful events and memories without becoming overwhelmed.

Another interesting characteristic is that securely attached people tend to express emotion openly and appropriately disclose personal information with significant others. They are perceptive about situational cues when determining how much they should disclose in a particular relational context. They tend to disclose about the same amount as others do to them, and they usually feel good about how much they disclose to others. Secure individuals also tend to be attracted to partners who disclose freely and who disclose personal information about themselves.[30] Secure individuals show wisdom in deciding how much to reveal to others, and they do this in a way that keeps them emotionally refueled and promotes a sense of connection with others.

Secure individuals develop effective ways to cope with stress and solve problems. These individuals tend to be curious and actively seek new information that helps them grow.[31] People with a secure attachment filter also tend not to get rigidly fixed on certain information so much that they discount new information that might cause ambiguity or confusion. Even if new information muddies the waters, people with secure attachments will still generally consider this new information. This includes information about relationships as well. Their internal secure base helps them to update their implicit sense of who they are and their

---

[28]M. Mikulincer and I. Orbach, "Attachment Styles and Repressive Defensiveness: The Accessibility and Architecture of Affective Memories," *Journal of Personality and Social Psychology* 68 (1995): 917-25.

[29]This is what happens with posttraumatic stress.

[30]M. Mikulincer and O. Nachshon, "Attachment Styles and Patterns of Self-Disclosure," *Journal of Personality and Social Psychology* 61 (1991): 321-32.

[31]M. Mikulincer, "Adult Attachment Style and Information Processing: Individual Differences in Curiosity and Cognitive Closure," *Journal of Personality and Social Psychology* 72 (1997): 1217-30.

gut-level expectations of others. As a result of this, securely attached individuals are typically more confident about their ability to flexibly adapt their beliefs to accommodate new information.

One of the ways secure individuals cope effectively is by seeking support when they need others to help them manage their emotions. For example, research shows that when secure women feel anxious, they are more likely to seek support than less secure women.[32] In addition, secure women tend to feel comforted by support from their romantic partners, whereas less secure women tend to withdraw emotionally and physically from their partners when they are distressed.

Secure individuals show a particular narrative pattern when they tell their story in the Adult Attachment Interview (AAI), which is a semi-structured interview about a person's attachment history.[33] Their stories tend to be coherent and collaborative. They tend to stay on track with the interview questions and with the context of the interview. In addition, when they tell their stories, secure individuals are able to access and convey the emotional meaning of their stories, and yet still structure them in a logical and coherent manner. Because they are emotionally engaged, their stories are believable.

One of the fascinating things about this research on the AAI is that secure individuals sometimes recount negative memories of their early attachment experiences. However, even when recounting painful experiences, the way they tell their stories marks it as a secure or coherent narrative. Secure attachment with a history of insecure attachment is referred to by attachment researchers as "earned secure attachment," which indicates that somewhere along the way, these individuals went through a healing process and developed a secure attachment through their relationships with significant others.

---

[32]J. A. Simpson, W. S. Rholes, and J. S. Nelligan, "Support Seeking and Support Giving Within Couples in an Anxiety-Provoking Situations: The Role of Attachment Styles," *Journal of Personality and Social Psychology* 62 (1992): 434-46.

[33]The AAI evaluates not so much the content of individuals' attachment story, but rather the way they tell their story. The scoring method is referred to as a narrative coherence approach. Carol George, Nancy Kaplan, and Mary Main, "Adult Attachment Interview" 3rd ed. (unpublished manuscript, University of California, Berkeley, 1996).

These individuals tend to show a sense of perspective and balance in talking about their past attachment relationships. In other words, they may recall painful experiences with an attachment figure, but they are able to recognize various underlying mental states and relational experiences, including with themselves, that may have contributed to the pain. In this, they often convey an implicit sense of forgiveness of those who have hurt them.

This balance shown by secure individuals reflects the concept of mentalizing, which appears to be an integral component of attachment security for both those who have had secure attachment tendencies throughout their lives and those who developed them later in life. Mentalizing, a concept developed by British psychoanalyst Peter Fonagy, refers to "the process by which we realize that having a mind mediates our experience of the world."[34] In other words, we mentalize when we hold in mind that others have a mind—their own internal experience—that is different from ours. This enables people to respond to their experience (of themselves and others) not just on the basis of external behavior but also on the basis of underlying mental states such as emotions and beliefs. This, in turn, enables insight and empathy, which promote healthy relationships.

Research suggests that a parent's capacity to mentalize is crucial to promoting secure attachment in the child, and secure attachment provides the key context for activating the child's own mentalizing potential. For example, one key study showed that parents with a high ability to mentalize were three to four times more likely to have secure children than those with a low ability to mentalize.[35] Among deprived mothers (e.g., parental mental illness, prolonged separation from parents, etc.) with a strong capacity to mentalize, every single one had secure children. In contrast, among deprived mothers with a weak mentalizing capacity, only one out of seventeen had a secure child. This

---

[34]Peter Fonagy et al., *Affect Regulation, Mentalization, and the Development of the Self* (New York: Other Press, 2002), 3.

[35]Fonagy, Steele, and Steele, "Maternal Representations of Attachment," 891-905. The ability to mentalize was measured with the Reflective-Functioning scale, which was developed by Fonagy and colleagues to measure one's capacity to mentalize.

finding reveals that a strong ability to mentalize could be a key mechanism in breaking the typical intergenerational transmission of insecure attachment.

Individuals with secure attachment tendencies typically do not become overwhelmed by pain when they recall painful events. They are able to stay in the present and remain emotionally engaged while describing such events. What is being revealed in all these studies is the individual's organized pattern for dealing with attachment-related information. Secure narratives are associated with the ability to develop healthy relationships.

In summary, the breadth of research on secure attachment filters reveals a strikingly coherent picture of an organized strategy for approaching relationships and emotional meaning. A secure attachment filter develops early on from repeated experiences with caregivers who are consistently emotionally available and responsive. Individuals learn from these experiences a strategy for regulating their emotions that allows them to be aware of their emotions and to use others in a balanced way for support. They learn that their own emotions will not overwhelm them and that expressing their emotions to others will lead to a positive experience of connection. They learn that they are capable of managing their own distress with the help of others who are there for them, and that others will provide comfort when they need it. These experiences are all recorded in implicit memory and then filter all relational experiences, particularly those involving some measure of close connection or attachment, including experiences of God.

These patterns are what individuals with secure attachment filters bring to their relationship with God. This does not mean there will not be difficult and painful times in their relationship with God. Rather, it means that they tend to expect God to be available and responsive, to genuinely care about them, and to welcome the expression of emotion, including negative emotions.

In our study mentioned previously, we found strong support for this. Secure individuals showed a stronger sense of connection to a spiritual community than any of the insecure attachment groups.[36] In addition, they experienced less anxiety in their relationship with God than preoccupied and dismissing individuals. This allows secure individuals to process difficult experiences in relationship with God and to stay connected to God even in the midst of dark and difficult times. Such times may be partially due to life situations, or they may just be times when God seems unresponsive—what Saint John of the Cross described as a "dark night of the soul."[37] Regardless of the nature of the difficult experience, a secure attachment filter provides a secure base to process and grow through trials.

In an interview study in which six secure attachment-to-God indicators were coded, Marie-Therese Proctor noted that three indicators were coded with high frequency: positive God concept, positive relationship with God, and valuing of relationship with God. Significantly less interview material was coded for the other three secure indicators: recognition of doubting as a part of a healthy relationship, comfort with questioning and examining beliefs, and integration (the ability to reflectively embrace and integrate positive and negative life experiences within one's spiritual framework and relationship with God).[38] Proctor highlighted the intriguing possibility that the results hint at a developmental progression in one's secure attachment to God. There may be a substantial range of developmental maturity within each attachment category with respect to relationship with God, and Proctor's results may be picking up on this.

For example, it may be that some individuals can have a foundational level of security and yet do not have the capacity to process doubts and trials in more complex ways. The theoretical question here is whether such capacities are *entailed* in secure attachment or whether secure attachment serves as a foundation for these capacities, which are distinct

---

[36]Hall et al., "Attachment to God and Implicit Spirituality," 227-42.

[37]Saint John of the Cross, *The Dark Night of the Soul: A Masterpiece in the Literature by St. John of the Cross*, trans. and ed. E. A. Peers (New York: Image Books, Doubleday, 1990). Saint John described two primary kinds of dark night experiences, but we are using the term here to refer in general to times when people feel like God is absent.

[38]Proctor, "God Attachment Interview Schedule."

from attachment. It seems likely that the capacities to regulate one's emotions and to view things from multiple perspectives are critical to more complex ways of processing doubt and painful experiences. Further research is needed to flesh out potential developmental pathways within each attachment category.

Preoccupied attachment filter. People with a preoccupied attachment filter expect others to be unreliable—sometimes available and responsive, and at other times not available and responsive. People with preoccupied attachment filters feel that they cannot predict how this will play out. They have developed a strategy of hyperactivating—shifting into high gear—their need for others when they become distressed. The strategy is to try to pull attachment figures into providing comfort and care. There is a tendency for people with this filter to become preoccupied with unresolved emotional pain and to demand—either implicitly or explicitly—that others take care of this pain. This self-preoccupation also makes it difficult to notice and attend to others' needs, which is necessary to effectively love others, thus linking attachment back to our core concern of spiritual transformation. We turn now to a closer look at what research reveals about preoccupied attachment filters.

A preoccupied attachment style typically develops from caregivers who are inconsistently available or responsive to an infant's physical or emotional needs.[39] In this relational environment, infants have a strong need for connection but an equally strong fear of rejection and separation. Due to inconsistent responsiveness, infants become preoccupied with staying physically close to their caregiver, because they have no internal sense of felt security. For them, being physically alone is equivalent to being emotionally alone. Hence, they develop an organized strategy for dealing with distress—they hyperactivate their attachment system, or their need for others. The result of this is that their emotional distress becomes elevated (often chronically), and they become totally focused on gaining support and comfort from their

---

[39]J. D. Green and W. K. Campbell, "Attachment and Exploration in Adults: Chronic and Context Accessibility," *Personality and Social Psychology Bulletin* 26 (2000): 452-61.

caregivers.[40] You can see this filter in the clingy child who is frightened to venture very far away from his or her mother.[41] Likewise, as adults these individuals may be experienced as "needy," which often drives others away, thus reinforcing the person's sense that attachment figures are not reliably responsive to their needs.

Preoccupied individuals have easy access to painful emotions; however, they have difficulty regulating their emotions. For example, preoccupied individuals recall negative memories more quickly and more strongly than people with any other attachment filter.[42] Preoccupied individuals also experience all emotions, regardless of whether they are the primary emotion associated with a particular memory, as very intense. For example, if they recall a predominantly sad memory, this will cause emotional flooding, bringing online other negative emotions, such as anxiety. They do not seem to be able to experience one negative emotion by itself without becoming overwhelmed with global negative emotions.

The way preoccupied individuals disclose information about themselves fits their organized strategy for dealing with attachment relationships and emotions. For example, they disclose about the same amount of personal information as securely attached individuals. However, they have difficulty adapting their level of self-disclosure to situational cues. They may tend to share too much information in indiscriminate ways. In addition, unlike secure individuals, they generally do not respond in kind to others by disclosing things on the same topic.[43] What is interesting, however, is that they tend to like high disclosure conversations. We see here a complex pattern of self-disclosure that represents an organized strategy for dealing with close attachment relationships, emotion, and distress. Preoccupied people tend to focus on their own needs and feelings, and can be somewhat oblivious to those they are disclosing information to, and to what the others have shared.

---

[40]P. R. Shaver and M. Mikulincer, "Attachment-Related Psychodynamics," *Attachment & Human Development* 4, no. 2 (2002): 133-61.

[41]In the infant attachment literature, this attachment tendency is called "anxious-ambivalent."

[42]Mikulincer and Orbach, "Attachment Styles and Repressive Defensiveness," 917-25.

[43]Mikulincer and Nachshon, "Attachment Styles and Patterns of Self-Disclosure," 321-32.

As we mentioned earlier, secure individuals tend to seek out new information and adjust their beliefs and expectations to accommodate new information. People with preoccupied attachment filters do not tend to do this. Instead, they tend to reject or ignore information that will cause ambiguity, and they have difficulty revising their implicit beliefs based on new information.[44] In fact, preoccupied individuals have a particularly difficult time revising their implicit beliefs about themselves and others. For example, in their evaluations of themselves, they focus on their weaknesses. This creates a lot of internal distress, which in turn exacerbates their negative view of themselves.[45] In addition, preoccupied individuals are less likely than secure individuals to revise their perception of their partner, even when their partner behaves in ways that do not fit their implicit expectations.[46] Preoccupied people seem to be resistant to taking in new information about their partners.

Individuals with preoccupied filters tend to tell their stories on the AAI in a way that lacks relevance. What this means is that they get off track from the specific topic or question, oftentimes because they become flooded with emotional pain. They have difficulty managing their emotions while simultaneously staying on task with the interview. They also provide very long and vague descriptions. Because of this it is difficult to follow their train of thought. They become wrapped up in their emotional pain and lose track of the context of what they are doing and the person to whom they are talking. It is not hard to see how this causes difficulties in relationships.

In summary, since their caregivers have not been emotionally attuned to them consistently, preoccupied individuals have difficulty regulating their own emotions effectively. They do have an organized strategy for attempting to do this, but it involves hyperactivating thoughts, feelings, and behaviors related to attachment relationships, which are

---

[44]Mikulincer, "Adult Attachment Style and Information Processing," 1217-30.

[45]M. Mikulincer, "Adult Attachment Style and Affect Regulation: Strategic Variations in Self-Appraisals," *Journal of Personality and Social Psychology* 75, no. 2 (1998): 420-35.

[46]M. Mikulincer and D. Arad, "Attachment, Working Models, and Cognitive Openness in Close Relationships: A Test of Chronic and Temporary Accessibility Effects," *Journal of Personality and Social Psychology* 77 (1999): 710-25.

predominantly negative. They have greater accessibility to negative memories than to positive memories, so they are prone to ruminate on their distress. As we mentioned previously, this tends to activate other painful memories, causing a cascade of painful emotions that are all mixed together. This, in turn, makes it more difficult for preoccupied people to be aware of and respond to others' needs. Overall, they tend to be less empathic than people with more secure attachments.[47]

What does all this mean for preoccupied people's relationship with God? Just as with secure individuals, preoccupied attachment tendencies also operate in one's relationship with God. These individuals are prone to feel abandoned by God and to experience their relationship with God as unstable. For example, we found that preoccupied individuals experience less of a sense of connection to their spiritual community and more anxiety in their relationship with God than secure individuals.[48] In addition, preoccupied individuals view God as less loving than those with positive views of themselves.[49] They tend to engage in clingy, help-seeking forms of prayer, desperately seeking to hold on to a bond that feels very fragile.[50] The pain they experience in their relationship with God becomes part of the entire package of global emotional pain in their lives. If they touch on a painful nerve in one area of their life, it tends to spill over into some aspect of their relationship with God, and vice versa.

Preoccupied individuals will tend to use God and their spiritual community to help them regulate their emotions. This is normal and healthy within certain limits, but it can become rather extreme with preoccupied individuals and may sometimes be experienced as ineffective. In order to grow, they need help regulating their emotions. This is something that can be provided in a healthy spiritual community, but it does not occur without challenges. In Proctor's study, those with a preoccupied profile

---

[47]Daniela Troyer and Tobias Greitemeyer, "The Impact of Attachment Orientations on Empathy in Adults: Considering the Mediating Role of Emotion Regulation Strategies and Negative Affectivity," *Personality and Individual Differences* 122 (2018): 198-205.

[48]Hall et al., "Attachment to God and Implicit Spirituality," 227-42.

[49]Kirkpatrick, "God as a Substitute Attachment Figure," 961-73.

[50]K. R. Byrd and A. Boe, "The Correspondence Between Attachment Dimensions and Prayer in College Students," *The International Journal for the Psychology of Religion* 11, no. 1 (2001): 9-24.

showed indications of self-doubt and concerns about their value to God.[51] In short, individuals with a preoccupied attachment tend to experience a significant degree of anxiety in their relationship with God.

Dismissing attachment filter. In contrast to those with a secure attachment filter, people with a dismissing attachment filter expect others to *not* be available and responsive to them—to be consistently unavailable. They expect emotionally barren relationships with significant others and tend to be emotionally distant in their relationships.[52] As a result, their brains have developed a particular strategy for dealing with this: to deactivate or shut down their need for God and others. This leads to difficulty feeling connected to others, being aware of their own feelings, and attending to others' needs. Let's take a closer look at what research reveals about this attachment filter.

A dismissing attachment style often develops from relationships with caregivers who are emotionally unavailable and unresponsive to an infant's emotional and/or physical needs. For example, dismissing parents are not very attuned to their infants' emotions. In other words, they do not intuit or sense what their babies are feeling or experiencing. As a result, they communicate in ways that are not contingent with their infants' needs. The nonverbal communication in which their words are embedded do not match their infants' nonverbal communication. This causes their children to develop a disconnect between their emotional experience (implicit knowledge) and language (explicit knowledge). Thus, instead of the two knowledge systems working together seamlessly, the rational system (predominant in the left hemisphere) comes to dominate the infant-caregiver relationship. The explicit knowledge system then functions relatively independently as a subsystem in the brain, rather than exchanging information with the implicit knowledge system and emotional centers of the brain.[53] As these infants record these experiences in their implicit memory system, they tend not to express affection or emotional need. In contrast, they deactivate their need for others.

---

[51]Proctor, "God Attachment Interview Schedule."
[52]Green and Campbell, "Attachment and Exploration in Adults," 452-61.
[53]Siegel, *Developing Mind.*

As mentioned previously, it is not that dismissing individuals do not feel; rather, they tend to be relatively unaware of their feelings. As we discussed in chapter four, structures deep in our brainstem monitor and regulate visceral changes in our bodies, which we experience as emotions. In order for us to become aware of our emotion, the orbitofrontal cortex (OFC), which monitors such visceral changes, needs to send this information to the right lateral prefrontal cortex where it enters the "chalkboard of the mind" in working memory. It has been suggested that a dismissing state of mind with respect to attachment involves a reduction in input from the OFC to the lateral prefrontal cortex.[54] This impaired linkage also appears to be associated with general right-hemisphere impairments in understanding the gist, or context of things, and in picking up people's states of mind that are expressed through nonverbal channels.

Since they do not develop a sense of felt security from their caregivers, these individuals find an alternate way to comfort themselves, one that does not require a positive relational environment. By deactivating their need for others, their brains become wired to regulate their emotions by themselves.[55] In other words, these individuals distance themselves from the source of distress and the potentially frustrating attachment figure, and they cut off negative emotions and thoughts. Likewise, they incorporate a conscious image of themselves as strong, highly self-reliant, and above needing other people. They tend to view others who need people as weak. From one perspective, we can see this as a creative adaptation to feeling emotionally alone. However, this strategy backfires in terms of their ability to process emotions, function in relationships, and process information in general. In other words, this unconscious strategy comes at a high cost.

Unlike securely attached individuals, who can bring their painful emotions online and tolerate them with ease, and preoccupied individuals, who tend to experience a flood of painful emotions when one comes online, dismissing individuals keep themselves at arm's length

---

[54]Siegel, *Developing Mind*.
[55]Shaver and Mikulincer, "Attachment-Related Psychodynamics," 133-61.

from their internal emotional world by keeping all emotions at bay.[56] This is a "front end" (automatic) defensive strategy. For example, dismissing individuals have less accessibility to memories of sadness or anxiety than either secure or preoccupied individuals. Interestingly, the memories dismissing individuals do tend to recall are devoid of emotion. This is likely due to the fact that they are not very attentive to emotional information as mentioned above.[57] This leads to emotionally barren memories. In other words, dismissing individuals make a subconscious, implicit, preemptive strike against emotional experiences in close relationships by disconnecting emotional information from conscious awareness more than do preoccupied or securely attached individuals.

In addition to the frontal assault on emotions, dismissing individuals also use a "back end" defensive strategy. They tend to deny experiencing anger and yet show more intense physiological signs of anger and hostility. There is a major disconnect here, and this is precisely the cost of their attachment strategy. If you ask them about anger, they will tell you that other people around them are angry, but they are not.[58] This is what psychologists call "dissociated anger" or "overcontrolled hostility." Another way to say this is that dismissing people show a disconnect between their conscious claims and their unconscious dynamics. For example, they report low levels of death anxiety on self-report measures and yet show high levels of death anxiety on a method of assessing this that bypasses conscious awareness of their emotional life.[59]

This defensive style serves to keep people with dismissing attachment tendencies from being aware of emotions that are experienced as dangerous to their (fragile) sense of self. However, implicit indicators of these emotions are still there, such as physiological arousal. Because they are also unaware of this implicit information, it can severely dysregulate

---

[56]Mikulincer and Orbach, "Attachment Styles and Repressive Defensiveness," 917-25.

[57]R. C. Fraley, J. P. Garner, and P. R. Shaver, "Adult Attachment and the Defensive Regulation of Attention and Memory: Examining the Role of Preemptive and Postemptive Defensive Processes," *Journal of Personality and Social Psychology* 79 (2000): 816-26.

[58]M. Mikulincer, "Adult Attachment Style and Individual Differences in Functional Versus Dysfunctional Experiences of Anger," *Journal of Personality and Social Psychology* 74 (1998): 513-24.

[59]M. Mikulincer, V. Florian, and R. Tolmacz, "Attachment Styles and Fear of Personal Death: A Case Study of Affect Regulation," *Journal of Personality and Social Psychology* 58 (1990): 273-80.

them without them realizing why this is happening. This style also fosters a paranoid and hostile stance toward others, which maintains the negative cycle of emotionally distant relationships.

Consistent with dismissing individuals' avoidance of close relationships, they do not tend to disclose personal information to others.[60] As we would expect, dismissing individuals are less satisfied with their relationships than secure individuals.[61] We also know that dismissing individuals avoid conflict more than people with a secure attachment filter and show more stonewalling (cutting off communication) behavior in romantic relationships.[62]

Dismissing individuals' strategy for regulating their emotions—to deactivate them—also has a negative effect on their thinking. For example, situations that bring out positive feelings often lead to new ways of thinking about things—new ideas and novel approaches to solving problems. Dismissing people miss out on this information that comes along with positive emotions.[63] They also miss out on information in other areas. Dismissing people tend to avoid emotional distress by lacking curiosity, not looking for new information, and discounting the importance of new information that may create ambiguity.[64] Because they are not open to new information, dismissing individuals tend not to transform and update their implicit beliefs and expectations about themselves, others, and the world. This keeps them in a negative cycle.

Dismissing individuals' views of themselves are also distorted in ways that are congruent with their deactivating emotion regulation strategy. For example, they rate themselves as lower than secure and preoccupied

---

[60]Mikulincer and Nachshon, "Attachment Styles and Patterns of Self-Disclosure," 321-32.

[61]J. A. Simpson, "Influence of Attachment Style on Romantic Relationships," *Journal of Personality and Social Psychology* 59, no. 5 (1990): 971-80.

[62]M. C. Pistole and F. Arricale, "Understanding Attachment: Beliefs about Conflict," *Journal of Counseling & Development* 81, no. 3 (2003): 318-28; J. C. Babcock et al., "Attachment, Emotional Regulation, and the Function of Marital Violence: Differences Between Security, Preoccupied, and Dismissing Violent and Nonviolent Husbands," *Journal of Family Violence* 15 (2000): 391-409.

[63]M. Mikulincer and E. Sheffi, "Adult Attachment Style and Cognitive Reactions to Positive Affect: A Test of Mental Categorization and Creative Problem Solving," *Motivation and Emotion* 24 (2000): 149-74.

[64]Mikulincer, "Adult Attachment Style and Information Processing," 1217-30.

individuals in their similarity to others.[65] In addition, they under-estimate how similar they are to others, especially when they are distressed. They react to threatening situations by inflating their positive view of themselves and perceiving others as different and less capable than they are. Part of how they appear to achieve this psychological sleight of hand is by attributing negative aspects of themselves to others.[66] This serves two functions: (1) it increases their sense of self-confidence in the face of distress, and (2) it increases distance, thereby decreasing connection between themselves and others. In short, dismissing individuals maintain a conscious, albeit fragile view of themselves as self-reliant and capable, and they short circuit their emotional experience, keeping others at arm's length.

In telling their story on the AAI, dismissing individuals tend to lack a sense of coherence because they make statements they are not able to support. For example, they frequently report that their childhood was very positive but then have difficulty providing memories that support this. They also tend to insist that they cannot remember much, if anything, from their childhood. This fits with the idea that dismissing individuals deactivate their implicit knowledge of attachment-related information.

This same pattern tends to play out in their relationship with God. They may consciously acknowledge needing God, but they rarely actually rely on God in difficult times. When distressed, dismissing individuals generally continue self-reliant coping strategies, keeping God and their spiritual community on the periphery, while focusing on explicit knowledge about God. For example, we found that dismissing individuals experience less of a sense of belonging to a spiritual community than secure individuals.[67] Compared to secure individuals, they also have fewer spiritual friendships that focus on spiritual growth and encouragement. In addition, dismissive people are less likely to believe in

---

[65]M. Mikulincer and V. Florian, "The Relationship Between Adult Attachment Styles and Emotional and Cognitive Reactions to Stressful Events," in *Attachment Theory and Close Relationships*, ed. J. A. Simpson and W. S. Rholes (New York: Guilford Press, 1998).

[66]M. Mikulincer and N. Horesh, "Adult Attachment Style and the Perception of Others: The Role of Projective Mechanisms," *Journal of Personality and Social Psychology* 76 (1999): 1022-34.

[67]Hall et al., "Attachment to God and Implicit Spirituality," 227-42.

and have a relationship with what they view as a personal God.[68] In other words, since they believe that intimate attachments are undesirable or dangerous, they do not think an intimate relationship with God is a possibility. It just does not show up on their radar because they do not have the experiential hooks—positive attachment experiences—on which to hang the experience.

One noteworthy finding is that dismissing individuals sometimes respond to a disruption in an important relationship by increasing religious behaviors or involvement. This contradicts their normal strategy. It seems likely that they may initially react to such distress with their typical strategy of deactivating their felt need for closeness. However, if the stress gets too severe and too disorganizing, this may neutralize their normal coping mechanisms of short-circuiting painful emotions, leading to a flood of painful emotions. This in turn may drive them to God and their spiritual community for support and comfort. We know that the hyperactivation and deactivation strategies both serve the same function of regulating emotions, and it may be that each strategy serves as a backup for the other when it becomes overwhelmed by high levels of stress that push a person out of their normal pathways of coping.

We also get a fascinating window into dismissing individuals' relationship with God through studies that have looked at prayer through an attachment lens. Dismissing people tend to engage in types of prayer that minimize a sense of closeness to God.[69] In fact, when they become more distressed and need support more (even though they don't show it), they spend even less time in types of prayer that foster emotional connection with God. In short, while keeping God at arm's length emotionally, dismissing individuals tend to relate to God through their explicit knowledge.

Fearful attachment filter. Fearful attachment can be viewed as a combination of the preoccupied and dismissing attachment styles.[70] Like the

---

[68]Kirkpatrick, "God as a Substitute Attachment Figure," 961-73.
[69]Byrd and Boe, "The Correspondence Between Attachment Dimensions and Prayer in College Students," 9-24.
[70]K. Bartholomew, "Avoidance of Intimacy: An Attachment Perspective," *Journal of Social and Personal Relationships* 7 (1990): 147-78.

preoccupied attachment filter, people with a fearful attachment filter want to have close relationships and need a lot of comfort and reassurance from others. However, like people with a dismissing attachment filter, fearful individuals tend to avoid close relationships, even though they desire them. Fearful attachment seems to develop from caregivers who tend to be inconsistently available. In addition, these caregivers tend to express negative and frightening emotions either in front of or toward their children.[71]

As these repeated experiences are encoded in implicit memory, it is natural that these children develop an implicit view of others as uncaring, or outright rejecting and hostile, and a view of themselves as unworthy and unloveable. Unlike preoccupied individuals who view themselves as bad, but view others as a source of potential comfort and security, fearful individuals view others as bad and expect others to make them feel worse if they get close to them.[72] While fearful individuals' view of others is different from preoccupied, their view of themselves is different from dismissing individuals. Dismissing individuals have, at least superficially, a conscious view of themselves as positive and self-reliant, whereas fearful individuals have a low self-esteem and need a lot of comfort from others. This is a very painful combination of conflicting needs. In short, their need for reassurance pushes them toward attachment figures, but their gut-level expectation of rejection causes them to avoid seeking support from attachment figures.

We don't know as much about the fearful attachment filter as we do about the other three. However, in summary, we can speculate that the overlap with both preoccupied and dismissing attachment filters may lead to a pattern of processing emotions like that of preoccupied people but avoidant behavior like those with a dismissing attachment filter. For example, fearful individuals are likely to be biased toward experiencing negative memories and painful emotions that then cause a cascade of

---

[71]Bartholomew, "Avoidance of Intimacy," 147-78.

[72]D. Griffin and K. Bartholomew, "Models of the Self and Other: Fundamental Dimensions Underlying Measures of Adult Attachment," *Journal of Personality and Social Psychology* 67 (1994): 430-45.

undifferentiated painful emotions (similar to preoccupied people). Yet, they are not likely to disclose much to others, much like dismissing individuals. Likewise, instead of their distress driving them to clingy behavior in an attempt to secure comfort from an attachment figure, it causes them to withdraw because they expect others to reject them. Thus, they end up isolating themselves but at the same time experiencing the intense pain of feeling unloveable and constantly fearing rejection.

In their relationship with God, we would expect fearful individuals to show this same pattern of being highly prone to experience a lot of pain, such as abandonment. And yet fearful individuals are likely to also avoid close emotional contact with God. They generally do not bring their pain to God in prayer, for example. In addition, they tend to not reveal much in a spiritual community. Our attachment-to-God study mentioned previously supports this picture. We found that fearful individuals looked the same as dismissing participants on spiritual community and the same as preoccupied individuals in their attachment to God.[73] This suggests that they show a similar pattern of behavior as dismissing individuals in terms of how they engage in spiritual community—they stay on the outskirts of the community. Yet, they showed the same level of anxiety in their relationship with God as preoccupied individuals, both of which were higher than secure individuals. This suggests that their experience of pain and fear of rejection in their relationship with God is similar to that of those with preoccupied tendencies. In short, fearful people desire a close connection to God and a spiritual community, but their implicit or gut-level experience tells them that seeking connection leads to rejection, so they stay on the periphery of the community and keep God at arm's length.

A caveat about categories. Given the emphasis on attachment categories in the research literature, it is important to clarify that people do not easily fit into categories. Attachment categories are an oversimplification of our relational tendencies, but they are still helpful in capturing a very real and meaningful picture of how we manage our emotions with

---

[73]Hall et al., "Attachment to God and Implicit Spirituality," 227-42.

respect to emotionally significant people in our lives. In discussing attachment categories in the context of psychotherapy, David Wallin reminds us that as we get to know people better, "we often feel less clear about exactly who the patient is—or, at any rate, that clarity is no longer reducible to a single classification."[74] As we develop relationships over time, we hopefully gain clarity on the particulars of the person's story, but those particulars fit less and less well into a categorical box. Attachment categories are heuristic mechanisms that can be very helpful, but it is important that we not think of people as fitting neatly in a category.

We mentioned earlier that under severe stress, people's typical coping mechanisms within their dominant attachment state of mind may break down causing them to switch to a different insecure attachment approach. Furthermore, even when people are not under severe stress, they may manifest different attachment tendencies in different contexts. Most people have multiple attachment filters that are triggered by specific meanings. For example, a client of mine who seemed predominantly preoccupied in the early stages of therapy would sometimes shift into a dismissing state of mind after her feelings of rejection in a relationship reached a certain point. Presumably when the hyperactivation of her attachment system failed to result in some modicum of emotional attunement, even if intermittent, her attachment system switched to a deactivating strategy. Attachment categories can be helpful in understanding people's relational styles with close others and with God, as long as we keep in mind the particulars of each person's story.

Why Attachment Filters Are Stubborn

Jeffrey came to see me for therapy because he was struggling in his romantic relationships. His parents were quite distant and uninvolved, which led to an attachment filter that could be somewhat captured as "eventually, everyone will leave me." His attachment filters caused him to perceive women as not genuinely interested in him and to choose women who, in fact, were not that interested in him. In addition, he

---

[74]David Wallin, *Attachment in Psychotherapy* (New York: Guilford Press, 2007), 97.

would in turn respond by putting a wall up and subtly pushing women away until they eventually *did* leave. He also experienced God as very distant and struggled to maintain a sense of connection to God. Jeffrey's engrained patterns of relating and feeling, and the way he elicited rejection from others, made his attachment filter difficult to change.

There are several reasons why our attachment filters, like Jeffrey's, are resistant to change. First, our attachment filters are the only way we have to create a connection with others. Insofar as our attachment filters are insecure, they reflect strategies for adapting to less than ideal attachment relationships. These attachment filters were necessary when they originated in order to cope with and maximize a sense of relational connection with attachment figures. Jeffrey's attachment filter helped him cope with parents who abandoned him in different ways throughout his life. While our filters help us cope by adapting to the realities of our relational environment, they become entrenched in the pathways in our brain and soul. Repeated experiences with attachment figures become engrained in implicit memory through changes in the biochemical structure in the brain that make it more likely that the filter will be activated in the future.

As a result, we bring old adaptations to new situations and relational experiences with God and others because this is the only way we know how, at an implicit level, to connect with others. Furthermore, because we are prewired to connect, any kind of connection that is familiar, even if it is distorted and painful, gets tagged in our brains as being better than no connection at all. Thus, leaving our attachment filters behind can feel overwhelming and scary, and it is not an option under our conscious control because of the way our brains process implicit relational knowledge. The late psychoanalyst Stephen Mitchell contended that people cannot give up old, dysfunctional attachments until new, healthier attachments are formed to take their place.[75] Attachment filters are not something we opt into because we like our odds. Internal and external relations with others are, quite simply, part of the very fabric of what it means to be human.

---

[75]S. A. Mitchell, "Object Relations Theories and the Developmental Tilt," *Contemporary Psychoanalysis* 20, no. 4 (1984): 1-19.

Attachment theorist Mary Main's notion of "secondary felt security" provides a helpful angle on this concept.[76] Part of the reason insecure attachment filters are so stubborn is that, even though they are painful, they provide a sense of felt security in a strange, secondary kind of way. We are primarily motivated by human contact and connection—*even if it is painful contact*. The painful connection of an insecure attachment filter provides some form of security because it is emotionally familiar territory, and it is a territory of connection. Secondary felt security is better than no security at all.

Second, our attachment filters operate in such a way that they are *self-reinforcing*. As we just mentioned, our attachment filters are engrained pathways in our brains, so we are prone to process our relational experiences through these pathways. When this happens, it affects what we *perceive* from others in our relationships in such a way that we end up playing a role in reinforcing our own filters, as we saw was the case with Jeffrey. For example, depressed people have a decreased ability to detect facial emotion, and brain imaging studies show that depressed people have less blood flow in the right hemisphere where facially expressed emotion is processed.[77] Even if someone is supportive, depression will cause people to struggle to sense this at an implicit level, and so they become unable to use the facial expressions of others to help them feel better and change their filters. This further intensifies the person's depressed state and attachment filter, which may include a sense of themselves as worthless and a deep view of others as unloving.

Attachment filters not only affect our relational perceptions—how we interpret experiences at an automatic gut level—they also influence how other people relate to us. We respond to others based on the way our experiences are processed through our attachment filters. For example, the depressed person who does not pick up on contingent, supportive emotions on a friend's face then enters a state of mind of self as worthless

---

[76]Mary Main, "Metacognitive Knowledge, Metacognitive Monitoring, and Singular (Coherent) vs. Multiple (Incoherent) Models of Attachment: Findings and Directions for Future Research," in *Attachment Across the Lifecycle*, ed. P. Harris, J. Stevenson-Hinde, and C. Parkes (New York: Routledge, 1991), 127-59.

[77]Siegel, *Developing Mind*.

and others as unloving. This in turn may cause the person to either lash out in anger or withdraw. As you can imagine, when the friend tries to reach out and be supportive, and gets either a seemingly out-of-the-blue outburst of anger or withdrawal in response, it does not foster further relational connection.

In fact, it fosters just the opposite. The friend is likely to now respond to her depressed friend out of anger or by pulling away. This creates a negative cycle that reinforces the depressed person's attachment filters. She feels that, once again, people are not there for her. In short, when it comes to the negative aspects of our attachment filters, we all work against our own growth and healing because we are trying to connect in the only way we know how. This is not a conscious choice we are making; it is the only way we know how to connect. As we will see, we are dependent on God and others to *show us* a different way of connecting that is more healthy and loving. We can see, then, how these relational cycles play out over and over in our lives and are resistant to change.

Conclusion

We remember how important people in our lives feel about us in our emotions, bodies, and images—in an implicit type of memory and knowledge. Furthermore, memories of relational experiences with emotionally significant people are etched in our souls and become filters that shape how we feel about ourselves, God, and others, and how we determine the meaning of events in our lives. Attachment filters have broad implications for our daily lives. Because of the centrality of relationships in our lives, relational deficits have pervasive effects. A recent statistical summary of a large number of studies on attachment documented the negative effects of insecure attachment, not only on our ability to relate well to others but also on mental health and well-being,[78] and even on physical health.[79]

---

[78]Ashley M. Groh et al., "Attachment in the Early Life Course: Meta-Analytic Evidence for Its Role in Socioemotional Development," *Child Development Perspectives* 11 (2017): 70-76.

[79]Tara Kidd, "The Psychobiology of Attachment and the Aetiology of Disease," in *Improving Patient Treatment with Attachment Theory: A Guide for Primary Care Practitioners and Specialists* (Cham, Switzerland: Springer International Publishing, 2016), 157-76.

It should be no surprise, then, that attachment filters are related to our spiritual well-being. We bring our distorted relational filters into our relationships with God and spiritual communities. One study found that attachment to God was related to moral decision making.[80] In fact, this study found that attachment to God predicted moral decision making even after statistically accounting for adult attachment in general. Another study found that attachment to God predicted awareness of God, spiritual meaning, and forgiveness.[81] The emerging evidence is that insecure attachment hinders, and secure attachment fosters, our capacity to fulfill the greatest commandments of loving God and loving others.

The picture painted by research on attachment may appear bleak, as our insecure attachment tendencies, left on their own, perpetuate and reinforce negative relational cycles. Yet throughout this chapter we have hinted at the possibility of growth and maturation in our capacity for love. In the next two chapters we turn to the topic of loving presence as the goal of spiritual development. With a deeper understanding of the goal for which we are striving, we will then turn in chapter eight to the topic of how we change and grow from a relational perspective.

---

[80]David M. Njus and Katrina Okerstrom, "Anxious and Avoidant Attachment to God Predict Moral Foundations Beyond Adult Attachment," *Journal of Psychology and Theology* 44 (2016): 230-43.

[81]Brian D. Augustyn et al., "Relational Spirituality: An Attachment-Based Model of Spiritual Development and Psychological Well-Being," *Psychology of Religion and Spirituality* 9 (2017): 197-208.

The Nature of Loving Presence

Goodwill and Connection

LOVE IS CENTRAL to the Christian life and to spiritual growth. When asked what was the greatest, or first commandment, Jesus stated, "'Love the Lord your God with all your heart and with all your soul and with all your mind.' This is the first and greatest commandment. And the second is like it: 'Love your neighbor as yourself'" (Matthew 22:37-39 NIV). The same story is recounted in the gospel accounts of Matthew, Mark, and Luke, highlighting its importance. The command to love could not be clearer. But attempts to obey this command become very complex, very quickly. What does it mean to love? What is love? What is the source of love? Who should we love? How much should we love? We all have a felt sense of what love is, but the concept becomes remarkably elusive when attempts are made to define it and inhabit it in our lives.

In the preceding chapters, we laid the foundation for the notion that we are created to connect. We first argued that as human beings made in the image of God we are beings-in-relation. Love is the most centrally defining characteristic of God and is manifest in God's trinitarian nature and relations. We image God through our capacity for love and through our loving relationships with God and others. As we discussed previously, the being-in-relation model involves three organizing principles: the relational *nature* of human beings, the relational *goal* of loving presence, and the relational *process* of sanctification.

In the last few chapters, we fleshed out the idea of our relational *nature*. We introduced the two ways of knowing and emphasized the importance of implicit relational knowledge for spiritual growth. We then talked about how attachment filters shape our capacity to love. In this chapter and the next, we extend the implications of being created to connect (our relational nature) to the relational *goal* of spiritual growth, suggesting that *loving presence* is the ultimate goal of sanctification. In this chapter focused on the nature of love, we will discuss the centrality of love in the Trinity and sanctification, the relational core of love, and conclude with the two essential components of love. In the next chapter, we continue our discussion of love by focusing on the art of love.

The Centrality of Love in the Trinity and Sanctification

It seems clear that, as beings who image God, loving presence is the goal of spiritual development. In other words, the goal of the developmental process of being conformed to the image of God is to grow in our love for God and others. Jesus' love command is the foundation for Christian ethics, "the central ethical concept in the New Testament."[1] In commanding us to love God and others, Jesus drew on commands articulated in the Old Testament (see Deuteronomy 6:4-5; Leviticus 19:18). The centrality of love was further developed throughout the New Testament in the writings of James, John, and Paul. Galatians 5:14 elevates love to the highest place in the ethical life: "The entire law is fulfilled in keeping this one command: 'Love your neighbor as yourself'" (NIV). First Corinthians 13:13 places love above faith and hope. Colossians 3 urges the development of a host of virtues, but "above all," love, "which binds everything together in perfect harmony" (Colossians 3:14 NRSV). First John 4:7-8 situates love at the very center of God's nature and activity, and draws out the implications for us: we should respond to God and others by expressing love. If we do not love, we do not know God. It is clear, then, that we must love.

---

[1] Alexander Pruss, *One Body: An Essay in Christian Sexual Ethics* (Notre Dame, IN: Notre Dame Press, 2013), 8.

The elusive concept of love became concrete in the person of Jesus. As noted in chapter two, Jesus is the image of the invisible God; he demonstrates for us what it looks like to perfectly reflect God's image. Jesus called his disciples to love God and others, and lived a life that demonstrated God's love to the full. His love was, indeed, an extension of the mutual love among the three persons of the Trinity. Consequently, in pursuing the end goal of renewing the image of God in us, we seek to become more Christlike, which is to say more loving.

Sanctification has a direction or goal. This goal is love, and this love is demonstrated by Christ. Given the profoundly trinitarian nature of Christ's love, we need to unpack the love between the Father and the Son, and by extension the love among all three members of the Trinity, as the multifaceted foundation for the love that believers are called to have for God and neighbor. From this foundation we will see the unique characteristics of Christian love for which human beings were originally intended. We will later draw out the implicit elements in the mutual love between the members of the Trinity in proposing a model of love that is comprised of two core characteristics.

The love between the Father and Son as the foundation for Christian love. The love believers are to have for one another is intimately tied to God's trinitarian love and our participation in that love. More specifically, it is uniquely reflected in the love between Jesus and the Father, and by extension the love among all three members of the Trinity. We see a particularly focused expression of this in the Upper Room Discourse (John 13–16) and the High Priestly Prayer (John 17).[2] On the evening before his crucifixion, Jesus instituted with his disciples the practice we refer to as the Lord's Supper, or Communion. In so doing, he also provided a representation of a future deliverance he would bring about through his death and resurrection. During the Passover celebration, Jesus provided an example of the love they are to have for each other. In an act of profound humility, Jesus washed the disciples' feet. He then said to the disciples:

---

[2]We draw here from the work of Donald Fairbairn. See Donald Fairbairn, *Life in the Trinity: An Introduction to Theology with the Help of the Church Fathers* (Downers Grove, IL: IVP Academic, 2008), chap. 2.

> Now the Son of Man is glorified and God is glorified in him. If God is glorified
> in him, God will glorify the Son in himself, and will glorify him at once. . . .
> A new command I give you: Love one another. As I have loved you, so you
> must love one another. By this everyone will know that you are my disciples,
> if you love one another. (John 13:31-35 NIV)

This passage is pregnant with deep meaning about God's love as the foundation for our love.

Our love for one another is intimately connected to Christ's love for us, as we see in John 13:34-35, and implied in the first part of the passage about Jesus being glorified through his impending death. We can think about this link in three ways: the reason for our love, the model for our love, and the source of our love. At a very basic level, it seems reasonable to assume that Jesus means here that we should love God and others *because* he loved us. His love is the reason for our love, or the foundational motivation. Elsewhere, we read: "We love each other because he loved us first" (1 John 4:19). God's love fuels our love out of gratitude.

Second, we may wonder if Jesus means that we should love each other the *way* he has loved us. Jesus has just washed the disciples' feet—an act of utterly humble love. The disciples would have never expected Jesus, their master and teacher, to wash their feet. It seems that Jesus is providing a model for how we should love others. He did this on the eve of his crucifixion, knowing what was to come. This demonstration of love may have been meant to foreshadow the very essence of love, which was the cross. Thus, the model Jesus is providing for how we should love may be more profound than that of washing the disciples' feet. After this demonstration, he speaks the words quoted above in John 13:31-35 where he talks of being glorified in connection with his impending death. What exactly is the connection here between his glory and his death? Moreover, what does this say about how we should love?

Glory refers to God's greatness and consequent worthiness to be praised, but it also refers to God's presence with his people.[3] In the New

---

[3]For the first meaning, the Hebrew term *kabod* ("glory" and translated as *doxa* in the LXX) derives from a word meaning "to be heavy." Its primary meaning came to be the esteem or honor belonging to a person. In the New Testament, the term took on the meaning "divine and heavenly radi-

Testament, God's presence is made known directly in the second person of the Trinity—the Word—who is the exact image or likeness of God (2 Corinthians 4:4). In explaining the incarnation, John says, "We have seen his glory, the glory of the one and only Son, who came from the Father, full of grace and truth" (John 1:14 NIV). The glory of Jesus, then, is the presence of the Father in and through him. Donald Fairbairn captures this well: "When we see the incarnate Word, we see something of the unique presence of God with him, something of his unique relationship with God the Father."[4]

Yet, we are still left wondering why Jesus talks about his glory, or the presence of his Father with him, in association with his imminent death. Fairbairn suggests that "the impending death of Jesus is the supreme way in which God is present with us."[5] Paul states that Christ's death is a demonstration of God's love for us (Romans 5:8). Thus, we can suggest here that Jesus' death is also the supreme way in which God has loved us. God's glory, then, is both his presence *and* his love. What, then, does this mean for our love?

God went to great lengths to promote our highest good: God's relational presence with us.[6] He sacrificed his only begotten Son in order to remove the barrier of sin and enable us to be restored to relationship with him. We cannot atone for others' sin as Jesus did, and love does not always require the sacrifice of one's life. However, the unimaginable lengths God went to in his supreme act of love for us suggests two things

---

ance." Stanley J. Grenz, *The Social God and the Relational Self: A Trinitarian Theology of the Imago Dei* (London: Westminster John Knox Press, 2001), 205-6. The second meaning is evident in the Old Testament, where the pillar of cloud and pillar of fire were visible symbols of God's presence with the people of Israel (Exodus 13:20-22). After they wandered in the wilderness and grumbled against God, God's presence, signified in a cloud, was shown to the Israelites and specifically referred to as "the glory of the LORD" (Exodus 16:10). Glory and presence are connected to the incarnation in the New Testament. Fairbairn, *Life in the Trinity*, 19.

[4]Fairbairn, *Life in the Trinity*, 134.

[5]Fairbairn, *Life in the Trinity*, 19.

[6]Duvall and Hays argue that God's relational presence is the central theme of the entire biblical narrative. In other words, the purpose of God's activity throughout salvation history, from the Tabernacle in the Old Testament through God's singular presence in the person of Jesus, is for God to be present with his people. It can be suggested from this that God's relational presence is our highest good and the essence of love. J. Scott Duvall and J. Daniel Hays, *God's Relational Presence: The Cohesive Center of Biblical Theology* (Grand Rapids, MI: Baker Academic, 2019).

for the way we ought to love. First, we should promote others' well-being and always help people move toward their highest good: relationship with God. Second, we too should go to great lengths in our love for our neighbors and fellow believers when such lengths are required. We should humbly serve others, regardless of status, as Jesus demonstrated in washing the disciples' feet. We should be willing to sacrifice and love others with the intensity and purity that characterized God's supreme act of love for us, always willing to go to great lengths.

Third, Jesus' love for us, and the love between the Father and Son, is the *source* of our love. Jesus' love for others was and is an extension of the *very* mutual love he experienced with the Father. It is a sharing in that love. We see this in Jesus' words to his disciples in John 15:9: "As the Father has loved me, so I have loved you; abide in my love" (NRSV). Jesus mediated the Father's presence and love to us. In John 17, Jesus says to the Father, "You . . . have loved them even as you have loved me." He continues, "I made your name known to them, and I will make it known, so that the love with which you have loved me may be in them, and I in them" (John 17:23, 26 NRSV). Likewise, part of what it means for us to love as Jesus loved us is that we extend the *very* love of Christ to others through the Spirit. We express not just our own love to others but the exact love and presence of God in which we participate. We mediate God's love, just as Jesus did.

Finally, we would note here that our love being intimately connected to Christ's love is also inherently linked to how the world will know that we are followers of Christ. In the latter part of the John 13 passage noted above, Jesus says, "By this everyone will know that you are my disciples, if you love one another" (John 13:35 NIV). Our love for one another is supposed to function as a mirror, reflecting Christ's love for us. When the world sees the way we treat one another, it should make them think of how Jesus lived and loved. This is not just any love, nor is it merely a superficial love defined by our culture. This love that we inhabit, indwell, and pass on to others is specifically tied to the person of Jesus Christ, the Word, the only begotten Son, the second person of the Trinity.

Given the centrality of love in the Trinity, then, let us take a step back and consider what this means for us. While we have laid out the contours for how our love is intimately connected to Christ's, there is still much to be clarified. We have noted that the foundational reason for our love is that God in Christ first loved us. But when we turn to our own lives, we find it filled with people, some close, some far away, some in particular kinds of relationships to us, some with little or no relationship to us. Not being God, what does Christ's love in and through us look like? Who should we love, and why?

The basis for neighbor love. Since every person is made in the image of God, every person reflects God's goodness and is thus the proper object of love.[7] No one, then, is outside the scope of our call to love. The implications of this are that we do not fulfill the love command by loving a specific person because of good qualities that he or she may have. Nor do we fulfill it by only loving those who have a particular relational connection to us, such as a child. The basis for our choice to love any given person is that he or she, like us, is created in God's image to be in relationship with God and is loved by God. This is an unchanging quality of each person, regardless of how much the image of God has been actualized or renewed in that person. As C. S. Lewis so eloquently put it, "There are no *ordinary* people. You have never talked to a mere mortal. . . . It is immortals whom we joke with, work with, marry, snub, and exploit. . . . Our charity must be real and costly love, with deep feeling for the sins in spite of which we love the sinner—no mere tolerance or indulgence which parodies love as flippancy parodies merriment."[8]

In thinking about the reasons we love, it is helpful to differentiate between the *moral* reasons to love (because God loved us and created us in God's image to be in relationship with God) and the *psychological* reasons for loving another. These are distinct but related reasons. In fact, a variety of psychological motivations may be invoked in loving others. After all, if we are created in God's image with the capacity to love God and others,

---

[7]Eleonore Stump, *Wandering in Darkness: Narrative and the Problem of Suffering* (Oxford: Oxford University Press, 2010), 91.
[8]C. S. Lewis, *The Weight of Glory* (San Francisco: HarperCollins, 1949), 9.

it stands to reason that we do, in fact, have psychological capacities that allow us to do this well. Furthermore, these psychological reasons for love also vary according to our relationship with the loved one.

How are the moral and psychological reasons for love related? The moral reason for loving others—because God loved us and created us in God's image to be in relationship with God—should cause us to desire to love others. In other words, in order to love, we have to internalize the moral motive so that it becomes a psychological desire, causing us to engage in love in alignment with our will. We have then moved from a moral motivation to a psychological motivation or grounding for our love (i.e., desiring). At this point, our love for the other may have little to do with the particulars of that person (i.e., characteristics that are loveable), and everything to do with the more general characteristic of being made in God's image. Even when someone is quite unloveable in the ordinary sense of the word, we can still love that person through an exercise of our will. Similarly, when we are not in ongoing personal relationship with another, we can still love that person from an exercise of the will. We might call this the volitional account of love. For certain people we love, this may be the extent of the psychological motivations that are employed in loving.

However, should we sustain a loving presence with another person over time, the psychological mechanism for love in the form of the capacity for connectedness and attachment can be invoked. These are the mechanisms we have spent time exploring over the course of this book. Over time, we become connected through an "ongoing pattern of concern," as Niko Kolodny calls it.[9] In this case, the psychological motivation for loving the other is the relationship itself, and this is deeper than a volitional decision to love the other. For example, one of the reasons Liz and I love each other is our connection that has persisted over time and all of the interactions between us. We might call this the relational account of love. The relationship itself is the reason for our love. For many people in our life, this is the primary psychological

---

[9]Niko Kolodny, "Love as Valuing a Relationship," *Philosophical Review* 112 (2003): 149.

grounding for love. We might argue that, psychologically, these are motivational reasons that should come into play in the context of our close
relationships with others in our spiritual community.

We expect that our spouse or our children would find both volitional
and relational accounts of our love for them disappointing. It would not
be enough that we love them because we choose to love them as people
made in the image of God, nor that we love them because we have given
birth to them and raised them (in the case of our children). They would
also want us to love them in response to loveable qualities in them. There
are, in fact, specific things about each other and each of our sons that we
find loveable and, in response, love. We can call this the responsive account of love. There are probably a handful of relationships in our lives
in which we engage in love in this way.

Ultimately, the responsive, relational, and volitional accounts of love
fall short in accounting for the kind of love we are commanded to have
for all. There is nothing wrong with invoking these additional psychological motivations in love, and in fact, it seems right that these motivations should characterize our relationships, depending on the kind of
relationship. However, the most foundational grounding for love, and the
most universal, is the moral account of being loved by God and made in
such a way that we image God through relationship with God and others.

We commit to persevering in love because of this moral grounding of
love, but once we engage in responsively loving that person, the psychological mechanisms for connection are evoked and aid us in that task. As
we internalize the moral obligation to love others, we inhabit it on a
motivational, emotional, and even biological level. We are designed for
loving others. This is, in fact, the way that the developmental nature of
spiritual transformation manifests itself: the easier we find it to whole-
heartedly follow the love command, the more we reflect God's way of
loving others.

The Relational Core of Love: One Agapē, Many Forms

It seems clear that we have a moral obligation to love; love is the goal of
our spiritual development. But what is love? At the popular level, C. S.

Lewis famously wrote about the "four loves" present in Scripture—*philia, agapē, eros*, and *storgē*, corresponding to friendship love, divine love, romantic love, and parental or attachment love. On a more academic level, Anders Nygren similarly made a distinction between *agapē* as a selfless kind of love and other, more possessive kinds of love, such as *eros*.[10] These distinctions, and the characterization of *agapē* love as a divine, sacrificial form of love different from other kinds of love, have been widely adopted in the evangelical world. In the ancient Greek context, *agapē* connoted a love that was more deliberate and committed than the whims of our mood. Hence, Stanley Grenz notes that Jesus' free sacrifice of his life for sinful humankind "led the biblical writers to the previously obscure Greek word *agape* as the term that could best express the self-giving disposition of the God of the salvation story."[11] Upon closer inspection, however, these distinctions are not as clear as they seem. We need to take a deeper look at the way these various terms are used in Scripture in order to develop a more nuanced approach to love.

As we explore this terrain, it becomes quickly apparent that these various Greek words translated "love" do not seem to be used in the New Testament in ways that consistently differentiate between different kinds of love. While *agapē* and its derivatives are the most common way *love* is used in the New Testament, Alexander Pruss notes that *agapē* and *philia* are used in largely interchangeable ways that do not clearly mark a difference in meaning.[12] Furthermore, *agapē* is used biblically across a wide variety of situations. For example, some cases occur in a context where the typical understanding of *eros* would seem more appropriate (such as in the Septuagint Greek translation of Song of Songs; see Song of Songs 2:5), and in other cases a malformed love is in view (as when Jesus rebukes the Pharisees for loving the best seats in the synagogue; see Luke 11:43). This leads Pruss to conclude that *agapē* does not refer to a particular kind of love, but to love itself.[13]

---

[10]Anders Nygren, *Agape and Eros* (Chicago: University of Chicago Press, 1982).

[11]Stanley J. Grenz, *The Social God and the Relational Self: A Trinitarian Theology of the Imago Dei* (Louisville, KY: Westminster John Knox, 2001), 314.

[12]Pruss, *One Body*, 8.

[13]Pruss, *One Body*, 12-13.

The distinct types of love articulated by Lewis and Nygren also do not represent the full spectrum of love. The Greeks, for example, did not stop with four loves. They distinguished between eight different kinds of love.[14] Consequently, rather than taking a "four loves" approach to defining love, we follow Pruss in contending that "every form of love is *agape*," and that romantic, filial-attachment, and friendship loves are all forms of *agapē*.[15]

Toward a prototype of love. What, then, is *agapē* love? Before highlighting the definitional components of love, we want to suggest a refinement to the idea above that there are not four (or more) qualitatively different kinds of love, but rather one love that takes many different forms. While we hold this to be the case, we would suggest that parent-child love, what the Greeks called *storgē*, and what we might call attachment love, serves as a prototype for God's love for us and the love we should have for others. C. S. Lewis described *storgē* as "'affection especially of parents to offspring'; but also of offspring to parents."[16] This love is founded in a secure attachment bond. In fact, Mary Ainsworth, one of the cofounders of attachment theory, stated that "attachment is a synonym for love."[17] Lewis highlights the two correlative sides of attachment love: caregiving, which he also called "gift-love," and care receiving, which he referred to as "need-love."[18] God's love for us clearly seems to reflect the caregiving side of attachment, or gift-love, while our love for God generally takes the form of need-love. However, our love for other people reflects both sides of attachment at different times. We see evidence of this prototype in Scripture, the Christian tradition, and our experience.

Jesus compares God's love to the love of parents for their children: "If you sinful people know how to give good gifts to your children, how much more will your heavenly Father give good gifts to those who ask

---

[14]Stephen Post, *Unlimited Love* (West Conshohocken, PA: Templeton Press, 2003).

[15]Pruss, *One Body*, 12-13.

[16]C. S. Lewis, *The Four Loves* (New York: Harcourt, 1960), 31.

[17]Mary Ainsworth, "Object Relations, Dependency, and Attachment: A Theoretical Review of the Infant-Mother Relationship," *Child Development* 40 (1969): 969-1025, 1008, https://dx.doi.org/10.2307/1127008.

[18]Lewis, *Four Loves*, 1.

him" (Matthew 7:11). Jesus also referred to the paternal qualities of God, which we see in the Lord's Prayer (Luke 11:2-4), and to the maternal qualities of God, such as when he compares God's love to that of a hen gathering her brood (Luke 13:34; Matthew 23:37). He describes the kingdom of heaven as being like "a king who prepared a great wedding feast for his son" (Matthew 22:2). The parable of the prodigal son depicts God's love as the mercy, tenderness, and forgiveness of a parent. Jesus sees a picture of God's love in the parental heart.

In this vein, Stephen Post argues that the foundational emotional capacities for what he calls "unlimited love" are found in the parent-child relationship.[19] We know from our experience that parental love, at its best, is the most pervasive, constant, and purest expression of love, suggesting that it provides a model of the divine love of the Trinity, which we are designed to inhabit and extend. As we noted, this *agapē* love as the New Testament writers called it has its roots in parental love, or what the Greeks called *storgē*.[20]

The caregiving side of *storgē* provides protection and emotional security for children when they feel sad, alone, or generally distressed. Attachment love, or *storgē*, champions the child's growth, encouraging him or her to explore the world and become his or her true self. Parental love also celebrates the child's accomplishments and his or her unique personhood. Above all, a parent's love is personal and intimate, as it is responsive to the unique personality and needs of the child. Parental love, at its best, always seeks the best interest of the child. It cultivates an affectionate stance toward the child and actively responds to his or her needs.

Moreover, attachment love is steadfast even when the child is unloveable. The Hebrew term *hesed* can be translated as "steadfast love" and is most often illustrated in the Old Testament by the intimate love a parent has for his or her child. We see in this Hebrew concept of love a deep commitment that remains faithful despite the child being difficult to love. This is what an attachment bond does. It creates a disposition in

---

[19]Post, *Unlimited Love*, 104.
[20]Post, *Unlimited Love*, 106.

the parent whereby the parent loves the child for no other reason than the bond they share. This love is not founded on the child being likable, loveable, cooperative, or reciprocating. Rather, this love is willing to sacrifice at a moment's notice if that is what is necessary—whether the reason is due to the child's "unloveableness" or needs that require practical or emotional sacrifice.

We often hear parents say that if they could, they would take on some pain of the child so the child would not have to experience it. Many have experienced this. I think of various emotional struggles and injuries my two sons have endured. Whether it was the pain of a broken leg, or feeling emotionally alienated, if Liz and I could have taken these pains on for them, we would have. This parental impulse brings to mind God's greatest act of love for us: Jesus paying the penalty for our sins so we don't have to do so. We resonate with Post's conclusion in searching for a prototype for love: "In the final analysis, parental love is reasonably close to being paradigmatic for *agape*, as long as it respects the freedom and maturity of the other."[21] Given parental-attachment love as a prototype, how, then, might we further define love in its basic elements? We turn to this in the next section, but first we address two clarifications regarding emotion and sacrifice.

Two clarifications: the roles of emotion and sacrifice in love. Before turning to an elaboration of two essential components of love, two clarifications are in order. First, the issue of the role of emotion in our understanding of love should be addressed. Post's definition includes the idea that love is "affective"—it has an emotional component.[22] Other authors would strongly disagree. Pruss, for example, states that "*agape* cannot indicate a loving feeling or emotion," and denies even that it might be a disposition or tendency to feel an emotion.[23] In support of his position, he argues that we are commanded to love, but that we cannot control our emotions. He further notes that feelings are transitory and that feelings are not as intimately tied to action as is the will.

---

[21]Post, *Unlimited Love*, 112.
[22]Post, *Unlimited Love*, 19.
[23]Pruss, *One Body*, 9.

The problem with Pruss's position is that it ignores biblical evidence that a kind of emotion is, in fact, in view. Peter tells his readers to "love one another deeply, from the heart" (1 Peter 1:22 NIV). The use of *agapē* in Song of Songs is clearly referring to an emotion. In fact, stripping love of its emotional character takes away from the ordinary meaning of the word and results in a very strange reading of most passages where love is mentioned.

The desire to understand love as something other than an emotion is perhaps a reaction to contemporary societal tendencies to reduce love to merely a subjective feeling. This is clearly also not what we have in mind, as we would suggest (and elaborate on below) that love implies desiring and acting toward the good of the other, which includes motivational, attitudinal, and behavioral aspects. Building on our discussion in chapter four on relational knowledge, in full-orbed love, emotion is the physiological and psychological motive behind the behavioral expression. It carries with it loving-action tendencies. The action tendencies are an intrinsic part of the emotion. Emotion cannot be separated from love, and love never exists without emotion. This conceptualization does not require that the subjective experience of emotion be consistently present. As we noted, emotion is a more complex phenomenon than the subjective experience of it. Emotion is the automatic way we evaluate the meaning of events with respect to our well-being. Considered in this way, the emotional nature of love fits well with the framework we have developed in previous chapters, in which emotion is the foundation for implicit relational knowledge, which we draw on in being with others.

Pruss's objection that the command nature of love is incompatible with its emotional nature appears to be problematic as well. Many of God's commands are impossible to obey through sheer exercise of the will. For example, in the Sermon on the Mount Jesus tells his disciples, "Be perfect, therefore, as your heavenly Father is perfect" (Matthew 5:48 NIV). Fortunately, as persons made in the image of God, we are designed with the capacity for emotional, volitional, attitudinal, and behavioral love—distorted as that image might be. As we collaborate with the Holy Spirit in spiritual formation, the affective part of love comes into play, and we find that we can, in fact, obey the love command increasingly over time.

The second issue to be clarified is whether self-sacrifice is an integral part of the definition of *agapē* love. As noted earlier, Lewis and Nygren's characterization of *agapē* as a form of love distinct from other kinds of love has resulted in a view of *agapē* as a special kind of divine love, clearly differentiated from other kinds of more "human" love by its sacrificial nature. Furthermore, these authors suggest that *agapē* is not a mutual kind of love. According to this view, if we benefit from a loving relationship, and if it is not costly to us, it is not *agapē*.

The core of love certainly is giving of the self for the good of the other. Sacrifice, as Stephen Post notes, is sometimes required.[24] However, if we consider *agapē* to be love, and if we consider the other "kinds" of love not as qualitatively distinct types of love but simply different expressions of love, then conceptualizing *agapē* as always nonmutual and sacrificial becomes problematic.

The mistaken notion of *agapē* as always being selfless and sacrificial can be addressed on both theological and philosophical grounds. Theologically, Pruss notes that God's sanctifying gift of love is precisely the ability to reciprocate that love. Because of God's love for us, we can love God in return. God's love is intended to be mutual; it aims at that mutuality. Similarly, the grounding of love in the Trinity demonstrates that sacrifice and lack of mutuality are not defining characteristics of love. As evidenced in the love between the persons of the Trinity, love is essentially reciprocal and does not require sacrifice.[25]

Similarly, from a philosophical perspective, desiring the good of others in love will ultimately include the desire that the loved one be transformed into the image of God, able to reciprocate in love.[26] When we see ourselves as above needing the love of others, our love runs the

---

[24]Post, *Unlimited Love.*
[25]Pruss, *One Body*, 13.
[26]Thomas Jay Oord has argued, likewise, that there are numerous problems with equating *agapē* with self-sacrifice and selfless altruism. Thomas Jay Oord, *Defining Love* (Grand Rapids, MI: Brazos Press, 2010).

risk of becoming paternalistic, condescending, and prideful. Pruss concludes that far from being alien to *agapē*, reciprocation is crucial to it.[27]

While love does not always require self-sacrifice and may not be the core or essence of love, Jesus does emphasize sacrifice as the highest form of love in the Sermon on the Mount. He asks: "If you love only those who love you, what reward is there for that?" (Matthew 5:46). He calls us to go beyond that and to love our enemy. We find ourselves sometimes needing to love people who are our enemy or who are unloveable—a form of love that C. S. Lewis defined as charity. However, sacrifice is not a defining essence of love in general, or even of what we may think of as a distinctly Christian love. We will return to the idea of loving Christianly in the next chapter. We turn now to the two essential components of love.

The Two Essential Components of Love: Goodwill and Connection

We propose here that love consists of two components: desiring the good of the other and desiring union or connection with the other.[28] These are drawn from Aquinas's theory of love.[29] Pruss adds appreciation as a separate component, which we will consider as a facet of connection or union.[30]

While not an exact modeling, these two components are also implicated in the concept of perichōrēsis used by Greek church fathers to capture the divine love among the Trinity. Recall that perichōrēsis pictures each member of the Trinity as dwelling in the other two while maintaining individuality. This indwelling clearly suggests a deep union among all three members of the Trinity. This deep union, in turn, is the highest good each member of the Trinity desires for the other two. In the complex ways each member of the Trinity carries out a particular role in salvation history, their union entails appreciating and celebrating the

---

[27]Pruss, *One Body*, 14.

[28]Pruss, *One Body*, 23-27.

[29]Stump, *Wandering in Darkness*, 91.

[30]Pruss, *One Body*, 24.

other two persons of the Trinity. We turn now to further exploration of these two components of love.

Desiring good for the other. Nicholas Wolterstorff notes that among the diverse usages of the word *love*, one of the most prominent meanings is that of seeking to promote the well-being or good of another person not merely as a means to an end, but as an end in itself.[31] Similarly, Post's definition centers on affirming and delighting in the *well-being* of others.[32] What is in view here is not a hedonic view of happiness or well-being, but rather something closer to the Eudaimonic view of happiness. There are several different terms used to capture this component of love, including well-being, the good, goodwill, flourishing, and what we might call health of the soul. Whatever term we use, love is intrinsically about desiring and working toward what is objectively good for the other, according to God's design of human nature. The desire for the well-being of others is common to love in all kinds of relationships—friendships, romantic relationships, parent-child relationships, love of neighbor, and even love of enemy. Goodwill, as the name implies, involves desiring good or well-being for the other and acting on that desire to do good for the other in some way. This is the part of desiring the good that results in action. In desiring the good of others, we ultimately desire the highest good for them: what we might call shared loving union with God and others, reflecting a perichoretic trinitarian love.

Working toward the good of another requires enough knowledge of that person to know what it is that would be good for that person. We also need to bear in mind what kind of relationship we have with another person. As we will discuss later, the good we bestow must be appropriate to that particular relationship. Working toward the good of another also requires a secure attachment filter. When our attachment filters are insecure, even if we desire to act in loving ways, our actions toward others are often motivated by defense mechanisms that protect us from emotional pain.

---

[31]Nicholas Wolterstorff, *Justice in Love* (Grand Rapids, MI: Eerdmans, 2015).
[32]Post, *Unlimited Love*, 19.

If the good we wish on the loved one and the work to carry out the desire to love does not, in fact, lead to the good of the loved one, our love may well be lacking.[33] In this case, we may not have sufficient knowledge of the loved one, or we may not be attending to the kind of relationship we have with the loved one, and consequently our love for that person is inappropriate or falls short in some way. This is a very important distinction when it comes to parenting and attachment. For instance, when a mother thinks she loves her children by overprotecting them and making choices that should be theirs to make, the resulting helplessness and lack of agency points to a lack in love, even when the mother sincerely believes that she is exercising love. In *The Four Loves*, C. S. Lewis recounts a similar example of Mrs. Fidget.[34] She stayed up late for her children, made dinner for them, and generally attempted to meet their every need, even as they became adults. Her "generosity" was not offered freely; rather, it was forced on them, an implicit condition for relationship with them. Her insistence on complete dependence on her was ultimately serving her own interests and was not promoting the good of her children. As Alexander Pruss puts it, her love was not "humble."[35] It did not defer to the actual needs of her children and, therefore, ultimately was not loving.

Mrs. Fidget was not promoting secure attachment, which goes hand in hand with love in an attachment-type relationship. One of the main characteristics of secure attachment is repairing relational ruptures. This

---

[33]Eleonore Stump makes an important distinction between an intrinsic desire and a derived desire for an intermediary mechanism that is believed to promote the good of another. In the former case, the lover is presumed to not be acting in a loving manner (e.g., seeking to humiliate a child to teach him a lesson wherein the person subconsciously desires to humiliate the child) precisely because the lover desires the harmful thing in and of itself and not just as a means to the good of the other. On the other hand, if the lover desires a mechanism solely because he or she believes it will promote the good of the other—a derived desire—then even if that mechanism ends up harming the beloved, we would say the person was acting in love (e.g., the mother who gives a medication to her child that she believes will heal her child when it actually ends up harming the child). I would add to this that we are speaking here predominantly about ways of relating to the beloved, and the very nature of relationships suggests that when a way of relating ends up harming the beloved, the lover is much more likely to be implicated in that. In other words, there are likely unhealthy attachment filters and patterns that are causing the harm. Stump, *Wandering in Darkness*, 95.

[34]Lewis, *Four Loves*, 49.

[35]Pruss, *One Body*, 30.

requires understanding there may be a difference between our intention to love and the outcome—that is, the objective good or well-being of the other. Recognizing this requires humility, perspective taking, and empathy. This illustrates the centrality of relational capacities for love. Love is never a detached act, a rational calculation of what will promote the good of the other. In its purest form, love requires deep connection, and this also shows the integral relation between goodwill and connection.

While we can be mistaken about what will promote the good of another person, sometimes the person we love can be mistaken about what will be good for him or her. Loving others does not necessarily entail giving them what they want. Rather, it involves desiring and doing what we can to accomplish what is truly in the best interest of others and what really contributes to their flourishing. This is clearly seen in parenting and conducting psychotherapy. Children and clients, like all of us, often want things that are not good for them. For example, children may want certain freedoms or possessions that will harm them, despite what they think. Clients often, very understandably, want to avoid processing emotionally painful issues, which is not in their best interest in the long run. The loving parent limits the child's freedom to the extent that it is in the child's best interest. Likewise, the loving therapist gently guides the client into processing painful issues. In love, we provide what others truly need for their good, not necessarily what they want. This is often difficult and requires a great deal of wisdom, and sometimes sacrifice.

To say that one can be mistaken about his or her own good entails an assumption that what is good for a person is an objective state of affairs.[36] While it may not always be perfectly clear what the good is in any given situation, because human beings have a particular nature, this would suggest that there is an objective standard for what causes human beings to flourish, which will always be in accordance with God's design. All goods must ultimately promote union with God as the highest order.

Seeking the well-being of the other may take a number of forms, depending on what is lacking in the loved one. Where there are needs or

---

[36]Eleonore Stump follows Aquinas in this point. Stump, *Wandering in Darkness*, 93.

suffering, love will move us to respond with compassion, sometimes in sacrificial ways, to meet the need. Where there is injustice, love moves to promote justice, to provide and protect basic human rights that others deserve. Love seeks the well-being of the loved one in all its dimensions: emotional, physical, social, vocational, and financial. Eleonore Stump argues that the highest good, the thing that ultimately leads to the flourishing of the loved one, is union with God and sharing this union with others.[37] This is consistent with our relational account of the *imago Dei* and psychological theory and research suggesting that we are relational beings. As attachment theory suggests, we need attachment bonds with others to grow and develop. A secure attachment bond is, in turn, a reflection of our ultimate need for union with God.

Desiring connection with the other. The connection component of love is often referred to as *union* or *unity*. While these old-fashioned terms may not communicate much to our modern ears, the idea, expressed by Aquinas, is that unity involves striving to understand the loved one from the inside in order to understand that person's perspective and goals from his or her point of view.[38] In doing this, unity is achieved in that we care about good and bad things happening to the loved one as if they were happening to us. We seek to fulfill the loved one's goals as if they were our goals. We act on behalf of the loved one as if we were the loved one. We look not to our own interests but to the interests of the loved one, to paraphrase the words of Philippians 2:4. In other words, we internalize the desire for good for the other to the point that the other's good becomes our own good. If at all possible, we relate with the other around the good we both desire for that person. This promotes unity that begins to overlap with emotional presence, as discussed below. The desire for connection, or union, involves loving from the viewpoint of being inside the other's soul. Union involves three more specific, interconnected facets: (1) emotional presence, (2) mutual closeness, and (3) appreciation or celebration.

---

[37]Stump, *Wandering in Darkness*, 93.
[38]Pruss, *One Body*, 31.

Emotional presence. In addition to seeking understanding of the other and sharing his or her goals, union involves emotional presence.[39] We have all had the experience of someone being physically present with us but not emotionally present—that is, not attending to us in a way that promotes a sense of connection. We intuitively feel that this experience is not sufficient. We naturally desire a deeper form of engagement in which we "feel felt," as Daniel Siegel puts it.[40] We want to know that we've impacted the other. Emotional presence requires certain ways of being with the other. At a minimal level it requires a direct, immediate experience of the other in which we are aware of the other's personhood.[41] Beyond this, however, emotional presence stems from several forms of interpersonal engagement that are broadly captured under the concept of intersubjectivity in the relational psychoanalytic literature.

Intersubjectivity generally refers to the interaction of two subjectivities, or two minds. Psychologist David Wallin regards the concept of intersubjectivity as "the best umbrella term for an invaluable body of clinical research that has taken shape in the last twenty years, that both echoes and extends the clinically fertile insights of attachment theory and infant-parent research."[42] Attachment theory and infant-parent research have provided significant insights into emotional presence and thus this component of love. Psychologists have come to identify three hallmarks of intersubjective relatedness that provide the contours of what we are calling emotional presence: (1) shared intention, (2) shared focus of attention, and (3) affect attunement. These facets of emotional presence overlap in actual experience with a sense of mutual closeness, another aspect of connection or union that we'll discuss below. However, they are somewhat conceptually distinct and prior to mutual closeness, and so we discuss them first.

When I get together with a few of my close friends just to spend time together, and we genuinely experience union with each other, part of this

---

[39]I draw here on Eleonore Stump's notion of "personal presence." Stump, *Wandering in Darkness*, 117.

[40]Daniel Siegel, *The Developing Mind*, 2nd ed. (New York: Guilford Press, 2012).

[41]Stump calls this "second-person experience." Stump, *Wandering in Darkness*, 112.

[42]David Wallin, *Attachment in Psychotherapy* (New York: Guilford Press, 2007), 57.

experience is the sharing of intentions. We share a general intention to connect with each other and promote true dialogue and understanding. This shared intention is an important aspect of emotional presence. In and through our conversation, we sense our shared intention as we experience the process of knowing and being known by revealing important things to us, listening, and responding with empathy. The shared intention promotes and catalyzes the overall experience of emotional presence.

Likewise, in psychotherapy, there is a similar shared intention—at least when there is a good working alliance between therapist and client. With all my clients, my overarching intention is to help them feel understood, heal, and grow. Most clients share this general intention as well, and this is the basis for a therapeutic alliance. This is an implicit (and sometimes explicit) agreement and sense that we are working toward the same goal on a macro level (the entire therapeutic endeavor) and a micro level (any given conversation). For example, when the dialogue is deepening in a session, and together we are experiencing the edges of a new and deeper understanding of the client, this relational experience is what psychologist Diana Fosha calls "positive relational affect."[43] It is a core process in all forms of psychotherapy, and especially relational forms of therapy. The contrast is the feeling that we are working against each other. In these moments, the shared intention of working toward a mutual understanding is lost.

Most clients have lower order and even competing intentions within themselves, and so there is a continuum of strength of shared intentions, which is reflected in how strongly they feel a sense of union or love. For example, in the early phase of therapy Lynn's intentions were more focused on reducing her quite overwhelming anxiety. I joined with her in this and shared this intention because it was a pressing need. It created some measure of emotional presence, but it was somewhat thin because Lynn's anxiety clouded her from experiencing me sharing her intention with her. As therapy progressed and Lynn became better able to manage

---

[43]Diana Fosha, *The Transforming Power of Affect* (New York: Basic Books, 2000).

her anxiety, our shared intention has grown to be much broader and deeper. Our conversations are much more fluid now, and Lynn sees me seeing her in our shared intention. This produces a deep feeling of emotional presence.

As another example, I often help doctoral students complete their dissertations, which is one of the major requirements for their degree. Over the course of typically several years of working on the research project, we share the intention of helping the student complete the project and of learning key research skills along the way. This shared intention creates a bond that promotes a sense of emotional presence. Union is a good in itself, as we are relational beings. However, in this case, the emotional presence and union also promotes another good in the student's life— that of obtaining a graduate degree and the knowledge and skills to help others.

The sharing of intentions is quite closely linked to another aspect of emotional presence—the sharing of a focus of attention. When I get together with a few close friends, part of the experience of being emotionally present with one another is sharing our focus of attention. As our conversation organically unfolds, we all attend to the same thing, and this connects us to each other. We may share a focus of attention on one person in the group—his or her self or soul—or on something outside of the person but indirectly linked to that person, like an event or project. When we talk about and focus on the same thing, it promotes a feeling of being with each other—of emotional presence. In fact, conversations that end in gridlock are often caused by a lack of shared focus.

Shared attention relates directly to our prewired relational capacities. A growing body of research is showing how important shared attention is for secure attachment.[44] As we noted in chapter three, dyadic shared attention in the form of attunement begins early in the mutual gaze of an infant and a caregiver. This attunement evolves between nine and twelve months into the child's capacity to spontaneously use point gestures to call things to the attention of caregivers, thereby facilitating the shared

---

[44]Ed Tronick, *The Neurobehavioral and Social-Emotional Development of Infants and Children* (New York: W. W. Norton & Co., 2007).

attention on an object other than the self. These early developmental capacities, fostered by parents who embody secure attachment and who help their children reflect on their internal world, form the basis for the later ability to share a focus of attention in more complex ways that foster emotional presence.

Finally, emotional presence involves affect attunement or empathy. Emotional presence among friends, and between client and therapist, goes beyond a cognitive connection. When I get together with my close friends, we feel present with one another in love partly because we are attuned to each other's feelings. This means we do not just cognitively understand each other's feelings, we also feel each other's feelings. When I see on a friend's face that he gets what I am feeling, I feel a deep sense of personal or emotional presence. In this sharing of affect, there is a union that is part of the very essence of love. Likewise in psychotherapy, affect attunement is a core aspect of helping clients feel that their therapist is emotionally present and not just going through the motions.

Eleonore Stump clarifies that the concept of presence that is desired in love is not the same as the desire to be in the company of the loved one.[45] There may be things about the loved one that, at least in the present moment, do not make it desirable to be in his or her presence. Union, however, involves a second-order desire. Even if you do not desire to be in the other's presence now, you desire that at some point you and the other will mutually desire to be in each other's presence. In love, there is always an end goal of being with the other. Love ultimately desires presence and unity as part of its very nature.

Mutual closeness. Mutual closeness is a facet of union that overlaps with, and yet is distinct from, emotional presence. Mutual closeness requires several aspects to be present in each person in order to feel close to the other. For example, for my wife to feel close to me, the following is entailed: (1) I must have an intrinsic need for relationship with her and therefore be vulnerable to her; (2) I must actively reveal things about myself that are important to me; (3) I must desire that she accepts my

---

[45]Stump, *Wandering in Darkness*, 91-92.

need and vulnerability; (4) she must, to some degree, accept my need and vulnerability; and (5) I must have some measure of internal integration within myself.[46]

First, for my wife to feel close to me, I need to have an intrinsic need for relationship with her. This means that my need for her is not a means to some other end that matters to me. I do not simply need my wife in order to use her to get ahead in my career, for example. My need for her is necessary only for the fulfillment of the desire for relationship with her. A broad view of attachment captures this well. Defining attachment in a narrower sense, we all need a handful of people in our lives with whom we develop a full attachment bond that provides an internalized sense of psychological safety and comfort on the one hand (haven of safety) and a sense of empowerment to explore the world on the other hand (secure base). However, a wider view of attachment suggests that we all have intrinsic needs for social connection to others even if they are not full attachment figures for us. We need relational connection with many other people in our lives in order to flourish.

The high rates of loneliness we are currently seeing provides evidence that this is the case. In a recent article in *Harvard Business Review*, former US Surgeon General Vivek Murthy states, "Loneliness is a growing health epidemic."[47] He goes on to note that, despite being more technologically connected than ever, rates of loneliness have more than doubled since the 1980s. According to a recent national study of adults forty-five and older, over one-third (35 percent) reported feeling lonely.[48] It is unlikely that this phenomenon can be explained solely by attachment issues, narrowly defined. Intrinsic needs for attachment are foundational in many ways, as we discussed in chapter five, but our intrinsic need for social connection goes beyond this. We need genuine relational connection with family members, friends, members of our community, coworkers, and

---

[46]Stump, *Wandering in Darkness*, 120.

[47]Vivek Murthy, "Work and the Loneliness Epidemic: Reducing Isolation at Work Is Good for Business," *Harvard Business Review*, September 2017, https://hbr.org/cover-story/2017/09/work-and-the-loneliness-epidemic.

[48]C. Wilson and B. Moulton, "Loneliness Among Older Adults: A National Survey of Adults 45+," prepared by Knowledge Networks and Insight Policy Research (Washington, DC: AARP, 2010).

acquaintances. We can even experience meaningful connection in a conversation with a stranger. Barbara Fredrickson calls these brief moments of connection "micro-moments" of love.[49] This intrinsic need for relational connection makes us vulnerable to others to some extent by its very nature. We can see, then, that the intrinsic need for relationship appears to be prerequisite for closeness across all of our relationships.

Second, to continue the example of mutual closeness with my wife, it involves actively sharing thoughts and feelings that are important to me and reveal aspects of my personhood. It is difficult to imagine an experience of unity or connection with another if the other does not know things about you that are important to you. The things you share must be important to you in order for you to feel truly known, which requires vulnerability. When others hold back from revealing things about themselves that matter to them, and share only superficial information, we do not feel close to that person. However, when I, for example, reveal things about myself that are subjectively important to me, desire that my wife accepts this, and she does in fact receive my self-revelation and vulnerability, a feeling of closeness ensues. This is a characteristic of the union for which we are designed. As relational beings, emotional closeness is part of love.

When I get together with the close friends I mentioned above, this is why we feel a sense of closeness with each other. We do talk about current events and catch up on what is happening in our lives, but we also share things that are important to us—things that reveal who we are and who we want to become. We share triumphs, struggles, and desires with respect to our work, colleagues, friends, and family. This requires a level of vulnerability, so there is an emotional risk involved. What if the others don't respond well? What if they don't understand or judge me? Even with close friends I sometimes hear the faint whisper of these anxieties. I suspect many of us feel this way at times. Yet, the flip side of this risk is the feeling of closeness, the feeling of being known, understood, accepted, and loved. This only happens when we deliberately share

---

[49]Barbara L. Fredrickson, *Love 2.0: How Our Supreme Emotion Affects Everything We Feel, Think, Do, and Become* (New York: Hudson Street Press, 2013), 10.

something about our internal world. This allows the other the privilege of feeling close to us, which can be reciprocated and strengthened in mutual closeness. The feeling of closeness comes from seeing something of the other's internal world, and just as importantly, seeing that we are allowing or even inviting the other to see our soul. It is, indeed, a privilege, and that is part of the phenomenological texture of the feeling of closeness.

Sharing something important to you, especially something emotionally painful, is by definition vulnerable. When something is important to you, it is part of your identity, and thus constitutes sharing the very core of your being. This is why we feel connected to the protagonist in a story who is vulnerable by sharing something important or painful with someone. In order for a story to work, the hero must be relatable, which requires being vulnerable. The hero must reveal important things about him or herself in order for the audience to feel close to the hero. Often these revelations take the form of painful self-doubt.

Mutual closeness can be asymmetric in a certain way. Eleonore Stump suggests that one person can feel close in a relationship while the other person does not feel close. An example she gives is that a priest can be close to a family in crisis he is helping, while the family is not close to the priest. While I am not a priest, I have helped many families and couples in crisis in my role as a psychotherapist. I can readily think of numerous couples that came to therapy in a crisis. In one couple, the wife wanted to leave the marriage, and in another, the husband was having an affair. When these couples shared their hurt, pain, and desperation with me, I did feel close to them in a certain way. They were very vulnerable with me, even if it was out of desperation. I suspect that they did not feel close to me in the same way. However, part of the reason for this is that they were in the midst of a crisis and much more focused on their pain than our relationship. Having said that, it does seem that a certain asymmetry like this is possible.

However, other attachment-type relationships suggest that asymmetric roles do not necessitate asymmetric closeness but rather lead to different forms of closeness. We can see this in the therapist-client relationship and parent-child relationship. With my long-term clients, there is certainly an asymmetry in roles and in how much each of us shares or reveals about ourselves. I know far more about my clients than they know about me. However, even though I don't reveal a lot of facts about myself, or even other things outside the therapy context that are important to me, this does not mean that my clients do not feel close to me. Clients I've seen for multiple years often directly express feeling close to me. What is different in our experiences of closeness is the way they feel close to me and vice versa. They feel close in a similar way to which a child feels close to a parent, even though they are adults. They do know me in very meaningful ways, and this often becomes a topic of discussion. For example, they have come to learn my mannerisms, how I tend to respond emotionally, how I think, and how I feel toward them. In more in-depth work, they also come to know some of my own struggles to some extent because they experience these struggles playing out in our relationship.

What have I revealed about myself in order for them to feel close to me in this way? The primary thing, as an attachment figure, is that I reveal how I feel toward them and how I hold them in my mind and heart. This invites them into my internal world in a way that is appropriate to the type of relationship we have.

We can see many parallels in the parent-child relationship. We reveal things about us to our children that are important for their growth and development and that allow them to become securely attached to us. Thus, self-revelation that allows another person to feel close to me does not just take the form of my own struggles and goals related to work or peer relationships. It also takes the form of revealing my attachment to those in my care. It involves revealing how others have impacted me in ways that help them grow. This point also shows that mutual closeness, and love, is always responsive to the type of relationship, as well as the specific person, points to which we will return in the next chapter.

Finally, we would note that mutual closeness requires some measure of internal or psychic integration. Eleonore Stump describes this in terms of consistency between higher- and lower-order desires for relationship.[50] If, for example, John has a first-order desire for relationship with Jane, but has second-order desires that conflict with those desires, this hinders Jane's closeness to John because it hinders John's ability to reveal himself to her in a pure way. Part of John's psyche is working against his own desire for closeness. Given our brokenness as fallen human beings, some measure of internal conflict within the psyche is inevitable.

People who experience dissociative phenomena and have separate "parts," or even full-blown personalities, provide a clear example of this due to the extreme nature of their disintegration. I had a client who had many "parts," including a mediator (who related to me and mediated contact between me and her other parts), victim childlike parts, and aggressive/abusive parts. In an extreme example like this, it was very clear to me that my client's lack of internal integration hindered her ability to be emotionally close to others. It was difficult for me to feel close when the nature of her self-revelations fluctuated wildly from one session to the next. She had desires to be close to me and also conflicting desires to sabotage me and our work together. She could not self-reveal a coherent internal world for others to grasp and relate to because one did not exist. Also supporting this point, as my client became more internally integrated over time in therapy, I felt closer to her. Her desires to sabotage our work lessened substantially, and so her desire for closeness with me consequently became more integrated or pure. This fostered a deeper sense of mutual closeness.

Appreciation and celebration. We noted earlier that love has an affective component: a positive emotional stance toward the other that we might call appreciation or celebration. Appreciating or celebrating another is a relational act that promotes connection and thus can be considered a facet of connection. Stephen Post emphasizes gratefully delighting in the well-being of others.[51] I would extend this by suggesting that connection as defined here entails gratefully delighting in the personhood of the other. Appreciation requires cultivating delight in the

---

[50]Stump, *Wandering in Darkness*, 124.
[51]Post, *Unlimited Love*, 21.

other. It is about our affective stance toward the other, which is cultivated over time. It is difficult to imagine desiring connection with another without a positive affective stance toward the other.

Appreciation involves knowing and expressing particular ways in which the loved one is good; it is a specific valuing of the person.[52] Appreciation may take the form of celebration of the person, delighting in the other by seeing and communicating what is lovely in the person. This requires knowledge of the other. In order to appreciate what is good in the loved one, we must know the particular ways in which that person is good. When we specifically value another, it promotes mutual closeness. For example, if I communicate to a friend that I appreciate something specific about who he or she is and how he or she relates to me, the friend will feel closer to me due to feeling seen and valued. To the extent that my friend receives my appreciation, I will likewise feel closer to him or her.

Closely related to appreciation is celebration, which is intertwined with connection as we noted earlier. Stump contends that the antidote to shame is a celebration of the life of the shamed person.[53] Celebration is critical because shame is intrinsically linked to the desire for connection or union in that the person who feels shame believes that others actively reject a desire for connection. Shame, then, moves against connection, and to the extent it is internalized, it hinders the shamed person from being open to receiving others' desire for connection. In contrast, a person whose life is celebrated is someone who has something lovely about him or her.[54] Those who celebrate with that person have, and show that they have, a desire for that person, and a desire for some form of connection that is intrinsically fulfilling. Seeing the beauty of the other's personhood entails desiring connection or union with the other, and so promotes love.

Conclusion

Love is central to the Christian life because love is the foundational dynamic that exists within the triune God, in whose image we are created.

---

[52]Pruss, *One Body*, 25.
[53]Stump, *Wandering in Darkness*, 147.
[54]Stump, *Wandering in Darkness*, 147.

God is a community of love who has existed throughout all eternity, and God invites us to participate in this very love by receiving it and then passing it on to others. As we do this, we are loved into loving.

While there is only one love rather than qualitatively distinct types of love, our love may take on many different expressions because it seeks to be responsive to the needs of the other and the relationship with the other. While our love may look very different in various situations, involving combinations of friendship (*philia*), appreciation and longing (*eros*), attachment (*storgē*), and sacrifice (*agapē*), familial-attachment love serves as a prototype of God's love and ours.

The essential components of love are seen most clearly in parent-child or attachment love, which bears a striking resemblance to God's love for us. Like God's love for us, this love is an affectionate one that delights in our well-being. It seeks a deep connection whereby the good of the other becomes our own good. It is not a distant love that seeks to somehow promote well-being while keeping others at arm's length. True love is not unable or unwilling to receive from others, even as part of the self-giving process of loving others. Rather, attachment love focuses on the good of the other, which always involves relational connection, and ultimately a shared union with God. When connection occurs, we benefit from the delight inherent in that connection, and thus we receive as part of a mutual process. However, the focus is never solely on our own gain; it is on promoting the good of the other, which includes a mutual sense of connection. Moreover, this attachment-based love is steadfast like God's love. The love among the Trinity in which we participate motivates us to create a bond with others—whenever possible—which in turn moves us to love others even when they are difficult to love.

As image bearers, we are relational beings, which is to say we are born to love. The essence of love, captured well in the prototypical attachment-based love, is comprised of two interconnected components—seeking the good of the other and seeking connection or union with the other. The notion of *loving presence* combines these two components into one unified reality that is relational in character. In love, we seek to be present with others in a way that promotes their well-being, according to God's design.

The Art of Loving Presence

Responsiveness to the Other

WHILE THERE IS ONE UNITARY CONCEPT of love, as we have suggested, it takes on many forms or expressions. To love someone well requires that the love have an appropriate form, depending on the kind of relationship and on the characteristics of the loved one. Another way of saying this is that love is an art that requires responsiveness. Love is not generic or abstract; rather, it adapts to love each person well.[1] In this vein, Stephen Post notes that love can take many forms, including celebration when someone demonstrates good character or a noteworthy accomplishment, active compassion when someone is suffering, forgiveness when someone needs reconciliation, care when someone is ill, companionship when someone is feeling lonely, and correction when someone is promoting ill-being.[2] These are just a few examples, but the point is that knowing when to employ any given form of love is an art that requires responsiveness and wisdom. In this chapter, we build on the nature of love in the last chapter by discussing the art of love, with a focus on the responsiveness that is required to the relationship and to each person. We then discuss the priorities of love, or the necessity to balance competing priorities in our call to love others. We close the chapter considering what it means to love Christianly.

[1]Eleonore Stump, *Wandering in Darkness: Narrative and the Problem of Suffering* (Oxford: Oxford University Press, 2010), 97-100.

[2]Stephen G. Post, *Unlimited Love: Altruism, Compassion, and Service* (Philadelphia: Templeton Foundation Press, 2003), 5-6.

The Art of Love: Responsiveness to the Relationship and the Person

There are two major factors that impact the good we seek for others and in particular the connection or union we desire to have with others: (1) the "office of love" or type of relationship, and (2) the characteristics and needs of the other. Love also requires a finely tuned responsiveness. Because the various demands for love are sometimes competing, they require us to be responsive in the right way at the right time. They require us to respond with wisdom such that our responsibilities to love are rightly ordered. Historically, scholars have referred to this issue as the "order of love."[3]

Love, then, is inherently responsive to the nature of a relationship, to the nuances of a particular relationship, and to the particular needs of a person and what will promote his or her flourishing. Because of this, we can think of love as an art, a description used by C. S. Lewis.[4] I take his meaning to refer to the intuitive or implicit knowledge involved in knowing how to love a person in the context of the specific relationship and in a way that is responsive to the person's particular needs at a given moment. Below, we elaborate on what it looks like for love—and connection or union in particular—to be responsive to the nature of the relationship, the needs of a person, and the order of love. All of this represents the art of love—the process of discerning the best way to promote well-being and connection with others, and overall, in a particular context.

Responsiveness to the nature of the relationship. The good we seek, the depth of understanding of another's perspective and goals that we can achieve, and the ways in which we actualize unity in emotional presence, mutual closeness, and appreciation will vary according to the nature of the relationship. The nature of a relationship and corresponding type of love is what Eleonore Stump calls the "office of love."[5] Love calls for different types of connection or unity with strangers, spouses, friends, and

---

[3]Post, *Unlimited Love*, 123-29.
[4]"Every love has its art." Lewis, *Four Loves*, 44. See also Lewis, *Four Loves*, 55.
[5]Stump, *Wandering in Darkness*, 98.

children, to name a few types of relationships. These various types of relationships also delimit and circumscribe what love can look like with a particular person. It may seem that this would restrain love from its full expression. I would suggest, however, that the nature of a relationship provides the very shape of its full expression. As love must be responsive to the nature of a relationship, it cannot ignore that shape but rather must be informed by it. Instead of limiting love, then, relational characteristics provide the contours of love. We elaborate on this idea below.

Clearly there are differences in our ability to gain knowledge of others in desiring unity depending on the type of relationship we have with them. We may exercise our love of a sister in Christ in an impoverished part of the world solely through our understanding of what it means to be a human being. We may not know anything else about her or have a means of gaining more information. Merely on the grounds of knowing she is a human being made in the image of God, we can understand her need for food and shelter, her need to protect and provide for her children, and also her need for human dignity and autonomy.

My ability to gain knowledge of and thereby achieve unity through presence and closeness with my wife is quite another matter. Not only do I know her well because of our common life together, but we continue to spend a great deal of time in conversation, which enables me to grow in my understanding of who she is and what she needs. This allows for the kind of emotional presence and mutual closeness more appropriate to this kind of relationship, and informs my loving actions toward her. For example, we can experience emotional presence and mutual closeness that come from parenting our children together. When we share attention on our personhood in the context of parenting, it promotes a certain texture of emotional presence that is deep and not possible in other more superficial relationships. When I reveal to my wife things about myself as a parent that are important to me and vulnerable, it likewise promotes a mutual sense of closeness that is shaped by the nature of our relationship.

In addition to the spousal relationship, parenting, therapy, friendship, and teacher/mentor-student relationships are examples of other offices of love that impact how we share in others' perspectives and how we experience presence and closeness with them. These types of relationships have certain parameters for love built into them. Parenting is familiar, and the role of therapist has many parallels to it. We do not love our children in the same way we love our friends or spouses. When my sons were younger, I didn't reveal many aspects of my own struggles with them, even though they were important to me, because I believed it would not be in their best interest to do so. They would likely not understand the meaning of what I was sharing, and/or it might have caused them to feel confused or emotionally overwhelmed. This type of relationship precludes certain forms of mutual closeness that would be disordered and carries within it a structure for other forms of mutual closeness that must be sought in love.

This sort of sharing is generally not appropriate in a parent-child relationship because it does not promote the good of the child. An essential reason that it does not do so is the very nature of the relationship. Children need their parents to manage their own emotions so they can help manage the child's emotions in order to develop a secure attachment and the capacity to love. This is the emotional parallel to the instructions we hear on airplanes to "put your own oxygen mask on first, then assist your child." In contrast, I might share certain struggles with a friend, or with my wife. It is appropriate within these relational contexts, but it is generally not appropriate, helpful, or loving within a parent-child relationship. To take an extreme example, sex within the confines of a marriage relationship is appropriate and can be loving, but it is always a gross violation of a parent-child relationship. This is, in fact, why incest causes so much damage to a child: it violates the very nature of the relationship and so it cannot be considered an act of love precisely because it cannot and does not produce sharing in a good, emotional presence, or mutual closeness. On the contrary, it causes internal fragmentation in both parties.

While there are unique features to the therapist-client relationship, there are many similarities with parenting as well. For example, while I may share some aspects of my experience of the relationship in order to help a client grow, in love I will not share my own internal struggles in such a way, or to such an extent, that it leaves a client feeling insecure or overwhelmed. Once again, certain forms of emotional presence and mutual closeness are not possible, but others are possible, and in fact unique to a therapeutic relationship. Friendship, likewise, has certain parameters of love built into it. Friendship calls for us to be committed to the other's well-being, to share activities and experiences, and to self-reveal certain kinds of things that are important to us, but not quite in the same way as in a spousal relationship. Sexual intimacy and certain types of emotional intimacy are limited—in love—to a spousal relationship. While love must be responsive to the nature of a relationship, it must also be responsive in a more nuanced way to the particular needs of a person given his or her overall context and development.

Responsiveness to the needs of a person. The unity that is sought in a relationship is impacted not only by the kind of relationship but also by the characteristics of the person that is being loved and the person's particular needs. For example, a person with an abusive background may react negatively to physical touch. I had a client, Amelia, for whom this was the case. While I sometimes shake hands with clients, Amelia could not shake my hand due to her history of abuse. Over the course of numerous years of therapy, she was never able to shake my hand, even though part of her wanted to do so. A form of loving presence that involved shaking hands was not possible for Amelia at that time, and so it would not have been loving for me to try to engage in this form of contact.

Likewise, a loved one may have a very limited capacity to share attention on the self and/or self-reveal in ways that promote mutual closeness. This could be, for example, someone who is developmentally delayed and has a limited capacity to know his internal world and reveal important things. Regardless of our desire to be emotionally close with this person, and the appropriateness of it in the context of our relationship, his capacity may limit the union we are able to achieve. In this case we promote whatever kind of union is possible for this particular person.

The practice of love. Any particular situation requires wisdom and discernment in how to love well given the relationship, the person, and the broader context. This is a constant process we engage in almost daily. The examples could be endless, but the art of love is revealed in the particulars of a given situation, so I offer a few examples here.

A while back a student of mine encountered a difficult relational experience with another person in a meeting in which I was involved. My response required a delicate balance to take into account his needs, our relationship, my relationships with colleagues, and the department as a whole. Since I was his adviser, I decided to reach out to him to see if he wanted to meet and process this experience. We met and I attempted to listen and validate his experience and praise him for how he handled the situation, while at the same time honoring my relationships with colleagues involved and not taking sides. I also attempted to discern what he needed given his level of development as a graduate student in his mid-twenties. I believed he needed support and empowerment, and that it was also good for him to deal directly with the others involved without my being in the middle. I also felt he needed to feel connected to and valued by our community at that time, and so I attempted to promote this. In terms of the various forms of love, I attempted to provide my student value, understanding, empowerment, and communion.

Responding to our children in love also requires responsiveness to their particular needs and developmental level. To take just one example, on one occasion when our younger son Aiden was a teenager, he got very mad at me for telling him something he believed was not true. From my perspective, what I said was true, but he interpreted it too literally. I tried to explain this but to no avail. He explicitly accused me of lying. I in turn got offended and mad, and an argument ensued with some fairly heated yelling on both sides. I realized I needed to end the argument and cool down, so I left the room.

As I was processing what had happened, I realized that in my response I was focused on myself. I was offended that my son would think I could have lied to him. This made me look bad. I realized that as his father, I needed to focus on his needs, an insight informed by the nature of our relationship. More specifically I realized that what Aiden needed at that moment to promote his good and our connection was for me to initiate repair, show empathy regarding his feelings of being lied to, and provide the emotional security of knowing that being trustworthy is of utmost importance to me. My assessment was based on our relationship, the situation, and his developmental level. A little while later, I talked to him and tried to convey these things. I got the sense that he took this in, and that it did indeed promote his good and our connection. Love, then, needs to be responsive to the nature of a relationship and to the particulars of the other. Yet how do we love well when competing demands for love vie for our attention? We turn now to the priorities of love.

The Priorities of Love: Balancing Competing Responsibilities in Loving Others

In the last chapter we noted that because all people are created in the image of God, our call to love extends to everyone.[6] This aligns with one of the five dimensions of love identified by sociologist Pitirim Sorokin: what he called extensivity. Sorokin defines this dimension of love in this way:

> The extensivity of love ranges from the zero point of love of oneself only, up to the love of all mankind, all living creatures, and the whole universe. Between the minimal and maximal degrees lies a vast scale of extensivities: love of one's own family, or a few friends, or love of the groups one belongs to— one's own clan, tribe, nationality, nation, religious, occupational, political, and other groups and associations.[7]

The dimension of extensivity points to the discussion of what is sometimes called the "order of love" (*ordo amoris*).[8] This refers to the tension in balancing love for those closest to us, such as family and friends, with love for those "out there"—all of humanity and particularly the poor and marginalized of the world. We all experience the range of possibilities for directing our love at some point in our lives. There are clearly times when

---

[6]Portions of this section have been adapted with permission from Todd Hall, "3 Practices to Love Your Little Corner of the World, and Beyond," Connection Culture, October 3, 2015, https://www.connectionculture.com/post/3-practices-to-love-your-little-corner-of-the-world-and-beyond.

[7]Pitirim A. Sorokin, *The Ways and Power of Love: Types, Factors, and Techniques of Moral Transformation* (Philadelphia: Templeton Foundation Press, 2002 [original 1954]), 16.

[8]Post, *Unlimited Love*, 32.

various extensivities in our purview compete for our limited resources, and we must make choices to extend our love to some but not others.

We clearly see an emphasis on loving the poor and the marginalized in Scripture. Yet we also see the special importance of loving family. It is possible to become out of balance on both ends of the spectrum. Some love only those in their inner circle and show no concern for people outside of their inner circle who are in need. On the other end of the spectrum, Stephen Post rightly notes that it is "possible for someone to be so focused on the needs of all humanity that the importance of special relationships is missed."[9] How, then, do we go about balancing various extensivities—those in our inner circle and those far outside of it?

There are risks on both sides of this issue: neglecting those closest to us, and neglecting the needs of wider humanity, particularly the poor and needy within our reach. However, as a general ordering principle, it seems prudent to start with our little corner of the world as a foundation and extend this love where possible, which requires great wisdom in practice.[10] Building on the right foundation for love is critical. We are embodied and relational beings. We are located in a particular place and time, and we can only extend ourselves so much. We relate most deeply to those in our little corner of the world. We have a profound responsibility to the people we interact with day in and day out, and even more so with those who rely on us for care: our children, spouses, partners, employees, friends, coworkers, and those who are hurting in our communities. Infants, for example, rely on their parents to literally regulate their emotions through eye contact and nonverbal communication. These early attachment experiences shape the very structure of their sense of self and impact every aspect of development. Furthermore, a parent as an attachment figure is not replaceable in providing for the emotional needs of his or her child. When parental attachment figures abandon a child, others can fill in the gaps, but some degree of emotional trauma will occur, which will have lifelong and far-reaching effects for

---

[9]Post, *Unlimited Love*, 32.
[10]The phrase "our little corner of the world" is drawn from Nicholas Wolterstorff, *Justice in Love* (Grand Rapids, MI: Eerdmans, 2015).

that child. When parental love is closer to the ideal, it promotes secure attachment, which is foundational for the one love of *agapē*. Although we cannot develop full attachment relationships with everyone, this is the type of love we seek to extend outside our little corner of the world.

As we noted earlier, attachment relationships are the prototype of love. The parent-child love between God the Father and God the Son is held up as a model for our love of others, and we are similarly encouraged to relate to God as our Abba, the most intimate of designations for a father. The story known as the parable of the prodigal son illustrates dramatically God's love in the form of a father's love. Furthermore, as we will explore in chapter nine, our relationships with others in the church are to be those of a family. From a psychological perspective, we learn to love in the context of our closest attachment relationships. Our later ability to love is generalized from these first patterns. Our earliest years are the most formative in this regard, establishing attachment filters that shape us throughout our lives. Good parental love results in secure attachment filters and the ability to confer this kind of love to others. Parental love is characterized by the "sustained emotional tendency toward the good of another that is almost always replete with helping behaviors."[11] It is often sacrificial in nature. It is the most intense and abiding love with which we are familiar.

A fascinating study supports this idea that extensive love is rooted in deep attachment love. Samuel and Pearl Oliner interviewed more than seven hundred people who lived in Nazi-occupied Europe, including those who rescued Jews, those who chose not to rescue Jews, and Jewish survivors. In contrast to the nonrescuers, the rescuers exhibited a deep sense of relatedness. "What distinguished rescuers," the Oliners note, "was not their lack of concern with self, external approval, or achievement, but rather their capacity for extensive relationships—their stronger sense of attachment to others and their feeling of responsibility for the welfare of others, including those outside their immediate familial or communal circles."[12] This deep sense of relatedness developed during childhood. For

---

[11]Post, *Unlimited Love*, 108.

[12]Samuel P. Oliner and Pearl M. Oliner, *The Altruistic Personality: Rescuers of Jews in Nazi Europe* (New York: Free Press, 1988), 249.

both rescuers and nonrescuers, their early family lives revealed that their "respective wartime behaviors grew out of their general patterns of relating to others."[13] Rescuers generally experienced strong and cohesive family bonds during childhood, whereas nonrescuers more often reported poor family relationships. For those who risked their lives to rescue Jews, extended love started with attachment love in the family.

This has important implications for how we address the priorities of love in our lives. While the risk of neglecting those closest to us may be less common than neglecting the needy and poor, it is nonetheless possible, especially for those heavily involved in service. When we invest in loving our children and those under our care in special ways, this has a ripple effect in preparing them to extend a deep love to others. The rescuers in the Oliners' study would not have been emotionally and psychologically equipped to engage in bold acts of love had they not received and internalized attachment love from their parents and families. It is important to be mindful of the deep ramifications of our responsibilities to love those closest to us. In addition, as we noted, attachment figures become irreplaceable in the psychological and emotional economy of the child. Providing occasional financial resources and emotional support for an abandoned child does not take the place of a lost attachment figure, as helpful as that is. There is something weighty about this responsibility for those entrusted to our care in this way. Because of this psychological reality, which reflects God's relational design of human beings, I would concur with Stephen Post in noting that "it is reasonable to first meet the genuine needs of those closest to us for whom we are particularly responsible, for example, as parents."[14]

This, however, does not negate our current responsibility to extend love to broader humanity, especially those who are poor, oppressed, and marginalized. This is perhaps the greater risk for most people. It is easy to become complacent by narrowly focusing on our inner social circle, treating all others as outsiders. While there are always tensions involved in balancing the competing demands for our love, I would suggest that it is not, ultimately, an either-or situation. Instead, we must

---

[13]Oliner and Oliner, *The Altruistic Personality*, 186.
[14]Post, *Unlimited Love*, 127.

live in the tension between loving our little corner of the world and extending that love to the broader world. Attachment love is the basis for the capacities of a broader universal compassion. However, we must extend this basis by reaching out beyond those who are near and dear with an attachment-type love that represents and embodies the very love of God. We cannot be a parent to everyone, but we seek to extend this quality of love to the family of God and to all people.

In a foundational way, Christians do this by extending this love to build the new family of God, which we discuss in more detail in chapter nine. Adoption provides a theologically rich picture not only of salvation but also of extending this intimate family-type love to those beyond our immediate biological family in forming the new family of God. Through faith in Christ we are adopted as sons and daughters of God, and into the family of God (Romans 8:15, 23; Romans 9:4; Galatians 4:5; Ephesians 1:5). People who were formerly outside the family based on biological lines became part of a new family of God. The concept of family, and the attachment-type love entailed in family, described a new reality for first-century Christians. This new, radically reenvisioned family now crossed socioeconomic, cultural, and ethnic lines in order to show God's character of love more clearly. The new family of God was to be a contrast-society living out a new social order of love.[15] Thus, when we wrestle with extending attachment love, or *storgē*, beyond our immediate biological family, we must first redefine what family means within a new kingdom reality. Our brothers and sisters in Christ *are* family, every bit as much as our biological family. While this does not eliminate some measure of tension between our responsibilities to our biological family on the one hand, and believers who are part of our local church and the universal church on the other hand, this new reality should inform how we wrestle with these tensions and balance our love.

Beyond the family of God, especially those in our local fellowship, we face tensions in how to extend love to all of humanity, especially the poor and needy. Garth Hallet frames the order-of-love issue by discussing a

---

[15]Gerhard Lohfink, *Jesus and Community* (Philadelphia: Fortress Press, 1982).

hypothetical case in which a father has to choose between providing a college education for his son or using these resources to save people from famine.[16] He concludes that the father should give preference, to the extent he can, to the starving. He also highlights Suzie Valadez as an exemplar for her work caring for impoverished Mexican people living in the Ciudad Juarez garbage dump. He notes that her children were required to make very real sacrifices due to their mother's work. How do we evaluate such situations in light of the priorities of love?

Thomas Oord argues that love needs to promote "overall well-being" or the "common good," meaning that love should include justice.[17] In other words, justice is the fairness component in promoting overall well-being. For example, granting excessive goods to the self or the few at the expense of the many is to act unjustly. It resonates that this must be in view in our ethical deliberations regarding the order of love. Oord eschews a strict utilitarian understanding of promoting overall well-being, noting that "precise calculation by localized individuals of the greatest good for the greatest number is inherently impossible."[18] His solution is that we "must make rough assessments of how our actions might affect the whole."

There is something right about this sentiment. We must somehow take justice and the greater good into account in ordering our love. Are our actions detrimental to some, even while promoting well-being for a few, and particularly the few who are closest to us? In such cases, the wisdom of love would suggest that we consider other approaches that will not harm some people. At the same time, even a rough assessment of how our actions affect the whole still seems overly abstract and very difficult to calculate, thus not providing substantive guidance. What does *the whole* mean? This starts to sound like the "greatest good for the greatest number of people," which lands us back in a strict utilitarian approach. In addition, this abstract approach to the "common good" runs the risk of suggesting that we have equal responsibilities to love those closest to

---

[16]Cited in Post, *Unlimited Love*, 123.
[17]Thomas Jay Oord, *Defining Love* (Grand Rapids, MI: Brazos Press, 2010), 60.
[18]Oord, *Defining Love*, 61.

us and all others who constitute humanity. While all people are worthy of our love, this brings us back to our general principle of the order of love: we do have a special responsibility to a few who are closest to us, such as our children.

This notwithstanding, there is something to be commended in Oord's sentiment and direction of thought. I take it to suggest that we must cultivate a wider and more holistic view of the impact of our actions than just the direct recipients of our love. Even if we can't assess the impact on the whole, we can consider ever-widening circles of impact as we consider how to best order our love. For Suzie Valadez, as she has come to know and be involved with the Mexican people living in the Ciudad Juarez garbage dump, they now come into view as she considers how best to order her love. They are no longer part of an abstract notion of humanity but rather particular people she knows who are now part of her circle of love.

Every situation is different and there are no formulas for discerning the best way to prioritize our love in any given situation. We must consider our responsibilities before God, seeking the guidance of the Holy Spirit and wisdom. I would simply note here that Jesus strongly emphasized caring for the poor, the widow, and the outsider. We would do well to follow suit, knowing this will often require sacrifice that is not sanctioned by our secular culture. At the same time, the details of how we are treating those closest to us, and how they are experiencing relationship with us, matter greatly. It is possible for Suzie Valadez, for example, to approach the sacrifice necessary for her children in a deeply loving way that engenders closeness to her and simultaneously models an ethic of service. On the other hand, it is possible for her to have little compassion for her children's experience of sacrifice and to not take into account their developmental needs for emotional connection and support. This could cause her children harm even as she promotes the well-being of the poor people living in the garbage dump. This latter case presents a tension we would do well not to dismiss. Instead, it behooves us to fully experience this tension and seek wisdom as we navigate it. I concur with Stephen Post, who suggests that "Christian spouses and their children must be brought into greater intimacy through the spiritual harmony of purpose that emerges from the challenges of serving the world."[19] Children can be included in our service in a way that is integrated with the family of God, creating a holistic dynamic that both promotes the well-being of the children and those the family serve. At the end of the day, we seek to love those in the new family of God with an attachment-type love, and to wisely extend this love to all people, especially the poor and oppressed.

Loving Christianly

Previously we noted that Nygren's work in particular represents a line of thought suggesting that *agapē* is a special kind of divine love, distinct from other forms of human love. More specifically, distinctively Christian love (*agapē*) on this view is defined by its sacrificial and nonmutual nature. We suggested several reasons that make this view less than compelling: (1) that love does not necessarily include sacrifice, (2) that the love shared among the Trinity is mutual, and (3) that love aims for mutuality and reciprocation. This, then, raises the question of whether there is a distinctively Christian love, and if so, what differentiates it from what we might call "natural love." In other words, should following Jesus in general, and in our day-to-day lives, make our love different? Moreover, should the love of Christians in general be somehow distinct from the love of those who are not following Christ?

I would suggest that the answer to this is both yes and no. Following Jesus should make the love of believers different and distinct in some ways from nonbelievers. However, this is not to say that Christian love is a special form or facet of love, such as sacrificial love, compassion, forgiveness, or correction. Rather, all forms of our love in all different kinds of situations and relationships should be *infused with God's love*, and thereby transformed into what C. S. Lewis called "charity."[20] Christian love is always done for the glory of the Father, in the name of Jesus, and by the power of the Holy Spirit, reflecting trinitarian love or perichōrēsis.

---

[19]Post, *Unlimited Love*, 124.
[20]Lewis, *Four Loves*, 116-41.

Christian love is not a type or class of love; rather, it is a certain quality that permeates all forms of love, in which our love is in Christ and reflects our abiding in Christ. Perichoretic love means that we love others as a participation in God's love.

In this vein, Alexander Pruss argues that *agapē* is "a qualitatively new deepening of the different forms of natural love" that becomes divine love when "we recognize the neighbor as someone created and loved by the triune God. In appreciating that neighbor, we appreciate the Trinity who created him, an appreciation only possible in grace."[21] When we approach loving others in this way, according to 1 John, our love comes from God, expresses to others who God is, and ultimately is a form of loving God. In this way, Christian love is a participation in God's love. As we participate in God's love, our natural human love continues and retains its essential character but is elevated to something beyond itself by God who is Love. C. S. Lewis describes this transformation of natural love into "charity" in this way: "The Divine Love does not substitute itself for the natural—as if we had to throw away our silver to make room for gold. The natural loves are summoned to become modes of Charity while also remaining the natural loves they were."[22]

While all forms of our natural love are transformed, Lewis emphasized the transformation of gift-love and need-love, the two correlative sides of attachment love. This is consistent with our suggestion that attachment love provides a prototype of love. As God enables divine gift-love, we increasingly desire "what is simply best for the beloved."[23] While *natural* gift-love is directed toward things that are intrinsically loveable, *divine* gift-love, in contrast, enables us to love what is not naturally loveable—both in action and in general character.

For example, a friend of mine, John, provided ongoing support and mentoring to a young man named Bill who was recovering from drug addiction. Bill had become a Christian and was trying to get his life back

---

[21]Alexander Pruss, *One Body: An Essay in Christian Sexual Ethics* (Notre Dame, IN: Notre Dame Press, 2013), 18.
[22]Lewis, *Four Loves*, 133.
[23]Lewis, *Four Loves*, 128.

on track. In some ways, he showed great fortitude, taking the bus long distances to work at a low-paying job. At the same time, he was impulsive, irritating, and often went against John's guidance, which led to yet another relapse and financial destitution. Bill was not easy to love. It would have been much easier for John to give up on him after the first bad decision or relapse. Instead, John continued doing whatever he could to help Bill with practical and emotional support until he eventually left the area and cut off contact. John's love was not merely a natural gift-love; it was infused with the very heart of God, which is what sustained it through many challenges and little to no appreciation (even though that was not John's main motivation) or visible long-term effect.

Lewis notes that God also enables gift-love toward himself. While God does not need our love in an ontological sense, God does need our love in a certain relational sense since we can freely choose to reject him. We offer gift-love to God, then, by freely and joyously giving our hearts to God even as our hearts are infused with, and empowered by, the very same God to whom we offer our love. In addition, we offer gift-love to God when we feed and clothe the stranger on God's behalf.

God grants us a transformed or supernatural need-love of God and others. First, with respect to our need-love of God, Lewis contends that our natural tendency is to believe, somewhere deep down, that we don't really need God in the most basic way. We cover this up by thinking that God loves us "not because He is Love, but because we are intrinsically loveable."[24] Even as we grow out of this belief, a subtler version of it takes hold. "Beaten out of this," Lewis suggests, "we next offer our own humility to God's admiration. Surely He'll like *that?* Or if not that, our clear-sighted and humble recognition that we still lack humility."[25] We can all recognize the contours of these natural tendencies at work in our hearts. In Christian need-love, God's transforming work in our hearts enables us to gradually gain the ability to fully accept our dependence on God. In place of our natural need-love,

---

[24]Lewis, *Four Loves*, 130.
[25]Lewis, *Four Loves*, 130.

"Grace substitutes a full, childlike and delighted acceptance of our Need, a joy in total dependence."[26]

With respect to our need-love for others, our natural tendency is to want to be loved for that which is good in us—our strengths, beauty, skill, and virtue. To be loved in the very midst of our unloveliness makes us vulnerable. This love, while healing, also stings. It's like putting alcohol on an open wound. It disinfects and heals, but it hurts at the same time. It is simply difficult to receive when we are vulnerable. This dynamic is even more heightened for those who have been consistently wounded by others in their vulnerability. This is where psychotherapy can play a pivotal role in not only healing but also in the transformation of natural love into Christian love or charity. Part of how our love is transformed as Christians, then, is that we become more able to fully and joyfully receive the caregiving love of others. Reflecting on the transformation of our love into Christian love, or charity, leads us to the question: How does this process happen?

I would suggest that participating in the love among the Trinity, allows our love to be transformed in the three interrelated ways we mentioned earlier: God's love is the *reason, model, and source for the transformation of our natural love into Christian love or charity.* This infusion of God's love in our love captures the notion of grace-filled love—charity (*caritas*), as Lewis called it—that goes beyond what feels good to us in the moment. This notion is what the New Testament authors sought to develop in co-opting the Greek word *agapē* to represent Christian love. To the ancient Greeks, *agapē* connoted a love that transcends immediate emotions and reflects a higher order principle by which we deliberately live.[27] Our love should be different from the love of people not following Christ. However, it is not a distinct type of love. Instead, our love should be different regardless of the recipient and situation.

First, participating in the love among the Trinity should give us a more profound reason and motivation to love others. We can see some

---

[26]Lewis, *Four Loves*, 131.

[27]Stanley J. Grenz, *The Social God and the Relational Self: A Trinitarian Theology of the Imago Dei* (Louisville, KY: Westminster John Knox, 2001), 313.

examples of this in stories of believers who forgive and seek the good of people who have seriously harmed them. Frank and Elizabeth Morris lost their only son when a drunk young man plowed into his car two days before Christmas.[28] Elizabeth began visiting the young man, Tommy, in prison, and found her hatred of him softening into compassion. Her husband, a part-time preacher, ended up baptizing Tommy. They now attend church together, and most Sundays Frank and Elizabeth take Tommy out to eat. In an interview, Frank said, "I knew God required me to forgive Tommy at some point, but I could have dropped it after that and probably would have felt more comfortable. But I felt that forgiveness required me to go the second mile and see what I could do for him."[29]

The reason for our love is that God first loved us when we did not deserve it. "But God showed his great love for us by sending Christ to die for us while we were still sinners" (Romans 5:8). This is the deepest reason a human being could possibly have to love another person. The reason for our love was enacted in the paradigmatic and most powerful love ever demonstrated—Jesus dying on the cross for our sins. We participate in God's love when we accept God's gift and experience the forgiveness of our sins, which in turn empowers us to love beyond our natural love. God's love within us motivates us to offer gift-love to others even when they are unloveable.

We are meaning-making beings, and without Christ we are limited to loving in a way that makes sense within the narrow confines of our natural tendencies and this life. However, participating in the love of the Trinity greatly expands the possibilities for our love. In Christ, our love is no longer limited by the gain we can receive from our love or by the natural attractiveness or loveliness of others (or ourselves). We have the motivation within us to love others even when they are not loveable. Our love is also no longer limited to making sense on the world's terms or

---

[28]William Plummer, "In a Supreme Act of Forgiveness, a Kentucky Couple 'Adopts' the Man Who Killed Their Son," *People*, August 26, 1985, https://people.com/archive/in-a-supreme-act-of-forgiveness-a-kentucky-couple-adopts-the-man-who-killed-their-son-vol-24-no-9/.

[29]David McCormick, "After Couple Forgave Son's Killer, All Three Were Able to Start New Life," *Los Angeles Times*, September 1, 1985, https://articles.latimes.com/1985-09-01/news/mn-25735_1_drunk-driver/2.

the terms of our fallen psychological processes. Christian love provides the motivation—the energy for action—to love beyond reason and beyond what makes sense in the short term. Our love is empowered by that which makes sense in the economy of the kingdom of God—the grand salvation story that connects us to God's love. This makes Christian love different.

Second, this motivation stems in part from the model of Jesus' love. The difference in our love is tied to the specific person of Jesus, who is God incarnate. Recall the passage in John we highlighted in which Jesus washed the disciples' feet. As we noted, this may have foreshadowed the great lengths God went to make his presence available to us. In all he did, Jesus sought to promote the well-being of others and sought union or connection with others. Moreover, he gave his life to make union with God possible, which is our greatest good. In Jesus, we have the ultimate model of love that transforms our natural love into a heavenly realm.

Finally, God's love is also the source of our love and, therefore, the source of the transformation of our natural love into charity. Alexander Pruss notes that this deepening of our natural love is only possible "in grace."[30] God as the source of Christian love is implicit throughout Lewis's discussion as well. For example, he notes that when people are receiving charity, they are loved because *"Love Himself" is in those who love them.*[31] As we noted earlier, Jesus loved others with the very same love he shared with the Father: "As the Father has loved me, so I have loved you; abide in my love" (John 15:9 NRSV). Jesus invites us to abide in his love, which is a sharing or participation in the love between the Father and Son. Divine love, then, is the source of our love. We pass on the very love and presence of God that lives within us. It is a power—or Person—within us that elevates our natural love to a heavenly love.

The implication of all of this for our sanctification—our growth in love—is that we need to engage in spiritual disciplines that train us to: (1) access God's forgiveness and our gratitude for this as our deep motivation for love, (2) gain a deeper understanding and appreciation of Jesus'

---

[30]Pruss, *One Body*, 18.
[31]Lewis, *Four Loves*, 133; emphasis added.

love for others as a model for our love, and (3) cultivate an awareness of the Holy Spirit who guides our thoughts and actions with the very love of the Trinity. May our love be more and more transformed by the love of the Trinity until that day when all our love will be worthy of heaven.

Conclusion

There is an art to loving others well, which requires wisdom. We have to discern what will promote the well-being of the other in the current situation and within the parameters of our relationship. This requires seeing and knowing the other as much as possible, understanding God's design for our well-being, and wisely discerning how this applies to a specific person and context.

As we seek wisdom in responding to the needs of others and balancing the demands of love with our limited resources, we strive to love our little corner of the world—those who depend on us the most—and to extend this attachment-type family love to those outside our inner circle and especially to the poor and oppressed.

In all our efforts to love, we strive to *love Christianly*—that is, to infuse our love with God's love. The New Testament depicts the love between the Father and Son, and by implication the love among all three members of the Trinity, as the reason, model, and source for our love. This provides the divine motivation to delight in others, and to love beyond reason, immediate gain, and what makes sense in the short-term economy of this life. Simply put, we love because God first loved us with an extraordinary, intimate, and sacrificial love. Our experience of this love, and gratitude for it, fuels a divine dynamic in our love. As we share in God's love—often through the body of Christ—it becomes our own, and we then pass it on to others. We share God's love foundationally within the body of Christ and extend this family love to the world. As we do this, the love of individual believers adds up to something greater than the sum of its parts—a mutual sharing in God's loving presence, which reflects the image and glory of God.

PART 3

The Process of Spiritual Transformation

Transformational Change

The Relational Dynamics of Spiritual Transformation

OUR SPIRITUAL JOURNEYS are a winding road, and we often feel like we can't see that far ahead. In speaking to Nicodemus of being "born again," Jesus emphasized the unpredictability of the Spirit-filled life: "The wind blows wherever it pleases. You hear its sound, but you cannot tell where it comes from or where it is going. So it is with everyone born of the Spirit" (John 3:8 NIV). There are moments in our lives when something inside us is transformed in a flash; however, the overall process of growing into Christlikeness requires time, patience, and difficult internal work behind the scenes. Both incremental and more sudden, transformational changes can be viewed as working together in an overall dynamic process of change.

We have discussed how our attachment filters shape how we experience ourselves and relate to God and others, and how we automatically evaluate the meaning of events in our lives. If this is the case, then transformation needs to take place at the level of our implicit relational knowledge. Anything short of this level of change is a spiritual shortcut that simply won't work in the long run. Changing our implicit sense of self or attachment filters is the only way we can truly grow in our capacity to love God and others. The focus of this chapter, then, is not on superficial external change or merely incremental change; rather, our goal and focus here is on deep internal change that we'll refer to as transformational change.

We can clearly see this focus on deep internal change in many of Jesus' teachings. For example, Jesus tells us, "A good tree cannot bear bad fruit, and a bad tree cannot bear good fruit" (Matthew 7:18 NIV). In addition, we see this in Jesus' response to the Pharisees in Matthew 23:25-26 (NIV): "Woe to you, teachers of the law and Pharisees, you hypocrites! You clean the outside of the cup and dish, but inside they are full of greed and self-indulgence. Blind Pharisee! First clean the inside of the cup and dish, and then the outside also will be clean." The Pharisees cleaned virtually everything except their relational capacity to love God and others.

This brings us to the pressing question of this chapter: How do our attachment filters change so that we become more like Christ in living out the greatest commandments—loving God and neighbor while participating in the love of the Trinity? How do we develop our capacity for loving relationships, the end goal of development, which involves every aspect of our being? In exploring these questions, we first explore the kind of change that leads to deep internal growth in our ability to love—*transformational change*. With this framework in place, we then consider several relational processes of change, including how story integrates the two ways of knowing and how we grow through suffering. We then explore the practices of change, with a focus on the benefits of mindfulness.

Transformational Change

Sometimes we do the work to grow spiritually and develop healthier, more loving relationships, and yet nothing seems to happen. This is also a common frustration of clients in psychotherapy. Often, deep internal change seems to occur at a snail's pace and is invisible to clients. In fact, one of my most important tasks as a therapist is to highlight—to make visible—the gradual incremental changes that are occurring internally in my clients. These discussions always feel very meaningful and typically encourage clients to stay the course.

While difficult to see, these incremental changes are important and build on each other until they coalesce into something qualitatively new. When this occurs, there is a transformation in the internal landscape of our soul. Our attachment filters reorganize, leading to a new experience of the self and new ways of relating. Such transformational change is more visible and sometimes referred to as a tipping point. A tipping point is when a small input has a large and unpredictable effect. Tipping points are an example of what scientists call "nonlinear" or "discontinuous" change, which is drawn from nonlinear dynamic systems theory.[1]

There are several defining characteristics of nonlinear dynamic systems that explain why fundamental changes in the way we relate happen in this unpredictable way.[2] One of the most important principles here is that our brains and souls self-organize. Basically this means that development involves increasing levels of order and complexity. This happens as lower order, less complex meaning systems become integrated or coordinated in a way that produces the emergence and stabilization of new, more complex, and higher order forms of organization. In this process, each level of organization builds on the previous one. For example, a two-year-old infant who experiences a conflict with his mother may learn to soothe himself using a variety of single relational-emotional capacities (e.g., turning to his favorite blanket). This may then be coordinated with another relational capacity to engage in playful games with his parent, leading to a coordinated, higher-level relational capacity to "repair," or to move from an emotionally disconnected and conflicted state to a state of positive connection.[3] Overall, the process of self-organization allows emotional information to be processed more rapidly and completely, enabling more integrated and healthy relational capacities.

---

[1]Nonlinear dynamic systems theory applies systems thinking to the way organisms change and develop. Allan Schore, *Affect Regulation and Disorders of the Self* (New York: W. W. Norton & Co., 2003), 89.

[2]The defining characteristics of nonlinear dynamic systems theory include: open systems, changes in psychobiological meaning states, self-organization and emerging complexity, developmental constraints on the complexity of organization, concurrent developmental pathways, and nonlinear shifts in organization. Schore, *Affect Regulation and Disorders of the Self*, 89; Richard E. Boyatzis, "An Overview of Intentional Change from a Complexity Perspective," *Journal of Management Development* 25, no. 7 (2006): 607-23.

[3]Karlen Lyons-Ruth, "The Two-Person Unconscious: Intersubjective Dialogue, Enactive Relational Representation, and the Emergence of New Forms of Relational Organization," *Psychoanalytic Inquiry* 19, no. 4 (1999): 576-617.

In our context of psychospiritual growth, repeated encounters of relational attunement or resonance (particularly with attachment figures) lead to processing the meaning of relational experiences (based on our relational filters) in less rigid and more complex ways. This complexity is good because it enables us to integrate more emotional information (often more positive information that doesn't easily stick), regulate our emotions, and ultimately develop a more secure internal attachment filter.

For example, people who suffer from borderline personality disorder (BPD) often experience others as all good or all bad, a defense mechanism referred to as "splitting." When I was a graduate student, I co-led a therapy group at a day treatment center. There was a female patient, Sharon, in the group who had been diagnosed with BPD. During one session when I attempted to empathize with her, she screamed at me and berated me in a very condescending manner. Something had caused Sharon to experience me as "all bad" (perhaps my relative inexperience and her perception that my statements didn't accurately reflect her emotional state), and she could not take in anything "good" from me. The way Sharon processed that experience and related to me was not complex or fluid; instead, it was rigid and compartmentalized. She likely experienced me, as a male authority figure, as similar to her abusive father. At an emotional level, she could not differentiate me from her father. In addition, she could not hold onto, or integrate, contrasting pieces of emotional information at the same time. She was not able to experience me as both missing the mark in a comment and yet showing genuine care for her at the same time. Those two things could not be integrated in her mind because of the lack of complexity.

A more mature, complex manner of processing would have led Sharon to experience some good in me along with the bad. This in turn would lead to more regulated emotions and healthy patterns of relating. For example, she may have felt frustrated by a particular comment, and yet expressed this in a direct but contained manner that would have facilitated a more productive dialogue.

The main point for our purposes is that deep internal change in our attachment filters involves incremental changes that, over time, coalesce into qualitative or transformational changes, which lead to new ways of being and relating. We can see an example in Jeffrey's story, a client we discussed in chapter five. To refresh your memory, Jeffrey came to see me for therapy because he was struggling with an on-again, off-again romantic relationship. Due to the loss of his mother in early childhood, he experienced a lot of anxiety and fear of abandonment, which tended to overwhelm others, causing them to withdraw and reinforcing his fear of abandonment.

While the anxiety, loss, and relational difficulties didn't go away completely during the early part of therapy, there were incremental changes. For example, Jeffrey developed the ability to manage his anxiety a little bit better. When something upset him, instead of it leading to panic, he was able to hang on—just enough—to the feeling that I would be there for him and everything would be okay. Instead of calling me and needing to schedule an extra session, he was able to wait until our next session to talk through things. Instead of avoiding his grief and feeling only anxiety (his mind's way of signaling the impending danger of loss), he gradually developed the ability to talk about and feel the sadness of the loss of his mother, even if only for short periods of time.

Despite these incremental changes, anxiety and unhealthy relational patterns persisted. At a fundamental level, Jeffrey still felt alone in this world. At times, he despaired over whether he would ever experience substantial growth and change. He would ask me if his life would ever be *really* better. Despite his despair, somewhere deep down I had faith that our relational connection was growing deeper roots and that this was preparing the way for change. I just didn't know how, and I couldn't predict when we would see transformational change. I persisted week after week trying to attune to Jeffrey's emotions and help him feel that I was with him in this journey. Jeffrey also persisted in doing the difficult internal work of processing painful issues week after week. We kept plugging away through the difficult "working through" phase of therapy.

Then at one point in the therapy, seemingly out of the blue, a tipping point occurred in Jeffrey. In a way, nothing had changed in the way we were working together. There was no dramatic event that happened, and we had been talking about the same issues every week. But (seemingly) all of a sudden, over a period of several months, I noticed that he was different. He still struggled, but Jeffrey had changed. He felt differently about himself—more secure and confident—in a very deep way. His gut-level expectations of others had shifted. He felt more secure in my care for him; he began to truly trust and deeply feel that I was for him. He also developed more healthy relationships with women. The walls had come down substantially, and he began to experience more meaningful connections with people and with God. You may have experienced this kind of internal shift in yourself and/or witnessed it in others. We move through our daily lives, and then in the midst of a deep connection with a friend, a time of quiet prayer, or communal worship, the internal landscape of our soul shifts. It may be a small input or shift, but it leads to a big change—transformational change that affects our core sense of self.

Understanding that spiritual growth involves, most fundamentally, a transformational or nonlinear model of change helps us understand why we sometimes experience spiritual growth and other times feel like we're stuck or moving backward. Two units of spiritual input do not necessarily result in two units of immediate spiritual growth. In fact, spiritual growth may not be evident at the time of the input. This can be confusing and frustrating if we hold to linear models of spiritual growth. In addition, a transformational model helps us understand how we can do our part in facilitating spiritual growth in our own lives and communities.

How, then, do these transformational shifts in our attachment filters take place and how do we intentionally promote this kind of growth? Because relationships are the mechanism of change, they are somewhat out of our control. We cannot control how God and others engage with us. However, there are some things that are in our control. We can do our part to facilitate certain relational *processes* that lead to transformational change. In addition, we can cultivate certain *practices* that facilitate transformational change. One of the key processes in transformational change is the integration of the two ways of knowing, which is facilitated by story.

Story and the Knowledge Spiral

A key process in transformational change is bringing together the two ways of knowing—explicit knowledge and implicit relational knowledge—so they work together in harmony. Wilma Bucci describes this process as "referential activity" (as each system *refers* to the other in a back-and-forth process), and we referred to it as "referential integration" or the knowledge spiral in chapter four. In this integrating, back-and-forth process, we create and discover meaning through a story process. This happens in two ways, although in reality they are both part of one overall dynamic process of reorganizing or remixing our experiences and knowledge. On one level, we *interpret our own experience* through telling our story to ourselves and others. On another level, we *feel an idea* as we hear stories that work our explicit knowledge into our hearts. Both of these micro story processes are part of the knowledge spiral and both go through four phases—preparation, incubation, illumination, and interpretation—just with different starting points.[4] In explaining the way story unifies ideas and emotion, Robert McKee provides a helpful vantage point on the knowledge spiral, which he refers to as the process of reorganization. He states, "Your intellectual life prepares you for emotional experiences that then urge you toward fresh perceptions that in turn remix the chemistry of new encounters."[5] Regardless of where you start in the process, we can see here that each way of knowing mutually shapes and informs the other. Below we'll consider the knowledge spiral from the vantage point of both starting points: interpreting our experience and feeling an idea.

---

[4]Wilma Bucci described the way in which the two types of knowledge integrate in the context of the scientific discovery process. She delineated this with four phases: preparation, incubation, illumination, and interpretation. These phases also apply to the emotional discovery process and transformational change. Wilma Bucci, *Psychoanalysis and Cognitive Science* (New York: Guilford Press, 1997).

[5]Robert McKee, *Story: Substance, Structure, Style, and the Principles of Screenwriting* (New York: HarperCollins, 1997), 110.

Interpreting our experience. Earlier we referenced the concept of "un-thought knowns"[6] as a picture of our relational way of knowing.[7] These are things we know, yet they remain unthought and unformed. They are emotional meanings that do not exist in words that can be thought and communicated to others. This is part of why changing our attachment filters is so profoundly difficult. The very nature of our attachment filters is that they are *unspeakable*, and when they are painful they are even more difficult to be aware of and communicate to others. When they remain unspeakable, they are very difficult to transform because they do not come into relational contact with God or others to bring new emotional information to bear on them. Yet our unthought knowns can become speakable through a translation process that links our raw, implicit knowledge with words and ideas. This translation happens through the process of telling our story, which involves the four phases mentioned above.

A fascinating thing about narratives is that telling coherent stories about our experiences requires a harmonious working relationship between the right and left sides of the brain, and between the two ways of knowing. The interpretive left side of the brain is predominantly responsible for recounting the logical sequence of events, whereas the right side is predominantly responsible for the emotional meaning of the events.[8] Thus, when both of these ways of knowing are working together, you get a logical *and* emotionally meaningful—or coherent—communication of a person's sense of self.

We will illustrate this process with my client Jeffrey, mentioned previously. During the beginning of therapy, he held a deep, unarticulated experience of anger toward his father for not helping him process the

---

[6]This phrase was apparently coined by Christopher Bollas in the context of psychoanalysis. He may have been drawing from Freud, who quoted a patient as saying, "I've always known that, but I've never thought it." Christopher Bollas, *The Shadow of the Object: Psychoanalysis of the Unthought Known* (New York: Columbia University Press, 1987); Sigmund Freud, quoted in David Wallin, *Attachment in Psychotherapy* (New York: Guilford Press, 2007), 115.

[7]Portions of this section are adapted with permission from Todd W. Hall, "Psychoanalysis, attachment, and spirituality Part II: The spiritual stories we live by," *Journal of Psychology and Theology* 35, no. 1 (2007): 29-42.

[8]Allan N. Schore, *The Science of the Art of Psychotherapy* (New York: W. W. Norton & Co., 2012).

loss of his mother. The *preparation* for this experience to be interpreted and transformed involved the ongoing work of therapy. As Jeffrey experienced resonance and attunement from me, and gradually became attached to me, this prepared him to feel safe enough (through an internal secure base) to begin to feel anger at his father, despite the risk of loss. The preparation phase can also involve explicit knowledge or ideas that shape our experiences. Jeffrey had read quite a bit about psychological growth and, more specifically, attachment. While this knowledge didn't directly change his experience, it was part of the preparation that facilitated a richer experience of our relationship and work together. We will return to this idea below.

All of this prepared the way for Jeffrey to begin to *incubate* his inchoate experience of anger toward his father. In the incubation phase, we continue to reflect on our experiences in the background of our mind and soul. Our implicit knowledge system processes our relational experiences and filters—our sense of connection and expectations in relationships. The rules that govern this processing are not known, and all of this happens behind the scenes, outside of our awareness. It is the place where we form new connections about the meaning of our experiences, about our sense of self in relation to others. It is the place where new story lines are forged.

At the beginning of therapy, Jeffrey did not feel consciously angry toward his father, but when the subject of how his father handled his loss came up, Jeffrey would feel a palpable discomfort and change the subject. Gradually, he began reflecting on this experience in the back of his mind. He began bringing it up on occasion in our sessions. Through our discussions, stronger emotions emerged, but they were still difficult to define.

This morphed seamlessly into the *illumination* phase, in which Jeffrey transitioned from a vague sense of discomfort about how his father handled his loss to a more focused feeling of irritation and confusion. In illumination, the connections forged in the incubation phase make themselves known, as if coming from the outside. In the context of transforming our attachment filters and capacity to love, illumination is the tipping point in which new gut-level meanings about ourselves, God, and others are crystallized. These new meanings, or attachment filters, may have existed in a nascent form, but now they come into clearer focus in our conscious awareness. Jeffrey became increasingly aware of feelings of anger toward his father and the need for distance. These feelings were there in the background previously, but now they became clearer and conscious. This led to a concomitant experience of a stronger sense of self as he became more his own person, less defined by his father's need to avoid loss. These feelings became a focus of our work for a significant period of time during this illumination phase.

This moved into the next phase, *interpretation*, in which Jeffrey began to interpret these new implicit experiences by translating them into words and ultimately into his story. Here, we give shape and form to the illuminations, which gives us more access to these implicit meanings within ourselves. The very process of interpreting our experience transforms it. In this phase, Jeffrey was able to capture his experiences more precisely in words. For example, at one point he told me, "I needed my dad's support as a child, but he let me down by making it unsafe to talk about our loss." This interpretive process enabled him to see the overall impact this had on his life and to feel not just anger toward his dad but also a new sense that it was okay to feel angry. This is part of how interpreting his previously inchoate experience changed the experience. It was now much more defined, and it led to a new overall experience of self that his feelings are okay and that he is worth loving. This ultimately led to a growing forgiveness of his father and a new sense of security with God.

The point of all this is that part of working toward spiritual growth is telling your story about your important relationships with God and others to significant people in your life. When you do this, two things happen that facilitate the spiritual transformation process. First, telling your story is like working a muscle. Although your story may not be totally coherent, the act of narrating your relational experiences causes the two hemispheres of the brain to work together, as noted above. Second, telling your story makes your implicit experiences explicit and brings them into contact with God and others. This allows more deliberative processing to transform the experiences. The very act of narrating your experiences changes your perception of the experiences, allowing them to provide a loving connection that will bring growth and healing.

Feeling an idea: aesthetic emotion. The second way the two ways of knowing come together through story is when we feel an idea—a concept we noted in chapter four. Through story, an idea or meaning becomes fused with our emotions and implicit knowledge, thus transforming it. How does story change us? It does so by conveying explicit knowledge in the implicit realm through the structure embedded within it.

Screenwriter Robert McKee tells us "the exchange between artist and audience expresses idea directly through the senses and perceptions, intuition and emotion."[9] Story doesn't explain its view of life—its explicit knowledge—in abstract ideas. Instead it creates what McKee calls *aesthetic emotion*—the feeling of an idea. This is a more structured form of implicit knowledge—a knowing that exists in our emotions and experience that is organized around an idea. Aesthetic emotion is a very important concept because it exists at the borderline between implicit and explicit knowledge, coming very close to a fusion between the two.

Stories carry knowledge within them, housed in the very structure of the sequence of events and the experiences we live through vicariously. Regardless of genre, the idea or meaning of a story is expressed or dramatized in the emotionally charged story climax. The hero comes to a moment of decisive choice—a true dilemma—at the story's climax. The hero's choice at the climax reveals the controlling idea of the story. Movies communicate ideas directly through the medium of visual story. You see an idea played out in the structure of the events that occur. More specifically, you feel the idea as you see it visually dramatized. It's a deeper and more direct form of knowledge than grasping a proposition in an intellectual sense.

---

[9]McKee, *Story*, 111.

For example, in the movie *Martian Child*, science fiction writer and widower David Gordon adopts an orphaned boy, Dennis, who thinks he's from Mars. Throughout the film, the negative value (or human experience) of the story is dramatized, and we feel a profound idea about our own relationships: *loss profoundly hinders our ability to love.* After a series of relational breakthroughs and setbacks between David and Dennis, Dennis finally runs away and climbs a tower to wait for his Martian people to come take him home. David finds him, climbs the tower, and reaches out to Dennis with an emotional plea: "Dennis, you're my son, you belong to me, and I will never, ever, ever, ever, ever, ever, ever leave you." At this moment Dennis faces a dilemma—continue to hope that Martians will come take him home or give up his defenses and take the risk of trusting David. As Dennis runs into David's arms, we immediately feel the controlling idea: *love overcomes loss when we face our fears and reach out to one another.*

The same principles apply to stories in Scripture and stories we might hear in our spiritual communities. Jesus taught truths through story to help us feel and experience them. The parable of the prodigal son is a well-known example. In this parable, we read about the son who squanders his inheritance and yet returns home and humbly seeks his father's forgiveness: "Father, I have sinned against both heaven and you, and I am no longer worthy of being called your son" (Luke 15:21). The father, who represents God, has a choice in his response: reject his son, or forgive him and welcome him back into the family. When we read that the father was filled with love and compassion when he saw his son a long way off, and then threw a party to celebrate because his son "was dead and has now returned to life" (Luke 15:24), we feel the idea: *God is infinitely gracious and delights when we seek to reconcile with him.* Jesus' parables are designed to help us feel God's truth so we know and inhabit it in a deeper way than just intellectually.

In our spiritual communities, we often share stories of spiritual growth and faith because they, too, help us to feel an idea. Such "God stories" help us see what faith looks like in a real-life context and add richness to our implicit relational knowledge and faith in God. For example, recently my mother-in-law, Rosa, shared that she got a message from the daughter of a woman, Estella, who attended a Bible class for children in the slums where she had taught when she was a teenager. Every Sunday afternoon for six years, Rosa and two others would go to the slums and bring children to a local storefront and teach Bible stories and encourage them. As a result of this, Estella and her family became Christians, including her parents, grandparents, two sisters, husband, and children. Her daughter is now studying to become a missionary. Hearing this story of my mother-in-law's faithful commitment to sacrifice her time, energy, and talent for these children helps our family to feel a profound truth: *the greatest contribution we can make in God's economy is to serve others.*

While stories help us to feel ideas and integrate them with our implicit relational knowledge, study of biblical truths and relevant topics can do the same. As noted previously, Robert McKee contends that our intellectual life shapes our emotional experiences, creating fresh new perceptions.[10] This process happens through the same phases in the knowledge spiral outlined above, but in a different way. For example, we might consider the theological theme that God is relationally present with us through Christ and the Holy Spirit.

In the preparation phase, we study this theme and gain more explicit knowledge of the details of how God's relational presence is the cornerstone of the entire biblical narrative.[11] This then moves into the incubation phase, in which our mind processes this knowledge in the background, perhaps involving some form of meditation, making connections with other experiences and concepts. In contrast to the process of interpreting an experience, what is incubated here is not a raw emotional experience, but explicit knowledge. This transitions into the illumination phase, in which connections are formed regarding God's relational presence, which then shapes and impacts our experience of

---

[10]McKee, *Story*, 110.

[11]As noted previously, Duvall and Hays argue that God's relational presence is the central theme of the entire biblical narrative. J. Scott Duvall and J. Daniel Hays, *God's Relational Presence: The Cohesive Center of Biblical Theology* (Grand Rapids, MI: Baker Academic, 2019).

God. As we pray, for example, we become more aware of God's presence in the here and now because the meaning of this experience takes on new dimensions in light of the illumination from the richness of this concept throughout Scripture. This propositional truth, with the help of the Holy Spirit, begins to take root more in our heart, and we begin to experience God's presence in new ways.

It is easy to neglect taking the time to sit quietly with the great truths of Scripture, yet we are repeatedly exhorted to do so in Scripture. "Whatever is true, whatever is noble, whatever is right, whatever is pure, whatever is lovely, whatever is admirable—if anything is excellent or praiseworthy—*think about* such things" (Philippians 4:8 NIV, emphasis added). With time and processing, these truths will make their way from our heads to our hearts.

Growth Through Suffering

While suffering is not something we wish on ourselves or others, it does bring with it the potential for spiritual growth in ways that are difficult to experience otherwise. Suffering has a way of shaking up our implicit view of ourselves in relation to God and others, opening up the possibility of transforming it. Given the pervasiveness of sin and suffering in the world, suffering has been explored extensively from both Christian and psychological perspectives. There is much to say about suffering, and more specifically about suffering and growth.[12] We limit ourselves here to briefly showing how suffering fits within the overall framework we have been developing in this book.

Suffering provides the impetus for growth because it is emotionally arousing, heightens awareness of our implicit attachment filters, and frequently challenges our explicit and implicit beliefs about the world and our place in it. Because of these factors, it provides the opportunity for an accelerated learning curve. In fact, a large body of psychological literature documents reports of growth following all kinds of sources of

---

[12]M. Elizabeth Lewis Hall, "Suffering as Formation: The Hard Road to Glory," in *The Holy Spirit and Christian Formation: Multidisciplinary Perspectives*, ed. Diane Chandler (New York: Palgrave Macmillan, 2016), 69-88.

suffering.[13] Suffering also holds a privileged place in the Bible as a source of growth. The theme of growth in suffering takes on the unique form of a promise from God to work all things (including, one might assume, painful and traumatic experiences) together for good for those who love God and are called according to his purpose (Romans 8:28). Similarly, James ties suffering to growth, encouraging believers to "consider it pure joy" when they face suffering, because of the outcome: "so that you may be mature and complete, not lacking anything" (James 1:2-4 NIV).

Suffering is disorienting. It challenges our beliefs about our identity, the way the world works, and possibly even our beliefs about God. It often disrupts our sense of purpose, interferes with our daily goals and strivings, and takes away things that make our life feel meaningful. This disruption is necessary for growth. In fact, some researchers believe that growth actually requires disorientation—that our foundational assumptions about the world and our place in it need to be shaken up. These overarching beliefs about the world, often referred to as "worldviews,"[14] consist of deep-seated, often unconscious beliefs about the world and our place in the world. They provide a sense of order and stability to our lives, structuring the way we interpret our experiences and providing guidance for our overall goals and daily choices. At a conscious level, they consist of our explicit beliefs about the world, which may be informed primarily by our Christian faith. We believe certain things to be true about God, the world, and our place in the world. At an unconscious level, worldviews include all of our implicit knowledge, including our attachment filters.

For suffering to produce change, it must shake or shatter our beliefs, what we know to be true, either explicitly or implicitly. For example, the death of a loved one may challenge people's largely implicit assumptions that the world is a good place and that people get what they deserve.

---

[13]Lawrence G. Calhoun and R. G. Tedeschi, "The Foundations of Posttraumatic Growth: An Expanded Framework," in *Handbook of Posttraumatic Growth*, ed. L. G. Calhoun and R. G. Tedeschi (Mahwah, NJ: Erlbaum, 2006), 3-23.

[14]Also called global meaning systems; see Crystal L. Park and Ian A. Gutierrez, "Global and Situational Meanings in the Context of Trauma: Relations with Psychological Well-Being," *Counselling Psychology Quarterly* 26, no. 1 (2013): 8-25.

When people's worldview beliefs are shaken up, the resulting meaning-making can allow people to rebuild their assumptions about themselves and the world, facilitating growth. In fact, several studies have reported that the greater the threat, the greater the reported growth.

Psychologist Crystal Park noted that there are two levels of worldview beliefs that are relevant to suffering.[15] The first level is *global meaning*, which refers to the worldview assumptions noted earlier. Global meaning focuses on beliefs about the nature of the world and global goals, which are the desired outcomes that motivate people in their lives. The second level of worldview beliefs is the *appraised meaning* of specific events. These have to do with the meaning that is attributed to the stressful event itself. For example, the event may be perceived as a loss, a threat, or a challenge. The appraised meaning of an event also includes beliefs about why the event occurred. According to Park's model, distress occurs when someone's appraisal of a specific event doesn't fit with his or her global assumptions or worldview.

The discrepancy causes people to engage in an active process to attempt to reduce this discrepancy. This is where processing comes in, as people adjust either their specific appraisals about the suffering event or their global assumptions to reduce this discrepancy. Research suggests that processing the suffering cognitively and emotionally facilitates growth.[16] In early stages, this processing may be unintentional, as the suffering event is remembered through intrusive thoughts. While distressing, this early processing allows the individual to come to grips with the reality of the situation. This unintentional processing facilitates a more intentional way of processing. When this occurs, the person's focus transitions to identifying coping methods and wrestling with issues related to meaning and implications for one's worldview. This latter, intentional processing, which Crystal Park calls "meaning making,"[17] is the kind of

---

[15]Crystal L. Park, "Religion as a Meaning-Making Framework in Coping with Life Stress," *Journal of Social Issues* 61, no. 4 (2005): 707-29.

[16]Calhoun and Tedeschi, "Foundations of Posttraumatic Growth," 3-23.

[17]Jeanne M. Slattery and Crystal L. Park, "Meaning Making and Spiritually Oriented Interventions," in *Spiritually Oriented Interventions for Counseling and Psychotherapy*, ed. Jamie D. Aten, Mark R. McMinn, and Everett L. Worthington (Washington, DC: American Psychological As-

processing that is critical for growth to occur. Research suggests that the amount of growth one experiences is directly related to the amount of intentional engagement with the trial.[18]

The need for meaning making offers the opportunity to engage in focused referential integration that weaves the two ways of knowing together. As our conscious and unconscious beliefs about the world and relationships are challenged and rearranged, the opportunity presents itself for our knowledge—implicit and explicit—to become more integrated, more complex, and more in line with reality. The disruption to our usual ways of viewing and experiencing the world can be very painful, but it allows for something new and more robust to emerge.

In fact, people who have grown through trials report changes in three interrelated domains: worldview, perception of self, and experience of relationships with others.[19] In terms of worldview, people report a deeper appreciation for life, including the simple moments in everyday life and relationships that are often taken for granted. They also report positive changes in priorities and a renewed sense that time and relationships are precious. Along with this, many report a renewed and strengthened spiritual vitality. For many people, suffering initiates a spiritual search for significance. For some people this search ends in a decline in spiritual vitality. For many, however, the process of making sense of their suffering causes an initial decline in spirituality but eventually leads to a stronger spirituality. A stronger sense of spirituality can provide several benefits: (1) a sense of control over circumstances that feel uncontrollable, (2) comfort, (3) a deeper intimacy with God, and (4) a sense of meaning in and through their suffering.

Significantly, the changes in views of the self and relationships that people report are relevant to transformational change in attachment

---

sociation, 2011), 15-40.

[18]M. Elizabeth Lewis Hall, "Suffering as Formation: The Hard Road to Glory," in *The Holy Spirit and Christian Formation: Multidisciplinary Perspectives*, ed. Diane Chandler (New York: Palgrave Macmillan, 2016), 69-88.

[19]Calhoun and Tedeschi, "Foundations of Posttraumatic Growth," 3-23; Stephen Joseph and P. Alex Linley, "Growth Following Adversity: Theoretical Perspectives and Implications for Clinical Practice," *Clinical Psychology Review* 26 (2006): 1041-53.

filters that we have emphasized throughout this book. The most common changes in the view of self have to do with seeing the self as stronger, wiser, and more resilient.[20] People may also report greater acceptance of their vulnerabilities and limitations.[21] Suffering challenges our assumptions of control, allowing for the possibility that in our helplessness we can learn to be more dependent on God's Spirit and more connected to the love shared among the Trinity. It is noteworthy that an acute sense of helplessness is linked with the greatest growth in the posttraumatic stress literature. Only in this state do we fully recognize ourselves as creatures before a powerful God—but a God who is also merciful and loving. Character changes are reported frequently as well.[22]

With respect to relationships, suffering often results in a greater valuing of relationships, which may pave the way for more intimacy as the individual increases self-disclosure and emotional expressiveness. People may also gain a new sense of empathy and compassion for the suffering of others.[23] One study found that while all forms of prayer were positively correlated with growth in suffering, contemplative forms of prayer had the strongest relationship.[24] This type of prayer may facilitate a meaning-making process in God's presence, which is necessary for growth.

While suffering can positively impact our relationships, our relationships with God and others play a critical causal role in growing through suffering. We need others to help us in the process of meaning making. We need a balance of support and challenge in order for growth to occur. On the one hand, without sufficient support, we feel overwhelmed, making it difficult to digest painful experiences. On the other hand, without sufficient challenge, we may settle for unhealthy ways of coping.

---

[20]Calhoun and Tedeschi, "Foundations of Posttraumatic Growth," 3-23; Joseph and Linley, "Growth Following Adversity," 1041-53.

[21]Joseph and Linley, "Growth Following Adversity," 1041-53.

[22]Christopher Peterson et al., "Strengths of Character and Posttraumatic Growth," *Journal of Traumatic Stress* 21, no. 2 (2008): 214-17.

[23]Calhoun and Tedeschi, "Foundations of Posttraumatic Growth," 3-23; Joseph and Linley, "Growth Following Adversity," 1041-53.

[24]J. Irene Harris et al., "Coping Functions of Prayer and Posttraumatic Growth," *The International Journal for the Psychology of Religion* 20 (2010): 26-38.

We also need to bring our suffering to God. Hardships in our lives can cause people to distance themselves from God. Christ's example encourages us instead to struggle in God's loving presence. As Peter put it, Jesus "entrusted himself" to God (1 Peter 2:23 NIV). The verb tense used can be translated "kept entrusting" and indicates that this was a deliberate choice on Jesus' part.[25] In other words, Jesus kept his struggles before God, intentionally "handing [them] over" his sufferings to God.

Romans 8 is a rich and intriguing chapter focused on the suffering of the believer, culminating in the often-cited promise that "in all things God works for the good of those who love him" (Romans 8:28 NIV). This passage first talks about the "present sufferings" of the believer and then describes our "groanings" as we wait for the end of our sufferings and the "redemption of our bodies" (Romans 8:18, 23 NIV). However, we are not alone in our groanings, as we are told that the Spirit groans with us: "The Spirit helps us in our weakness. We do not know what we ought to pray for, but the Spirit himself intercedes for us through wordless groans . . . in accordance with the will of God" (Romans 8:26-27 NIV).[26] The Spirit aids us in bringing our suffering to the Father. In addition to this, the Spirit comforts us in our suffering by strengthening our Father-child relationship with God, which brings us into deeper participation in Christ's sonship with the Father. In other words, the Spirit guides us to experience and share in the love between Jesus and the Father in order to help us cope with, and even grow through, our sufferings in this life. "And by [the Spirit] we cry, '*Abba*, Father.' The Spirit himself testifies with our spirit that we are God's children. Now if we are children, then we are heirs—heirs of God and co-heirs with Christ, if indeed we share in his sufferings in order that we may also share in his glory" (Romans 8:15-17 NIV).

This passage in Romans 8 is particularly striking when viewed through an attachment framework. Paul uses the vivid imagery of the groanings

---

[25]D. Edmond Hiebert, "Selected Studies from 1 Peter Part 1: Following Christ's Example: An Exposition of 1 Peter 2:21-25," *Bibliotheca Sacra* 139, no. 553 (1982): 32-45.

[26]M. Elizabeth Lewis Hall, "Suffering as Formation: The Hard Road to Glory," in *The Holy Spirit and Christian Formation: Multidisciplinary Perspectives*, ed. Diane Chandler (New York: Palgrave Macmillan, 2016), 69-88.

of childbirth to describe the suffering, a picture of visceral, gut-wrenching pain made more difficult because it is nonverbal ("we do not know what we ought to pray for"). In an unimaginably intimate way, the Spirit attunes with our soul, taking on our groanings and bringing them to the Father. The secure attachment imagery in our experience of the Father is also clear here. In our distress, we cry out to the Father in the most intimate and informal way possible—"Abba!" or "Daddy!"—with the knowledge, reinforced by the Spirit, that God cares and responds. The possibilities for deep change to our attachment filter are striking.

Scripture gives us abundant guidance in the process of handing over our suffering to God, in the form of lament. The biblical practice of lament can be considered a kind of framework for meaning making and for referential integration of the two ways of knowing. Although lament occurs throughout Scripture, it is found in its purest form in the psalms, almost 40 percent of which are psalms of lament. Lament is not merely pouring out our heart to God, nor is it complaining or venting. Instead, lament has a specific structure. It is a stylized form of speech consisting of common elements that define a specific trajectory. The elements include: (1) an address to God, (2) a pouring out of our suffering to God, (3) a request to God to alleviate the suffering, and last but not least (4) an expression of trust in God.[27] The trajectory involves a transformative psychological move from distress to praise. In praying through the lament, the structure of the lament begins to restore some sense of order in the midst of chaos and pain. The shape of lament causes our verbalized experience to be molded by encountering the reality of God and his character in a powerful form of referential integration. When we express our experience in the form of lament, and allow our experience to be shaped by the words of the lament, our experience itself is transformed.

The Practices of Transformational Change

The last few decades have seen a resurgence of interest in ancient spiritual practices aimed at cultivating an intimate relationship with God. For

---

[27]Glen Pemberton, *Hurting with God: Learning to Lament with the Psalms* (Abilene, TX: Abilene Christian University Press, 2012), 65.

centuries, prayer, lectio divina (spiritual reading of Scripture), meditation on Scripture or contemplation of God, solitude, silence, and worship have been employed to experientially collaborate with the Holy Spirit in order to experience God's relational presence. Dallas Willard defined discipline as "an activity within our power—something we can do—which brings us to a point where we can do what we at present cannot do by direct effort."[28] As we have noted previously, the spiritual disciplines do not directly affect our ability to love God and others. However, they impact our growth indirectly by facilitating the relational processes that facilitate transformation in our souls.

The Christian practice of mindfulness, or mindful awareness, goes back centuries in the contemplative tradition.[29] Interestingly, the Christian practice of contemplation declined in the sixteenth and seventeenth centuries, largely as a result of an emphasis on scientific objectivism and mechanistic rationalism.[30] In other words, Christianity lost touch with the contemplative practices during the split between explicit theology and implicit spirituality, which we traced in chapter one. Reclaiming this contemplative tradition is consequently an important part of bringing these two ways of knowing back together in a relational spirituality paradigm.

Rather than focusing on individual spiritual practices, the intent here is to highlight how these disciplines can pave the way for transformation by facilitating a certain kind of internal environment that is open to experiences of God and others. As psychologist Eric Johnson puts it, "Christians have to re-wire their brains for accessing glory."[31] In order to do this, we turn to psychological research on mindfulness. While the secular psychological literature does not address the ultimate purpose of Christian contemplative practices—intimacy with God—it

---

[28]Dallas Willard, "Spiritual Disciplines, Spiritual Formation, and the Restoration of the Soul," *Journal of Psychology and Theology* 26 (1998): 106.

[29]Stephen P. Stratton, "Mindfulness and Contemplation: Secular and Religious Traditions in Western Context," *Counseling and Values* 60 (2015): 100-18.

[30]Stratton, "Mindfulness and Contemplation," 105.

[31]Eric L. Johnson, "How God Is Good for the Soul," *Journal of Psychology and Christianity* 22 (2003): 78-88.

is helpful in describing why these practices may, in fact, result in that kind of relational intimacy.

The practice of mindful awareness has to do with focusing your attention on your direct experience in the present moment and fostering a certain orientation to your experience characterized by curiosity, openness, acceptance, and love.[32] In the Christian tradition, mindful awareness is practiced as a type of prayer focused on one's direct experience of God and Jesus through the Holy Spirit. It has to do with giving one's full, undivided attention to relating to God in a passive, nondefensive, nondemanding, open way.[33] Mindful awareness is not just being aware in a general sense. It has to do with being aware of yourself in the context of your relationship with God. Furthermore, it has to do with accepting your experience via active listening and openness to the experience of God's presence.[34] Thus, awareness and acceptance are the two key characteristics of contemplative practice.

The disciplines included in the contemplative tradition play an important role in facilitating the integration of the two ways of knowing. When the contemplative prayer practices are silent, imageless, and focused exclusively on being in God's presence, a bottom-up referential integration may be facilitated in which our experiences are interpreted. In this careful attention to oneself in God's presence in the present moment, images, gut-level sensations, and discrete emotions may surface and ultimately find their way into more specific ideas.

Sometimes practices in the contemplative tradition are more meditative in nature. In other words, rather than having no focus (other than being in God's presence), the focus is on a specific passage of Scripture, visualization, or short prayer. The combination of explicit knowledge with attentive meditation may result in a top-down referential process, in which we feel an idea. Explicit biblical teachings or characteristics of

---

[32]Daniel J. Siegel, *The Mindful Brain: Reflection and Attunement in the Cultivation of Well-Being* (New York: W. W. Norton & Co., 2007).

[33]Stratton, "Mindfulness and Contemplation," 109.

[34]Natasha Monroe and Peter J. Jankowski, "The Effectiveness of a Prayer Intervention in Promoting Change in Perceived Attachment to God, Positive Affect, and Psychological Distress," *Psychology of Religion and Spirituality* 3 (2016): 237-49.

God on which the practitioner is meditating can find their way into implicit knowledge. Regardless of the route of the referential integration, practitioners of contemplative practices often report that the outcome is an awareness of being deeply loved and loving in return.[35] In fact, several recent studies on contemplative practices have reported increased perceived closeness to God with centering prayer,[36] spiritual meditation,[37] and prayer involving asking God questions, then waiting patiently and silently for a response.[38] We might say that contemplative practices facilitate a secure attachment to God.

The psychological literature on mindfulness notes that the essential elements necessary to cultivate awareness are silence and solitude. In our contemporary world, we are constantly bombarded with some kind of stimuli. If we don't make an intentional effort, it is easy to never be alone with our thoughts or with God. Attending to the stimuli that bombard us from the outside is precisely the opposite of mindfulness. We give up control over what we focus our attention on, and the result is that we do not attend to our own inner experience. Moreover, our attention is scattered in such a state, making it difficult for new thoughts, new information, and new perspectives to emerge. Silence and solitude help us to focus our attention inwardly and to allow new experiences to emerge.

As we practice silence, we develop the capacity to be present in the moment. The present moment is the only place we begin to be aware of our sensations, our observations of our own mind, and a kind of knowing that has a more direct quality to it. This is a gradual process that takes intentionality, but as we develop the capacity to be mindfully aware—to be present in the moment—it leads to several beneficial outcomes: (1) we come to more easily hold multiple perspectives; (2) we become less reactive to our experiences; (3) we observe our sensations;

---

[35]Monroe and Jankowski, "Effectiveness of a Prayer Intervention," 111.

[36]J. K. Ferguson, E. W. Willemsen, and M. V. Castañeto, "Centering Prayer as a Healing Response to Everyday Stress: A Psychological and Spiritual Process," *Pastoral Psychology* 59 (2010): 305-29.

[37]A. B. Wachholtz and K. I. Pargament, "Is Spirituality a Critical Ingredient of Meditation? Comparing the Effects of Spiritual Meditation, Secular Meditation, and Relaxation on Spiritual, Psychological, Cardiac, and Pain Outcomes," *Journal of Behavioral Medicine* 28 (2005): 369-84.

[38]Monroe and Jankowski, "Effectiveness of a Prayer Intervention."

(4) we act with a deep awareness of our own mind; (5) we label and translate our experiences in a way that does not remove them from their experiential nature; and (6) we do not judge our experience automatically in an autopilot mode.[39]

Numerous benefits have been demonstrated to result from the practice of mindful awareness. Mindfulness improves relationships, possibly by improving the ability to sense others' nonverbal emotional signals and internal worlds. This is likely a core mechanism of empathy, which facilitates compassion for others. In fact, research has shown that mindfulness and secure attachment are related. The two dispositions have related neurological correlates, foster similar positive psychosocial outcomes, and may mutually influence each other.[40] Mindfulness practices have been found to decrease insecure attachment, perhaps by allowing for better emotional self-regulation and by decreasing defensiveness during conflict.[41] Put simply, these practices help us love others better.

The common neurobiological mechanism for these positive outcomes appears to be the middle prefrontal cortex, which has been shown to be activated during mindfulness. This part of the brain blocks the top-down flow that normally predominates automatically. It does this in part by providing an *integrative* function. The fibers from this area of the brain reach out and connect to distant areas of the brain, linking the various areas to provide a functional unity. Thus, areas that have their own special function come to function as a whole in combination with other areas. Neural integration involves the monitoring and influencing of firing patterns of various distinct regions of the brain.[42] These elements remain differentiated, but they now work

---

[39]Siegel, *Mindful Brain.*

[40]C. A. Pepping, P. J. Davis, and A. O'Donovan, "Individual Differences in Attachment and Dispositional Mindfulness: The Mediating Role of Emotion Regulation," *Personality and Individual Differences* 54 (2013): 453-56; P. R. Shaver, S. Lavy, C. D. Saron, and M. Mikulincer, "Social Foundations of the Capacity for Mindfulness: An Attachment Perspective," *Psychological Inquiry* 18 (2007): 264-71.

[41]R. M. Hertz, H. K. Laurent, and S. M. Laurent, "Attachment Mediates Effects of Trait Mindfulness on Stress Responses to Conflict," *Mindfulness* 6 (2015): 483-89; R. M. Ryan, K. W. Brown, and J. D. Creswell, "How Integrative Is Attachment Theory? Unpacking the Meaning and Significance of Felt Security," *Psychological Inquiry* 18 (2007): 177-82.

[42]Siegel, *Developing Mind*, 2012, 339-44.

together as one unit, able to accomplish things they could not accomplish by themselves.

This type of neural integration and coordination within the brain is actually an outcome of attuned relationships. This goes back to how God created us to connect. Secure, attuned relationships and being present in the moment in those relationships actually lay down the neural circuitry in our brains that facilitates emotional and relational security. Integration in the brain, in general, turns out to be a fundamental process in all aspects of well-being, and we can see how this notion of differentiated components functioning as one unit captures a core truth at many levels of reality: the brain, the self, relationships, families, communities, and organizations of all types require integration for health and well-being. In fact, it may be that this aspect of our functioning reflects something of the trinitarian nature of God. *Perichōrēsis*, or the sharing of divine love among the Trinity, can be conceptualized as the prototype of integration.

One of the mechanisms involved in mindfulness helps us understand the positive outcomes it engenders. Richard Davidson has shown that mindfulness helps people regulate their emotions by approaching them.[43] He found that when people encounter emotion-provoking stimuli, there is a shift toward left anterior prefrontal activity, and this part of the brain is believed to be associated with positive affect and with approach. It appears, then, that being present in the moment and being mindful of our own mind helps us to approach our emotions with a positive stance— perhaps one of curiosity and acceptance. This in turn helps us to regulate our emotions and understand their meaning. This is likely a fundamental process involved in referential integration, or integrating the two ways of knowing.

One of the biggest challenges to being present in the moment is the top-down patterns of brain activation that keep us on automatic pilot. Cars provide an analogy here. I have a friend who likes fully automatic cars. He doesn't want to know or feel when the car is shifting gears. His

---

[43]Richard J. Davidson, "Well-Being and Affective Style: Neural Substrates and Biobehavioral Correlates," *Philosophical Transactions of the Royal Society of London B*, 359 (2004): 1395-1411.

father, in contrast, liked sports cars in which he could feel the road. When we are on autopilot due to top-down patterns, we do not feel the road of life. Our automatic reactions pull us out of direct, immediate experience. We just glide along, unaware of when we shift gears. This narrows the scope of our awareness. We become aware of only the result of our automatic pilot rather than being aware of what our mind is doing and that we are separate from the operations of our mind rather than embedded within them. These habitual top-down patterns are highly selective and cause us to grasp onto preconceived notions about the way things should be, which causes an inherent tension with the way things actually are.

Mindfulness undermines the dominance of our explicit, verbal networks involved in these top-down processing circuits. The role of mindful awareness is to help us discern the nature of the mind itself, which seems to be a precondition for the insight that preconceived ideas and emotional reactions to events are not the same as one's self. This activates and provides access to our implicit relational knowledge of our sense of self. It helps us grasp the idea that there is something deeper to the self that stands under our reactions and emotions. This experience of our core self is a type of implicit relational knowledge. This is the domain in which transformational or nonlinear change occurs. The net result is that mindful awareness loosens the grip of our attachment filters. It makes them more flexible and less rigid, which is a core indicator of psychospiritual well-being and maturity.

Being present in the moment is a core part of what it means to find our identity in Christ and to express this identity through service, rather than finding our identity in the doing of our service. In other words, mindful awareness is central to help our doing flow from our being. Only when we are present in the moment can our doing flow from our being. If we are not present in the moment, we operate on automatic pilot, and there is little sense of being. Doing is operating on its own, apart from any conscious, attending "I," and apart from the Holy Spirit. When this happens, we live in the past or the future. When we are present, however, we begin to break the top-down patterns of brain activation that keep us on autopilot. We begin to rewire these circuits in a way that frees us up to receive new information, to be surprised by new perceptions that were ruled out by our previous top-down patterns. We can fully be with others, which allows us to love them more deeply.

Perhaps this allows us to gain a greater glimpse of God. Much of our experience of God is colored by our attachment filters, which hinder our experience of the loving presence of God. The most profound tipping points occur when we see God more for who God really is. But God does not force us to be with him in a way that restructures our implicit knowledge of him. Instead, God invites us to be present in the moment and share in the very same love that flows between the Father, Son, and Holy Spirit, thereby receiving love into the core of our being.

Conclusion

We have articulated here a relational framework for understanding the process of spiritual growth. The foundation for this model is the nature of transformational change. As we strive to grow through relationships with God and others, incremental changes occur, but they are often difficult to see. Even when we don't see immediate results, we need to continue our intentional efforts to grow, knowing that the incremental changes will eventually combine to forge qualitative shifts in our attachment filters. This transformational or nonlinear change is what leads to deep changes in our ability to love God and others.

There are several processes that facilitate transformational change. One key process is the integration of the two ways of knowing through a story process. Our raw experiences become interpreted as we tell our story, which in turn transforms our emotions and experiences. Likewise, hearing stories of faith and growth helps us to feel an idea, working explicit knowledge into our hearts, which in turn leads to new explicit knowledge.

A second key process in transformational change is the meaning-making process that can occur as a result of suffering. As our deep beliefs about the world and relationships are challenged and reorganized, entrusting our suffering to God presents the opportunity for our implicit and explicit knowledge to become more integrated, complex and mature.

Finally, we turned to the practices that facilitate deep change. Spiritual disciplines bring intentionality to the process of change. The Christian practice of mindfulness, in particular, has the potential to hinder negative automatic cycles and promote the ability to be relationally present and intimate with God.

To this point, while emphasizing relationships, we have focused largely on the individual Christian. In the next and final chapter, we conclude our exploration of a relational spirituality paradigm with a focus on the relational communities that God established as the nurseries for our growth in love.

Spiritual Community

The Communal Nature of Spiritual Transformation

LET'S BEGIN WITH a thought experiment. What would happen if we took seriously the *relational nature* of being made in the image of God, the *relational goal* of sanctification as loving presence, and *relational processes* as the means of sanctification? We would engage intentionally with other Christians, allowing them to form us in loving ways, and participating deeply in their growth in loving ways. We would work through difficulties in relationships, and grow in perseverance, patience, and the ability to forgive as we dealt with each other's growing edges. Over time, attachment relationships like those experienced in families would develop, and the resulting communities would be living demonstrations of God's love to those outside of their communities.

This emerging picture of spiritual communities characterized by love should sound familiar, because it is a central theme in the New Testament, where it is referred to as the church. We tend to think about a church as a building, or perhaps as a set of programs centered around a Sunday morning service. However, the church is an *ekklēsia* as described by New Testament writers—in other words, "a people" or a community. As 1 Peter 2:9-10 (NIV) puts it, "You are a chosen people, a royal priesthood, a holy nation, God's special possession, that you may declare the praises of him who called you out of darkness into his wonderful light. Once you were not a people, but now you are the people of God."

In the New Testament, the church is described as a family created by God for a specific purpose: to collectively demonstrate God's love and be a visible sign of salvation for all nations. The church would draw the nations to itself by being a contrast-society living out a new social order of love.[1] The community of God would be a radiant city on the hill (Matthew 5:13-16).

While the idea of long-term, loving relationships in the context of the church is not a new idea, it is a radical idea. Unlike the context of the early church, our (Western) cultural context is one of radical individualism. We are socialized into independence, not healthy interdependence. We are socialized to think that we have the authority, and even moral obligation, to decide on our own values and tell our own stories. We are socialized to prioritize our own desires and subjective happiness over the good of whatever group we belong to, be that family, friends, or church. In this context, the norm is to think of church as a place to get my needs (as defined by myself) met. This typically results in a pattern of jumping from church to church in search of the perfect place. This is not the biblical picture of spiritual community, nor does it foster deep spiritual formation.

Spiritual formation occurs primarily in community. As we noted earlier, while we cannot directly control our spiritual growth process, we can be intentional about involvement in spiritual community. We can "put ourselves in the way of God." Involvement—ongoing, long-term involvement—in a spiritual community is the relational context for being transformed to become more like Christ.

If spiritual formation is primarily about learning to love, how can that pursuit be served by leaving relationships when they get hard or do not feel satisfying? The very opposite of this is taught throughout the New Testament; we are expected to lay aside our self-interests for our fellow Christians. This commitment to the community above the self is taken to the extreme of dying for the sake of our community. John told his readers, "This is how we know what love is: Jesus Christ laid down his

---

[1]Gerhard Lohfink, *Jesus and Community* (Philadelphia: Fortress Press, 1982).

life for us. And we ought to lay down our lives for our brothers and sisters" (1 John 3:16).

Throughout this book, our unit of analysis has been, in one sense, the individual (and dyadic relationships): how, as individuals, we image God; how our individual brains work; how we develop relational filters; and how we grow and change in the context of relationships. However, an integral part of the relational spirituality paradigm here is that the individual self is inextricably formed in relationships. As we have noted, our brain and soul are fundamentally social in their very nature. Thus, even as we have focused on the individual, our unit of analysis can never be strictly the individual. To truly understand the person, we must understand his or her social and community context. In this chapter, we will revisit many of the above themes, but from the vantage point of explicitly starting at the group level rather than the individual level. What is the importance of the church? What is its function? What are the characteristics of a spiritual community that facilitate spiritual growth so that individually and corporately we reflect who God is?

When we examine biblical teachings on the church, perhaps not surprisingly, many of the themes we have emphasized at the individual level also emerge as central. We concluded in chapter two that we bear the image of God as beings-in-relation. The image of God is participation in trinitarian love. This love is extended to the body of Christ as a more complete manifestation of the image of God and the love of God. As God is trinitarian, we image God most fully in community, which requires maintaining our individuality. The image includes the capacity for dyadic love, but it is most fully expressed in community. Simon Chan notes, "The spiritual life is essentially life-in-relation patterned after and sustained by the Trinity that assumes a definite shape within the church created by Christ."[2]

In chapters three through five we discussed how we, as individuals, need relationships—especially attachment relationships such as those

---

[2]Simon Chan, *Spiritual Theology: A Systematic Study of the Christian Life* (Downers Grove, IL: InterVarsity Press, 1998), 103.

found within a family. The New Testament describes the church as the new family of God. Chapters six and seven developed the concept of loving presence as the goal of spiritual development. As we will see, the primary characteristic of the New Testament church is love. In chapter eight we discussed the need for relationships in order to produce deep, internal transformation in our capacity to love. The New Testament repeatedly uses the metaphor of the body to describe the church as the primary context for growth.

Throughout this book, we have made the argument that we need others to grow. In this chapter, our focus is on who the others are: the church. In the remainder of this chapter, we will briefly highlight the biblical context for the importance of spiritual community. Following this, we will highlight four key characteristics of spiritual community that help us go about creating the kind of communities in which our hearts are transformed by connecting our stories to God's grand story. We conclude by pulling together some key implications for creating spiritual community together.

The Nature of Spiritual Community

Ecclesiology, the study of the church, occupies a prominent place in the teachings of the New Testament. This is especially true in the Epistles, where the biblical writers were concerned with establishing and strengthening the newly emerging spiritual communities resulting from missionary activity. Paul gave more attention to the concept of spiritual communities than any of the other biblical authors. He refers to aspects of community life in every one of his writings, and in a few, community is the primary focus.[3]

Paul frequently used metaphors to help early Christians understand the nature of spiritual community. He compared the church to a building or temple, to a field or grafting on a tree, and to dough. He showed a distinct preference for the metaphor of a body, developing it in several of his letters. However, his most significant metaphor for the church was

---

[3]Robert J. Banks, *Paul's Idea of Community: The Early House Churches in Their Cultural Setting*, rev. ed. (Grand Rapids, MI: Baker Academic, 1994), 1.

the church as a family.[4] We focus here on Paul's two primary metaphors for describing the church: the church as family and the church as a body. The first metaphor, the church as family, focuses on the bonds of love that should characterize our life together as sons and daughters of God. The second metaphor, the church as body, highlights the interdependence of the members of the body, particularly as it relates to the growth of the body. We will examine each of these in turn.

The church as family. Jesus promised those who left their families to follow him that God would be their Father (Matthew 23:9) and that they would have many mothers, brothers, and sisters (Mark 10:29-30). In this way, Jesus established the church as a new family, consisting of all who followed Jesus. This way of thinking about the church is the first and most foundational of the metaphors used by Paul. We might even say that it transcends a mere metaphor, describing a new reality. Brothers and sisters became the most common way of referring to, and thinking about, one another in the context of the church. This status as siblings was rooted in the common experience of being sons and daughters of God.

This was a new, radically reenvisioned family that crossed socioeconomic, cultural, and ethnic lines in order to show God's character more clearly. It was not merely a comforting new way of addressing each other; rather, it demanded a series of new obligations, some of them quite radical. For example, in Paul's letter to Philemon he relies on family ties to convince Philemon to release Onesimus from slavery and accept him as a fellow brother in Christ. Similarly, the book of Ephesians argues for the unity of Jews and Gentiles in the church in light of their common Father. "For through him we both have access to the Father by one Spirit. Consequently, you are no longer foreigners and strangers, but fellow citizens with God's people and also members of his household" (Ephesians 2:18-19).

The strength of this family metaphor is difficult for us to grasp given our current cultural context. As adults, even when we are close to our

---

[4]Banks, *Paul's Idea of Community*, 49.

families of origin, other commitments, such as those to our spouses and children, come first. Furthermore, many people maintain only superficial ties to their siblings, who may live far away geographically. This situation is far removed from the family understanding that Paul was relying on to develop his family metaphor.

Joseph Hellerman notes that in the Mediterranean world of the New Testament, the primary commitment was to the family of origin, rather than to the marriage.[5] Ties of common blood were much stronger than the "merely" contractual bonds of marriage. In other words, the strongest ties of loyalty and affection were not to the spouse but to siblings. In a world where marriages were formed in order to enhance the honor or wealth of the bloodline, the quality of the relationship of the husband and wife took a backseat. Consequently, in communicating a picture of committed and affectionate relationships, Paul used the stronger metaphor of the sibling relationship rather than the marital relationship. Paul used family imagery to communicate expectations regarding the emotional bond between community members, the unity among them, the sharing of resources typical of a family context, and the loyalty and commitment of the members.[6]

The new family ties were grounded in love. The use of the family metaphor seems to be driven by the emphasis on warm, interdependent relationships such as those found in families. Theologian Gerhard Lohfink notes that "in the New Testament . . . interpersonal love almost without exception means *love for one's brother in the faith, love of Christians for one another*."[7] He goes on to say, "There seems to be hardly anything else about the New Testament which is as intensively suppressed as this fact." He then lists twenty-four instances in which we are admonished to love those in the church. These instances are interspersed with allusions to family, in the form of encouragement to love our brothers and sisters and to love God's children. The centrality of love to the understanding of the

---

[5]Joseph H. Hellerman, *When the Church Was a Family: Recapturing Jesus' Vision for Authentic Christian Community* (Nashville, TN: B&H Publishing, 2009), 37-38.
[6]Hellerman, *When the Church Was a Family*, 78-79.
[7]Lohfink, *Jesus and Community*, 110; italics in original. Lohfink goes on to argue that different terms are used to describe concern for those outside the church, 110-13.

church explains why Paul can conclude that members of the community are to "let no debt remain outstanding, except the continuing debt to love one another" (Romans 13:8 NIV).

John's Gospel and letters expound on this familial love with particular clarity. First, we see that John reminds us that we cannot separate love of God from love of others: "For whoever does not love their brother or sister, whom they have seen, cannot love God, whom they have not seen" (1 John 4:20 NIV). Our relational connection with God is intimately tied up with our relational connections with others. True community flows from our relationship with God and reflects the very nature of our trinitarian God. In fact, it is somewhat misleading to speak of growth as something that happens solely inside the individual. The more we love, the more we identify with Christ's body, the church. The goal of sanctification is not only the pursuit of individual qualities but also the development of qualities that allow us to live well with our brothers and sisters in Christ.[8] The goal is not merely to increase one's individual capacity to love, but to love others well, particularly in the context of Christian community.

We see this intimate connection between loving God and others earlier in John's first epistle, in a passage that is worth quoting in its entirety:

> Dear friends, let us continue to love one another, for love comes from God. Anyone who loves is a child of God and knows God. But anyone who does not love does not know God, for God is love. God showed how much he loved us by sending his one and only Son into the world so that we might have eternal life through him. This is real love—not that we loved God, but that he loved us and sent his Son as a sacrifice to take away our sins. Dear friends, since God loved us that much, we surely ought to love each other. No one has ever seen God. But if we love each other, God lives in us, and his love is brought to full expression in us. (1 John 4:7-12)

God's love for us is the foundation of our love for others.

The church as body. In using the metaphor of a family, Paul emphasizes the basis and character of relationships in spiritual communities.

---

[8]Lohfink, *Jesus and Community*, 102-3.

However, when he uses the metaphor of the body, he seems more concerned with interdependence and consequent growth of the members of the spiritual community. In 1 Corinthians 12, Paul draws numerous analogies between the human body and the church. Like body parts, each member of the body of Christ belongs and has a function within the larger body. The intrinsic connectedness of the members of the body is also stressed in this passage. What happens to one member of the body affects the entire body. Paul does not say that it should affect the entire body; he simply states that it does (1 Corinthians 12:26). Similarly, Romans 12 stresses that we are one body *in* Christ; Christ is the source of that connectedness. We are intrinsically interconnected by virtue of our faith in Christ.

In Colossians, Paul connects the body metaphor to the idea of growth. Christ is identified as "the head, from whom the whole body, supported and held together by its ligaments and sinews, grows as God causes it to grow" (Colossians 2:19 NIV). Similarly, in Ephesians Paul says that members of the body are given a variety of gifts "to equip his people for works of service, so that the body of Christ may be built up until we all reach unity in the faith and in the knowledge of the Son of God and become mature, attaining to the whole measure of the fullness of Christ" (Ephesians 4:12-13 NIV). The passage further articulates the relational nature of the interactions that will lead to growth: "speaking the truth in love, we will grow to become in every respect the mature body of him who is the head, that is, Christ. From him the whole body, joined and held together by every supporting ligament, grows and builds itself up in love, as each part does its work" (Ephesians 4:15-16 NIV).

These passages make clear that we depend on each other in the body of Christ to help us grow into maturity. In living out deeply connected, familial relationships with each other and in interacting with each other in light of our gifts, we help others grow individually and corporately. This goes back to chapter three and the idea that we are created to connect. God designed us such that we need a deep sense of belonging and connection to a community, and the kinds of interactions that occur in these communities, in order to grow.

The concept of speaking the truth in love—authoritative speaking into our lives in the context of a caring relationship—is pervasive throughout the New Testament. For example, Peter instructs us that "Each of you should use whatever gift you have received to serve others, as faithful stewards of God's grace in its various forms" (1 Peter 4:8-10 NIV). Paul instructs us to comfort others with the comfort we have received from God (2 Corinthians 1:3-4). However, we are also instructed to hold each other accountable for our sin and to confront each other (Matthew 18:15-17). We are to help each other see the truth about ourselves and God. Yet, we are always to do this in the context of God's grace, with the other person's best interest in mind, which is love.

Another way of examining the New Testament emphasis on interdependence on each other for growth is seen in the frequent New Testament use of the reciprocal pronoun "one another." Paul, in particular, repeatedly exhorted the early church to engage with one another in a variety of ways. One of the broadest of these "one another" statements, 1 Thessalonians 5:11, says to "build one another up" (RSV). The point of this building up is not simply to contribute to the self-improvement project of the individual Christian, but to contribute to the building of the church, the community. The church as the focus of the "building up," as well as the role of communal practices in achieving this goal, are clear in another Pauline passage: 1 Corinthians 14:26 states, "When you come together, each of you has a hymn, or a word of instruction, a revelation, a tongue or an interpretation. Everything must be done so that the church may be built up" (NIV). What we do together in the context of our meeting as the church contributes to our growth.

Among the lengthy list of "one anothers," another deserves special mention: that of "admonishing one another." This command, found in Romans 15:14, is expanded on in Galatians 6:1: "Brothers and sisters, if someone is caught in a sin, you who live by the Spirit should restore that person gently" (NIV). When speaking of loving one another and building each other up, we may lose sight of the fact that love for others also involves seeking their good in the form of correction. The community love found in the New Testament is never a superficial love focused primarily on making others feel good; instead, it has expectations for its members and sometimes requires difficult interactions in the hope of promoting well-being or health of the soul.

Thus, as the family of God, we are to have loving, committed relationships with our brothers and sisters in Christ. As the body of Christ, we are interdependent on each other, and in the context of exercising our gifts, we grow and mature, individually and corporately, as the church. In the next section we will unpack these ideas further, drawing on some research from the social sciences to help illustrate the characteristics of a spiritual community.

Four Characteristics of Spiritual Community

We can think of a spiritual community as having four key characteristics, each discussed below: spiritual, relational, intentional, and authoritative.

Spiritual. First, a spiritual community is not just a community; it is spiritual by its very nature. The goal of a *spiritual* community is not just to foster general social connections. It is to glorify God by continually stimulating spiritual transformation among its members—transformation into the image of Christ. Stated differently, the goal is to glorify God by developing human beings who are fully human, imaging God. One of the ways in which spiritual communities do this is through what is sometimes referred to as the "means of grace."

Means of grace are the "ordinary channels . . . of the supernatural influences of the Holy Spirit."[9] They are the common ways the Holy Spirit uses to imbue God's transforming grace into our lives. The Holy Spirit can, of course, use any circumstance in our lives as a means of God's grace, but there are certain communal practices that are specifically mentioned in Scripture and modeled by Jesus that stand out as special vehicles of transformation. While the specific means of grace that are emphasized differ among the Christian traditions, given our particular

---

[9]Charles Hodge, *Systematic Theology, Volume III* (Grand Rapids, MI: Eerdmans, 1940), 217.

focus on relational transformation, we note three in particular: the Word of God, the Lord's Supper, and worship. Moreover, in this section we focus on the *communal* practice of these means of grace.

In chapter eight we noted spiritual disciplines in the contemplative tradition that can assist in integrating the two ways of knowing, and in our direct relationship with God. These types of disciplines are typically practiced individually. However, a biblical ecclesiology also recognizes the importance of communal spiritual practices in shaping us. Our individual spiritual practices should grow out of our participation in the life of the community. This is a fact that is often forgotten in our individualistic societies and Protestant contexts with their emphasis on personal devotions. Public reading of Scripture, the Lord's Supper, and communal singing are some of the major components of public worship in all Christian traditions. How do they contribute to our formation? These communal practices engage us with others as we more fully weave our stories together with God's story in physical, embodied ways.

One means of grace by which spiritual communities point us toward God is the Word of God—perhaps the most explicit way of putting our story in the context of God's larger story. As we hear God's Word, we are given the opportunity to open our hearts to God's grace. We see our lives in a different perspective. God's Word draws us into loving relationship with God and with one another. Eugene Peterson expresses this idea cogently: "The primary reason for a book is to put a writer into relation with readers so that we can listen to his or her stories and find ourselves in them, listen to his or her songs and sing along with them, listen to his or her arguments and argue with them, listen to his or her answers and question them."[10] Scripture makes clear that the Holy Spirit enables change through God's Word (John 8:43, 47; 1 Corinthians 2:14; James 1:18). When Jesus prays for his disciples, he prays, "Sanctify them by the truth; your word is truth" (John 17:17 NIV). Engagement with God's Word can lead to tipping points that change our experience of our lives in the here and now. This brings us back to the fundamental purpose of

---

[10]Eugene H. Peterson, *Working the Angles: The Shape of Pastoral Integrity* (Grand Rapids, MI: Eerdmans, 1987), 99.

our lives. Our two knowledge systems can then mutually influence one another in the knowledge spiral as we process God's Word and open our hearts to the work of the Holy Spirit. As Peter Toon puts it, "Christians are wholly involved in [the biblical] story because they are brought into union with the Father, through the Son and in the Holy Spirit. The story, which is ultimately the story of the Holy Trinity, becomes their story. They are involved in divine autobiography."[11]

What, then, is the role of community in God's Word as a means of grace? Isn't it sufficient to read our Bibles alone? Tod Bolsinger emphasizes that *who* reads the biblical stories and *how* they are read are as important as the fact that they are read.[12] The storytellers model the transforming power of the story and, through the powerful medium of face-to-face contact, communicate the emotion and meaning of the story. The relationships with the storytellers similarly influence the assimilation of the stories.

The Lord's Supper is an intrinsically relational practice, as we remember and celebrate the central story of Christianity: Jesus' death on the cross for us. We literally take in the body and blood of Christ, allowing it to nurture and sustain us. In this powerful gesture of dependent relationship, we are shaped by the story of salvation. Yet the Lord's Supper is also a communal event. First Corinthians 11:27-34 makes clear the profound importance of recognizing the communal implications of taking the Lord's Supper together. Commentators believe that the wealthier members of the congregation would arrive earlier and have a more bountiful meal, leaving the scraps for the rest of the community. This violated the unity that the meal was to represent and foster. Earlier in his letter, Paul had written, "Is not the cup of thanksgiving for which we give thanks a participation in the blood of Christ? And is not the bread that we break a participation in the body of Christ? Because there is one loaf, we, who are many, are one body, for we all share the one loaf" (1 Corinthians 10:16-17 NIV). The Lord's Supper was a concrete

---

[11]Peter Toon, *Our Triune God: A Biblical Portrayal of the Trinity* (Wheaton, IL: Victor, 1996), 62.
[12]Tod E. Bolsinger, *It Takes a Church to Raise a Christian: How the Community of God Transforms Lives* (Grand Rapids, MI: Brazos Press, 2004), 121-22.

representation of the unity of the body of Christ. Engaging in the ordinary, everyday behavior of eating and drinking together weaves our everyday lives together. The communal taking of the bread and wine is a regular practice intended to deepen the connection between members of the community around the story of the sacrifice of Christ.

Worship is yet another powerful communal means of grace. The primary point of worship is not personal transformation; it is to glorify God. Having said that, when we engage in worship, recognizing who we are in relationship to God, we are also opening ourselves up to being transformed by that experience. While worship is a very broad category, we focus here on one of the specific ways it has been practiced communally since Old Testament times: communal singing. Singing together in worship may be one of the most powerful means of grace for emphasizing our interrelatedness. Interestingly, psychological research on groups demonstrates that singing together produces an endorphin release and promotes a sense of cohesion.[13] In the context of the church, when we sing together, we are proclaiming historical events and signaling their significance for our lives in the present.[14] Simultaneously, we are weaving our story with the stories of those around us. In a summary that pulls together many of the themes we have been highlighting, James Torrance writes, "In worship, as at the Lord's table . . . we seek together, in a life of communion, to comprehend with the saints of all ages the Triune love of God in Christ."[15]

There are many means of grace in which spiritual communities engage, and many ways of going about them. The main point here is that a spiritual community is a particular kind of community that has a specific end goal—transformation into the image of Christ and building the kingdom of God. Because of this, spiritual communities must engage in particular kinds of activities together in order to achieve the end goal of being transformed into the image of Christ.

---

[13]Eiluned Pearce, Jacques Launay, and Robin I. M. Dunbar, "The Ice-Breaker Effect: Singing Mediates Fast Social Bonding," *Royal Society Open Science* 2 (2015): n.p.

[14]Bolsinger, *It Takes a Church to Raise a Christian*, 88.

[15]James B. Torrance, *Worship, Community & the Triune God of Grace* (Downers Grove, IL: InterVarsity Press, 1997), x.

Relational. It almost goes without saying, but a spiritual community is relational by its very nature. We often take this for granted, but if we think about this, it means that a spiritual community has to do things that explicitly foster relationships among its members. What kind of relationships, then, should be fostered? We noted earlier that attachment relationships are particularly important to change the deep structure of our attachment filters. These are people to whom we have an emotional connection, meaning that we can rely on them for support, comfort, and encouragement, particularly during difficult times.

There are increasingly fewer places where people can develop these kinds of close relationships. Sociological research relying on large, population-based data demonstrates that in the last four decades, our social networks of close ties have shrunk.[16] In 1985, when asked to name people with whom they have discussed important matters during the preceding six months, respondents offered an average of three others. Two separate studies in 2011 found that this number had decreased to only two. Similarly, in his groundbreaking book *Bowling Alone*, Robert Putnam argued that we have become increasingly disconnected from family, friends, and neighbors.[17]

There are two types of attachments we can foster in a spiritual community: specific attachment relationships between two people and attachment to the community itself. The first type we discussed in chapter five. Spiritual communities need to be structured such that people can develop meaningful connections with one another. This needs to take the form of small groups as one dimension of the community. We will return to the importance of group size shortly.

In addition, much like a family, a spiritual community is more than the sum of the individual parts. Every community has a set of social norms, values, and implicit/unspoken rules, as well as a particular feeling

---

[16]Matthew E. Brashears and Laura Aufderheide Brashears, "Close Friendships Among Contemporary People," in *Emerging Trends in the Social and Behavioral Sciences: An Interdisciplinary Searchable, and Linkable Resource*, ed. Robert A. Scott and Marlis C. Buchmann (Hoboken, NJ: John Wiley & Sons, 2015): 1-12.

[17]Robert D. Putnam, *Bowling Alone: The Collapse and Revival of American Community* (New York: Simon & Schuster, 2000).

or tone. We might capture this to some extent with the concept of *ethos*. Most of the ethos of a spiritual community is implicit and unspoken. All members of the community contribute to its ethos, but the leadership contributes a disproportionately large amount to it. As the leaders go, so go the people.

As noted in chapter four, John Bowlby, the founder of attachment theory, made an interesting point that attachment behavior is often directed toward groups and institutions, such as schools, colleges, work groups, and religious groups.[18] Such groups can actually become a secondary attachment figure, and in some cases a primary attachment figure. I found this to be the case when I practiced psychology in the Army for several years. It was commonly known among mental health officers that many soldiers would come to treat the Army as an attachment figure. In cases in which they were discharged due to psychological issues, these individuals exhibited many of the signs of separation and loss of an attachment figure. Bowlby noted that in most such cases, the development of attachment to the group occurs through attachment—sometimes symbolically—to a person (or persons) holding a prominent position within that group.

This has important implications for spiritual communities of all types. Leaders (whether explicitly defined as such or not) set the tone for the ethos of a spiritual community to which most members will be become attached to some extent. In addition, because leaders represent the group, individual members of the community develop an attachment to the group via the leaders. Leaders, then, bear a large responsibility to develop a healthy community ethos so that members can develop secure attachments to a community that models grace.

Intentional. Spiritual communities are intentional. Creating a context in which people tell their real stories, and develop deep relationships with each other and with God, does not happen accidentally. In fact, if we look at the landscape of our churches today, there is evidence that it is very difficult to develop true communities. For example, fewer than

---

[18]John Bowlby, *Attachment and Loss, Volume 1: Attachment*, 2nd ed. (New York: Basic Books, 1982).

one out of six Christians has a relationship with another believer that provides some level of spiritual accountability.[19] Our individual relationships with God and others require intentionality. This is even more the case for a community of people with different cultural backgrounds, personalities, visions, concerns, relational and spiritual histories, and levels of spiritual maturity and commitment. As we have discussed, we cannot control the process of spiritual growth, but we can create the conditions for growth by intentionally doing things that foster community. There is no formula for this. It can look as many different ways as there are communities. But we must be intentional.

One of the things we must be intentional about is the size of the functional units of our communities. Psychologist and anthropologist Robin Dunbar concluded from his research that the upper limit of an average person's social network is around 150 people.[20] In other words, "Dunbar's number" sets the upper limit on the number of individuals we can know as persons—that is, those with whom we have a defined personal relationship, and with whom we are bound because of a shared history or commitment to shared values and beliefs.[21] Not coincidentally, this turns out to be the typical size of personal social networks in contemporary society, as well as the most common number of friends listed on Facebook pages.[22]

Dunbar argues that this upper limit is related to the size of the human neocortex—the part of the brain responsible for abstract thought and reasoning. The more people in your group or community, the more relationships you have to monitor and remember. Relationships require investments of memory and empathy, and enough knowledge of others to predict their behavior. Relationships also require time investments for

---

[19]George Barna, *Revolution* (Carol Stream, IL: Tyndale House Publishers, 2005).

[20]Robin I. M. Dunbar, "Coevolution of Neocortical Size, Group Size and Language in Humans," *Behavioral and Brain Sciences* 16 (1993): 681-735. Note that Dunbar has also found that religious communities may be able to sustain cohesion at larger sizes more than secular communities: Robin I. M. Dunbar and Richard Sosis, "Optimising Human Community Sizes," *Evolution and Human Behavior* 39 (2018): 106-11.

[21]Robin I. M. Dunbar, "Cognitive Constraints on the Structure and Dynamics of Social Networks," *Group Dynamics: Theory, Research, and Practice* 12 (2008): 7-16.

[22]Robin I. M. Dunbar, "Mind the Gap; or Why Humans Aren't Just Great Apes," *Proceedings of the British Academy* 154 (2008): 403-23; S. Wolfram, "Science Data of the Facebook World," April 24, 2013, https://stephenwolfram.com.

their maintenance, and time is a limited commodity. Finally, relationships require emotional investments. Given these factors, as human beings, there are natural limits to the amount of relationships we can nurture and sustain.

Dunbar's number has important implications for our spiritual communities. It suggests that our churches and spiritual communities should be structured in functional units of 150 or less. If groups move beyond this size, even just slightly, the dynamics of the community change dramatically, rendering them more vulnerable.[23]

There are, of course, some individual differences in Dunbar's number. In fact, neuroimaging studies have demonstrated that some areas of the prefrontal cortex correlate with the size of face-to-face social networks, and with the number of Facebook friends.[24] The individual differences in our ability to manage social networks seems to be closely related to our experiences during our early formative years, which influence these parts of the brain.[25] As we detailed in an earlier chapter, our ability to connect with others at an emotional level and to understand the emotions of others is linked to our own experiences of being understood. In other words, we are loved into loving. This means that those who are particularly hindered in their ability to love may be able to handle significantly fewer than the average of 150 relationships. This, of course, has implications for the ways we structure spiritual communities and may require the provision of smaller groups to best accommodate those with significant struggles in life.

Dunbar has also done research into the structure of social networks within the community of 150. There are distinctions in levels of intimacy and contact within our social network. In the context of spiritual

---

[23]Dunbar and Sosis, "Optimising Human Community Sizes," 106-11.

[24]P. A. Lewi et al., "Ventromedial Prefrontal Volume Predicts Understanding of Others and Social Network Size," *NeuroImage* 57 (2011): 1624-29; J. Powell et al., "Orbital Prefrontal Cortex Volume Predicts Social Network Size: An Imaging Study of Individual Differences in Humans," *Proceedings of the Royal Society B: Biological Sciences* 279 (2012): 2157-62; R. Kanai, B. Bahrami, R. Roylance, and G. Rees, "Online Social Network Size Is Reflected in Human Brain Structure," *Proceedings of the Royal Society B: Biological Sciences* 279 (2012): 1327-34.

[25]Robin I. M. Dunbar, "The Social Brain: Psychological Underpinnings and Implications for the Structure of Organizations," *Current Directions in Psychological Science* 23 (2014): 109-14.

communities, we can think of the depth dimension of spiritual communities as a series of concentric circles or tiers. Research shows that each tier tends to be about three times bigger than the next smallest one, with each larger tier tending toward less emotional intimacy and contact frequency.[26] For example, all modern armies follow this structure: sections of approximately 15, forming companies of about 150, battalions of approximately 5,000, divisions of 15,000, etc.[27] In the next few paragraphs, we will unpack three layers of tiers and how they might function in a spiritual community.

The innermost circle represents a few close attachment relationships and/or a small group of about five people with whom we share our spiritual stories on a regular basis. From a psychological perspective, research shows that we tend to have about five close attachment relationships, and consequently these people provide the important functions of a safe haven and secure base. We can think of this as our first-tier community. This may be a small group of many types. It could be a small group in a local church context or a small group of friends that have been brought together through some other context.

For example, in a study in which my colleagues and I interviewed college students who attended a Christian college, we found that they frequently defined their primary spiritual community as a small group of college friends who live in close proximity to each other.[28] They often emphasized the fact that the group is not just a social group; rather, it has developed to have an explicitly spiritual focus and function. The important thing is that the focus of the group is on the spiritual growth of the members. This is the level of community at which spiritual values and morals are transmitted through relationships, particularly across generations. Ideally, this close circle of relationships occurs in the context of a local church community, as this connects the group to the body of Christ.

---

[26]Dunbar, "The Social Brain," 110.

[27]Dunbar, "The Social Brain," 112.

[28]Kendra Bailey, Brendon Jones, Todd W. Hall, David Wang, and Jason McMartin, "Spirituality at a Crossroads: A Grounded Theory of Christian Emerging Adults," *Journal of Psychology of Religion & Spirituality*, 8, no. 2 (2016): 99-109.

The next biggest group of about fifteen people, the second tier, are those whom we see regularly and can rely on for more costly kinds of emotional, social, and economic support, such as loans, help with projects, and child care.[29] These relationships, especially the most intimate ones, are referred to by David Benner as "spiritual friendships."[30] Benner cites five ideals of spiritual friendship: love, honesty, intimacy, mutuality, and accompaniment. Spiritual friends are those we share our spiritual journey with as it unfolds. A friendship characterized by the ideals Benner cites is clearly not a superficial relationship. It requires a deep mutual commitment to the spiritual transformation of the other. It also requires a strong sense of intentionality.

There are several fundamental aspects of what spiritual friends do with and for each other. First, they share their experience of God with each other and attempt to be with the other in this experience. This requires vulnerability and trust to share the sometimes dark and confusing places we experience with God. It requires an openness to the confusion and messiness of the spiritual transformation process and a stance of being with the other rather than trying to fix or solve a problem. Second, spiritual friends seek the Holy Spirit's guidance in speaking into the other's life in the context of their current experience of God. Finally, spiritual friends are committed to interceding on behalf of each other, with a specific focus on the other's spiritual growth.

The next circle in the depth of community typically involves a group ranging from about 15 to 150. This is our third-tier community. In reality, this might comprise a series of groups of various sizes. We might be part of a Sunday school class, and also sing in the choir, and serve in the high school ministry. This larger group is the next functional unit of community in terms of the depth of the relationships. Such a group is too large to develop close attachment relationships, and yet it is still

---

[29]A. J. Sutcliffe, R. I. M. Dunbar, J. Binder, and H. Arrow, "Relationships and the Social Brain: Integrating Psychological and Evolutionary Perspectives," *British Journal of Psychology* 103 (2012): 149-68.

[30]See David G. Benner, *Sacred Companions: The Gift of Spiritual Friendship & Direction* (Downers Grove, IL: InterVarsity Press, 2002).

possible to maintain some level of meaningful connection across a group this size.

It is possible to be a relationally connected community up to about 150 people. Such groups are very important, especially when they cross generational lines and provide the opportunity for the spiritualization of attachment—that is, for the transmission of spiritual values and morals. From a psychological perspective, research shows that these people provide support primarily in the form of information and less costly kinds of concrete support.[31] While we may not develop close attachment relationships with more than a handful of people, we will grow by hearing the stories of others and how God is working in their lives. These stories also model for us how to love God and others in various contexts. We also benefit from the gifts of those in the body of Christ in this level of community.

The next circle of community represents groups larger than 150, which we can think of as a fourth-tier community. Research shows that we can have up to 500 acquaintances, and a maximum of 1,500 people with whom we can match names to faces.[32] Beyond 150, there can still be some level of community, but it is less constituted by the matrix of relationships than it is by a sense of connection to a handful of leaders and a common vision and ethos of the community.

There are still benefits to larger communities such as this. They can provide resources, structures, and programs that facilitate the smaller communities' pursuit of the common vision of the larger community. However, the law of 150, as well as the importance of attachment relationships, suggests that when our communities grow this large, we must be intentional about dividing them and creating the smaller circles of community that foster deeper attachment relationships. In other words, fourth-tier communities will not foster any significant depth of spiritual transformation. Third-tier communities can facilitate some meaningful level of growth. However, generally, first- and second-tier communities— especially first-tier—are the fodder for deep healing and spiritual growth.

---

[31]Sutcliffe et al., "Relationships and the Social Brain."
[32]Dunbar, "The Social Brain," 110.

They are the context for relational experiences that mark our spiritual lives as "before" and "after." We must work to develop and foster first- and second-tier spiritual communities if we are to see true spiritual transformation take place.

It should be emphasized that these tiers have built-in cognitive limits; we can only maintain a limited number of relationships at a given level of emotional intensity. In other words, our love for others needs to differentiate between the different levels or tiers, simply because of our human limitations. We are called to love all, but the expression of that love may, and should, differ in different kinds of relationships as we noted in chapters six and seven.

The danger of ignoring this concept of tiers is illustrated in a study of ministry workers.[33] Because of the nature of their work, ministry workers often feel pressure to maintain a large number of personal relationships. Furthermore, they often spend a large portion of their time caring for others. These researchers found that ministers reporting fewer than twelve to fifteen relationships in their first and second tiers (combined) experienced higher burnout levels and lower perceived ministry effectiveness. Furthermore, those with *more* than fifteen relationships in their first and second tiers also reported greater burnout. These results suggest that there is an optimal range of the number of people that comprise our first and second tiers (around twelve to fifteen) and that deviation from this is likely to cause problems.

We must also be intentional about what happens in the smaller units in our congregations. While we must live life together, the spiritual purpose of the communities must not be forgotten. The purpose of our life together is not merely to feel good (although it does feel good to be deeply connected to others), but to help each other grow and to do God's work together. We must resist the temptation to turn our life together into nothing more than social activity. We must also function as salt,

---

[33]Candace Coppinger Pickett, Justin L. Barrett, Cynthia B. Eriksson, and Christina Kabiri, "Social Networks Among Ministry Relationships: Relational Capacity, Burnout, & Ministry Effectiveness," *Journal of Psychology and Theology* 45 (2017): 92-105. The ministry workers included national and international missionaries and youth pastors.

lamp, leaven, and mustard seed—small things with a disproportionately large influence.[34] The primary agent for change is precisely the love we are able to offer.

Authoritative. Fourth, spiritual communities are authoritative. What does it mean for a community to be *authoritative*? To provide some background on this aspect of community, we draw here on the work of a group of scholars and practitioners who treat children and do research on child development.[35] This group was commissioned to address the deteriorating mental and behavioral health of US children and to propose policy solutions to the problems. The Commission on Children at Risk concluded that the crisis stems from a lack of connectedness: close connections to other people and deep connections to moral and spiritual meaning.

After extensive research, they attributed the decline in children's mental and behavioral health to the weakening of "authoritative communities" in the United States and advocated for the strengthening of these kinds of communities. They defined authoritative communities as "groups of people who are committed to one another over time and who model and pass on at least part of what it means to be a good person and live a good life."[36] In other words, authoritative communities are communities that speak the truth in love.

It is not difficult to see the similarities between "authoritative communities" and the spiritual communities we are advocating here that comprise the body of Christ. Their description of an authoritative community includes, among others, the following six characteristics: (1) it treats others as ends in themselves, rather than as means to an end; (2) it is warm and nurturing; (3) it establishes clear limits and expectations; (4) it is multigenerational; (5) it reflects and transmits a shared understanding of what it means to be a good person; and (6) it is

---

[34]Chan, *Spiritual Theology*, 104.

[35]Kathleen Kovner Kline, ed., *Authoritative Communities: The Scientific Case for Nurturing the Whole Child* (New York: Springer, 2008), xiii-xiv.

[36]The Commission on Children at Risk, "Hardwired to Connect: The New Scientific Case for Authoritative Communities," in *Authoritative Communities: The Scientific Case for Nurturing the Whole Child*, ed. Kathleen Kovner Kline (New York: Springer, 2008), 9.

philosophically oriented to the equal dignity of all persons and to the principle of love of neighbor.[37] In essence, authoritative communities blend and integrate warmth and empathy on the one hand and moral structure on the other hand. They are neither permissive, with an anything-goes attitude, nor authoritarian, with a cold, rigid focus on rules. In contrast, these communities are supportive while at the very same time expecting certain behaviors, values, and character traits because they are good for the individual's well-being and for the community as a whole. Authoritative communities, then, help their members become a certain kind of person through intergenerational connection, warmth, and moral boundaries.

Much of the research supporting the value of authoritative communities comes from research on church participation. Hundreds of studies have supplied evidence that church participation exerts a protective influence on factors including mortality, hypertension, suicide, promiscuous sexual behaviors, drug and alcohol use, and delinquency.[38] In addition, participation in organized religion increases well-being, hope, purpose, meaning in life, self-esteem, and educational attainment. These findings support the premise that communities that establish moral expectations in supportive contexts decrease participation in problematic behaviors and increase prosocial behaviors, leading to positive outcomes.

Why is it that these kinds of communities are able to exercise a powerful moral influence on their members? Part of the answer comes from what psychiatrist Barbara Stilwell has called "the moralization of attachment."[39] Stilwell describes a process through which infant-parent attachment interacts to form a security-empathy-oughtness representation within the child's mind. In other words, implicit feelings of

---

[37]The Commission on Children at Risk, "Hardwired to Connect," 26.

[38]Byron R. Johnson, "A Tale of Two Religious Effects: Evidence for the Protective and Prosocial Impact of Organic Religion," in *Authoritative Communities: The Scientific Case for Nurturing the Whole Child*, ed. Kathleen Kovner Kline (New York: Springer, 2008), 187-225.

[39]Barbara M. Stilwell, "The Consolidation of Conscience in Adolescence," in *Authoritative Communities: The Scientific Case for Nurturing the Whole Child*, ed. Kathleen Kovner Kline (New York: Springer, 2008), 123-50.

security or insecurity are paired with the (often nonverbal and unconscious) messages from parents about which behaviors are pleasing or nonpleasing, prohibited or encouraged, worthy of attention or not worthy of attention. In this way, there is a biological readiness to moralize behavior, based on seeking parental connection. When people of various ages form part of a close-knit spiritual community, their internalization of the values of the community goes hand in hand with the emotional connections with members of that community.

As noted above, the local church, when it is functioning well, clearly fits the description of an authoritative community. When I was in high school, I had the good fortune to become a member of a church that functioned as an authoritative community. I was involved in a small youth group that fostered close relationships with my peers and several youth pastors. The youth pastors were encouraging, warm, and supportive, but I also internalized a set of values that I heard them teach and saw them live out. It was clear that there was a model of the "good life" we were striving for, and concomitant moral boundaries. Certain behaviors were out of bounds because they didn't promote the good life; that is, they didn't honor God or our brothers and sisters in Christ. I knew this based on the way my youth pastors (and the senior pastor) treated others with kindness and also the way they lovingly confronted problematic behaviors in members of our community.

For example, on one occasion one of my youth pastors, Spencer, and his wife, Rhonda, got into an argument, which led to him canceling an event. He could have covered this up, but instead he shared afterward how he felt he had hurt his wife and that he apologized and asked for forgiveness. They both shared openly, but appropriately, about their relationship and this event, and it led to meaningful discussions about the importance of humility and forgiveness. Perhaps more important than the discussions, as critical as they were, I saw warmth and moral structure modeled in their relationship. Hurtful interpersonal behavior was not condoned, and yet forgiveness was freely offered and warmth was quickly restored. Because I developed close relationships with my pastors and many adults (the value of intergenerational connections comes into play here), I wanted to please them and be accepted by them, which in turn caused me to take on their values as my own. This is the moralization of attachment in action.

In our overview of New Testament teachings on the church, we emphasized the importance of "speaking the truth in love." From a social science perspective, the research on authoritative communities concludes with the same bottom line: we need relationships, but we need specific kinds of relationships that will authoritatively provide us with a true story within which we can find our own story and identity.

Belonging: Building Spiritual Community Together

We all have an innate need to belong to a community. We need "our people" who understand us, support us, encourage us, and challenge us to grow. This is a human need. Secular communities fulfill some of these needs. Yet secular communities leave an unmet need in our sense of meaning and purpose. We know and feel that we're called to a community that has a deeper purpose and a higher good. The new family of God is rooted in the love of the Trinity and is therefore the paradigmatic expression of community and the ultimate group to which we desire to belong. As children of God, we belong to the body of Christ in an objective sense. However, we also desire to subjectively experience a sense of belonging to God's new family—to be part of not just a group but the ultimate family that is centered around God's love.

Yet this experience of belonging too often eludes us as we feel disappointment in our church communities. When this happens, it is natural to become disillusioned with our spiritual community. At times, we may feel overlooked, not included, or not valued. We may feel the community is not meeting our needs, doesn't reflect our values, or has too much conflict. I have worked with many clients who felt this way at times, and encountered such feelings in myself and others in my church. Communities in the early New Testament church also struggled with conflict and tension among their various members. When we become disillusioned, the temptation we face is to *disengage* in various ways: (1) we search for a "better" church community; (2) we stay on the edges of community; or

(3) we convince ourselves that we're better off practicing solo Christianity. These temptations are almost automatic due to the individualistic and consumeristic culture in the Western world. When we disengage from Christian community, it becomes fragmented, and we collectively fail to create a new social order of love and to shine God's light to the world.

This raises a crucial question: How do we go about building a sense of ultimate belonging in our spiritual communities, especially in the face of the conflict and disappointments that will inevitably occur? The answer is, in a word: *together.* We build spiritual community—a place of belonging—as we travel together along the journey. Moreover, this side of heaven, we will always be transforming our church communities so they increasingly reflect God and provide a contrast-society that shines God's light to the world. In this section, we briefly explore several components of belonging, while highlighting a few principles from the previous material to help shape our mindset and guide our actions toward building a sense of belonging to God's new family.

The structure of belonging. As we build God's new family, we must be mindful and facilitate the experience of three interrelated aspects that comprise the structure of belonging: a shared identity, a shared experience, and a shared purpose. First Peter 2:9-10 provides a brief but helpful picture of these aspects of belonging in the body of Christ. First, we share an identity as God's "chosen people" and as a "royal priests, a holy nation, God's very own possession" (1 Peter 2:9). As noted earlier, God's chosen people are described as a new family. We find our deepest identity or sense of who we are in being a child of God and sibling to our brothers and sisters in Christ. We share this identity with each other, and thus it is a significant aspect of what bonds us to the new family of God. We belong to the body of Christ because we are all children of God. In our gatherings, we need to practice reminding ourselves of our common identity to promote a sense of belonging that will in turn build commitment and mutual love.

Second, we all share the experience of having received God's mercy (1 Peter 2:10). While everyone's salvation story differs, we share the basic experience of receiving God's forgiveness and being adopted as a child of God. This is a very formative experience that bonds us together, and one that we re-experience throughout our lives. In addition, we share the experience of corporate worship as we sing, hear and respond to God's Word, pray, and receive communion together. As we gather in small and larger groups, we need to rekindle and remind ourselves of our shared experience. One powerful way of doing this is sharing our testimonies and other ways we have experienced God's mercy. In my Sunday school class, we have times devoted to sharing how God is working in our lives. In our worship services, we also periodically set aside time for people to share their testimonies and the ongoing work of God in their lives. It is always uplifting, and these times renew our shared experience of God's mercy and grace, as well as our shared identity as children of God. We belong precisely because we share a profound experience.

Finally, we share a common purpose to "show others the goodness of God" (1 Peter 2:9). This echoes what we have noted previously: the new family of God is to collectively demonstrate God's love and be a visible sign of salvation for all nations. God's plan is that his people would draw the nations to himself by being a contrast-society living out a new social order of love.[40] This new family of God is to be a radiant city on the hill (Matthew 5:13-16). Thus, our common purpose is to develop this new social order of love, which contrasts greatly with the values of secular society, and thereby reflect God to the world. This is something we can only do collectively.

When we gather as a local expression of the family of God, we need to explicitly remind ourselves of our common purpose. We do not belong merely to socialize with people like us and stay in our comfort zone. This would be a thin sense of belonging indeed. Rather, we experience belonging to the family of God in part because we are working on a mission together—the ultimate mission. We are working with God and each other to bring about the kingdom of heaven. Each local community plays its own role, but within our local spiritual community, we work side by side with each other to create a community characterized

---

[40]Lohfink, *Jesus and Community*.

by the mutual love of the Trinity and to offer this mutual love and be-longing to the world. We belong because we share the most important purpose of all.

The glue of belonging: commitment and mutuality. A healthy spir-itual community is the responsibility of all of its members, who must all work in cooperation with the Holy Spirit. Each of us is creating the very communities to which we desire to belong and from which we desire to receive support. This means we are all accountable for doing our part in building spiritual communities that: (1) we desire to belong to, (2) exhibit a new social order of love, and (3) display God's love to the world.

When we become disillusioned, our temptation is to focus on what we are getting (or not getting) from our community. This is understandable. We all feel this way at times, and we all need support and love from others in our community when we get stuck in such an emotional place. We may need to reach out and let others know how we are feeling. Making ourselves vulnerable requires great courage and is the fuel that drives authentic connection and transformation in community.

While we need this help from other members of the body, as we are all interdependent, we also need to do our part in refocusing our mindset, in concert with the Holy Spirit, on how we can help create the community that truly shines God's light. This requires a deep com-mitment to the community. In order to be part of building something larger than ourselves, we have to stay and remain engaged when things get difficult. As we noted, this goes very much against the grain of our individualistic society. It is much easier to leave, and this is almost normal in our culture. When we leave at the first sign of difficulties, however, we are more likely to repeat old, unhealthy relational patterns. Transformational change, in contrast, happens through long-term re-lationships that allow us to face our pain, with others, and become more securely attached. This is consistent with the family bonds that comprise our church communities.

The family of God is a new reality that both shines God's light to the world and foreshadows the fullness of heaven. This is not to say that there are not times we need to leave a local church community, but it is to say that allegiance to family in our spiritual community should be paramount in our decision making. As we consider our commitments to spiritual community, we would do well to remember that we are building something that foreshadows heaven and that will someday come to full expression in heaven.

With our commitment in place, part of our contribution is to be on the lookout for our brothers and sisters in Christ who may be feeling disillusioned or frustrated, or may just be hurting. Just as we receive support during times like these, we bring this love full circle by offering it to others in our community. As we are reminded of our shared identity, experience, and purpose, we find ourselves moved to love our brothers and sisters in Christ. We desire their well-being and we seek connection. As we noted earlier, this means we strive to understand what the other needs to promote their well-being.

As in any relationship, spiritual community requires mutuality, but at the collective level. This does not happen in a linear manner. Each person gives and receives to different people and subgroups, but at the collective level, everyone, and the community as a whole, grows. We must commit ourselves to the higher good of family members and to the community as a whole. When we do this, mutual love becomes a reality—a love that reflects the Trinity and shows the world who God is.

I have had the privilege of being a member of a Sunday school class that embodies this commitment and mutual love for over seventeen years. People tend to remain in the group for a long time. Many of the families have been a part of the group for over a decade, and we have experienced all facets of life together, including triumphs and tragedies. Most of the members of the group are committed to the group as a whole and volunteer their time and talents for the good of the group. While our community is certainly not perfect, and occasional frustrations and tensions arise, there is a distinct sense of mutual love in our class. People reach out and offer emotional and practical support to others. The central point is that, on balance, everyone takes responsibility for the community and invests in the good of the group. Because of that, we all receive even while we all give to the group, stimulating a mutual love that reflects the Trinity.

The unit of belonging: small groups. We noted previously the importance of attending to the size of groups in our spiritual communities. The first two tiers, up to five and fifteen members, respectively, are where attachment and closer relationships can develop, which have the potential to promote transformational change. In his work on building community, Peter Block echoes the importance of the small group, suggesting it is "the unit of transformation."[41] We might extend this idea to suggest that small groups are the unit of belonging. When we refer to small groups here, we do not necessarily mean a small group program. Rather, we are thinking of any small group that meets regularly within the larger context of the body of Christ.

Larger groups within our spiritual communities are important, but we must strive to connect people in first- and second-tier small groups, for these groups create the conditions for intimacy, authentic relatedness, a unique valuing of each person, and meaningful dialogue. As members of the community, we can each focus on creating the experience of belonging as we gather. This requires being present in the moment and recognizing that we are now inhabiting a sense of belonging to God's family. Within a smaller group, it is possible to foster intimacy, authenticity, and a more personal sense of belonging.

For example, in my Sunday school class, we structure time for sharing meaningful things about our lives, which engenders a sense of closeness. We strive to create an environment in which it feels safe to share struggles, promoting authenticity. We attempt to model for each other humility and an ongoing process of growth—the mindset that none of us has arrived and each of us needs God's grace every day. This creates an environment in which everyone is uniquely valued. There is an implicit understanding that each person is important, and this value is inhabited as the group is responsive to the needs of each person as they arise. Sharing struggles and important things about our lives, in turn, creates the safety for true dialogue.

---

[41]Peter Block, *Community: The Structure of Belonging* (San Francisco: Berrett-Koehler, 2008).

In our small groups, we must intentionally promote meaningful dialogue, which is all too often absent in our gatherings. Real dialogue, David Benner notes, is challenging because it goes beyond the simple exchange of ideas or opinions.[42] Dialogue, rather, is "exploration and discovery through conversational engagement."[43] It is designed to promote awareness and insight, and it seeks mutual understanding. Dialogue is an "I-Thou" encounter in which the purpose of the conversation is simply to meet each other. It requires an openness and surrender to the process. In dialogue we go with the process by attuning to the others' emotions, listening for their emotional truth, and sharing our emotional truth in turn. As we do this, something new is created and discovered within each person and the group.

Dialogue creates personal or relational knowledge of the self and other, which leads to an expanded and enriched capacity for love. In dialogue we experience something of the essence or core of the other person. As Benner puts it, "The 'other' becomes present, not merely in one's imagination or feelings, but in the depths of one's being."[44]

While time and structure to promote dialogue will only be one of the activities within a spiritual community, it is important that we create the space and psychological safety for this. Because dialogue involves risk and vulnerability, it requires safety, and this is best accomplished in small groups. We suggested in chapter six that love is comprised of goodwill and union, which further involves mutual closeness. Dialogue is a form of mutual closeness in which we reveal important things about ourselves and receive the revelations of others with care and compassion. Thus, dialogue is a form of love that creates the very fabric of our communities. Because of the power of this relational knowledge and experience, dialogue promotes a deep sense of belonging. We belong because we discover ourselves, others, and Christ anew within the small groups of our communities.

---

[42]David Benner, *Presence and Encounter: The Sacramental Possibilities of Everyday Life* (Grand Rapids, MI: Brazos Press, 2014), 87.

[43]Benner, *Presence and Encounter*, 87.

[44]Benner, *Presence and Encounter*, 88.

Conclusion

With this, we have come to the end of our journey together. In these chapters, I have sought to bring together theology and psychology to argue for a fundamentally relational way of conceptualizing who we are as humans made in the image of God. We have unpacked the implications of this for our growth into maturity, more fully reflecting God's image as we become increasingly like Christ. The core of this transformation has to do with love, as we reflect our triune God who is love. We suggested that attachment-type relationships, and the relational knowledge that undergirds them, are foundational for spiritual growth, as they shape our implicit self and capacity to love. We concluded with a call for life in community as the new family of God—the kind of spiritual community that provides the context for this growth, and that in itself becomes the goal, as together we more fully reflect who God is. We are, indeed, loved into loving in the context of Christian community. We end our journey with the words of Simon Chan, who in one sentence summarizes much of what has been said here: "Christian spirituality can be nothing other than living the Christian life in union with the Trinity in the church."[45]

---

[45]Chan, *Spiritual Theology*, 122.

General Index

Scripture Index

CAPS
INTERNATIONAL

An Association for Christian Psychologists,
Therapists, Counselors and Academicians

CAPS is a vibrant Christian organization with a rich tradition. Founded in 1956 by a small group of Christian mental health professionals, chaplains and pastors, CAPS has grown to more than 2,100 members in the U.S., Canada and more than 25 other countries.

CAPS encourages in-depth consideration of therapeutic, research, theoretical and theological issues. The association is a forum for creative new ideas. In fact, their publications and conferences are the birthplace for many of the formative concepts in our field today.

CAPS members represent a variety of denominations, professional groups and theoretical orientations; yet all are united in their commitment to Christ and to professional excellence.

CAPS is a non-profit, member-supported organization. It is led by a fully functioning board of directors, and the membership has a voice in the direction of CAPS.

CAPS is more than a professional association. It is a fellowship, and in addition to national and international activities, the organization strongly encourages regional, local and area activities which provide networking and fellowship opportunities as well as professional enrichment.

To learn more about CAPS, visit www.caps.net.

The joint publishing venture between IVP Academic and CAPS aims to promote the understanding of the relationship between Christianity and the behavioral sciences at both the clinical/counseling and the theoretical/research levels. These books will be of particular value for students and practitioners, teachers and researchers.

For more information about CAPS Books, visit InterVarsity Press's website at www.ivpress.com/christian-association-for-psychological-studies-books-set.